LAW OF THE LAND

Travel Guide for the LGBTQ+ Community

International Travel

By Michael L. Moore Esq.

DEDICATION

This book is dedicated to the memory of my late older brother, Kenneth Lee Moore, whose tragic murder at 15 years of age inspired me to write this series of books.

This book is also dedicated to my parents, John Henry Moore, and Edna Mae Moore, whose tremendous parenting skills kept me focused on the important things in life: being reverent, getting educated, and prioritizing family.

Finally, this book is dedicated to my beautiful family, my wife Royellen, my son AJ, and my daughter Karla. They inspire me every single day to be kind, patient, and compassionate.

IN LOVING MEMORY OF:

Belinda Joyce Moore Moss—my beautiful and wonderful sister, who supported me in every positive thing that I ever attempted to do.

Michael Eugene Baker—my dedicated and loyal friend and brother, who always wanted the very best for me.

Sylvia Joyce Hill—my eldest sister, who had a beautiful spirit and was like a second mother to me.

LAW OF THE LAND®
PUBLISHING for Tourists & Business Travelers

Travel smart. Stay legal. Stay safe.®

From local laws to medical guides we've got you covered world wide
in one digital platform.

PREFACE

My introduction to the justice system came when I was only 10 years old. My 15-year-old brother was murdered with a butcher knife by a 19-year-old in a simple argument over a torn shirt. I was devastated by his death and sought retribution for his fate that never came. The woman was initially charged with second degree murder, but after plea negotiations, she was convicted of manslaughter and sentenced to only five years in a youthful offender school and ordered to undergo psychiatric care. That was it. Nothing more. The judicial system had run its course.

My family knew nothing about the justice system, and we did not have the tools to advocate for ourselves. No one provided us with a written source to reference for guidance through this process. There was no easily accessible, easy to understand, definitive source to use to educate ourselves about the legal system that we suddenly and unexpectedly found ourselves immersed in after being victimized by such a violent criminal act.

As I got older, finished college, law school, and ultimately started prac¬-ticing law, it became clear to me that most people are not knowledge¬able about the law or how the judicial process works. If most people are uninformed here in the United States regarding the law and the legal process, how would they fare when in other countries? I realized that tourists and businesspeople who travel internationally needed access to information on how to navigate the legal system in other countries!

For many years, there has been considerable media attention focused on international travelers experiencing legal difficulties while traveling abroad. Most of these news stories gained attention in the United States and abroad because they involved American citizens facing punishment that was considered "unconventional" and "harsh" by United States' legal standards. I recall a news story in 1994 regarding Michael Fay, a young American male, who had broken the law in Singapore. He was convicted and sentenced to be caned and or whipped publicly. While the United States Government weighed in on the inappropriate and cruel nature of the punishment, the young American was beaten because he had been convicted under Singapore law.

Similarly, in recent years, international news stories have garnered head¬lines regarding foreign travelers and their issues with the laws of coun¬tries that were not their own. Amanda Knox, an American wom-an, was accused of murdering her roommate in Italy in 2007 and spent almost four years in an Italian prison before being definitively acquitted by the Supreme Court of Cassatio. Kenneth Bae, an American citizen, was ar¬rested in North Korea in 2012 and was convicted for hostile acts against the communist country. He was sentenced to 15 years hard labor but was released in 2014 after efforts by the U.S. State Department. More recently, United States Basketball Star, Brittany Griner was arrested in February 2022 at a Moscow airport on drug-related charges and de¬tained for nearly 10 months, spending much of that time in prison. Her plight unfolded at the same time Russia invaded Ukraine and further heightened tensions between Russia and the United States, ending only after she was freed in exchange for a notorious Russian arms dealer.

It was in 1994 that another personal tragic event occurred that finally inspired me to write this series of books. A dear friend and also client of mine was brutally murdered while on his second honeymoon in Jamaica. News of his murder shocked me and our local community. The legal hurdles his family had to overcome to see that justice was properly dispensed far away from home, in another country, with an entirely dif¬ferent set of criminal procedural rules and laws, was difficult to navigate.

As I was my friend's attorney at the time of his death, his family asked that I act as their "legal liaison" to the Jamaican Prosecutor's Office and to the Jamaican Police Department. I participated in multiple police in-¬terviews with my client's widow because she was the primary witness to his murder. As a former prosecuting attorney, I was also allowed by the

Court, as a professional courtesy, to sit at the prosecutor's table to consult with the prosecuting attorney during trial. What I observed about the Jamaican trial process from a front row seat was compelling enough to cause me to seriously consider educating the "world" regard¬ing what to expect and how to act appropriately when faced with legal issues while traveling abroad.

One of the realities in life is that, regardless of what country you are in, it is never a pleasant experience to run afoul of the law and be forced to accept that someone else will be making a decision about your pecuniary, proprietary, or penal interests (your money, your property, or your freedom).

It is important to know what the laws are, how they apply to you, and how to navigate the legal system if you are charged with a crime. It is also very helpful to know what resources are available to you if you are the victim of a criminal act. At the end of the day, an "ounce of prevention is worth a pound of cure," so the more knowledge you have, the more ammunition you possess, and the more likely you will have a positive outcome.

If you're traveling to any of the 30 countries discussed in this book, make sure to take along a copy of this book! It's packed with essential information and tips that will help you understand what to do (and what to avoid) to stay safe and have a smooth trip. Whether for business or pleasure, this guide will help you navigate the local LGBTQ+ scene and avoid any legal issues.

TABLE OF CONTENTS

INTRODUCTION

INTRODUCTION

As a practicing attorney for over 34 years, I have encountered numerous clients who travel often but are unaware of the laws of the land they are traveling to.

Therefore, many years ago, I decided to write a series of books that would explain the laws of specific countries. My focus was to explain the laws that may affect travelers in a straightforward manner, without all of the legal language that is sometimes hard for even seasoned attorneys to understand.

About This Book

The aim of this book is simple: to provide a clear, accessible understanding of how LGBTQ+ individuals are treated around the world, and to offer useful guidance for those navigating these realities—especially while traveling. In this book, I have provided context and background information to help paint a broad picture of the global landscape. You'll find examples of countries that are highly accepting and supportive—where rights are protected, visibility is celebrated, and communities thrive. You'll also read about places that are showing meaningful progress in their acceptance of LGBTQ+ individuals through legal reforms, shifting cultural attitudes, and growing public support. And then, there are regions where hostility remains deeply entrenched, where laws and societal norms continue to marginalize, criminalize, or even endanger LGBTQ+ lives.

To support this understanding, I've included snapshots of each country's political system, LGBTQ+ legislation, related crime statistics, and other key factors that can influence one's experience—especially when traveling. These sections are accompanied by practical, common-sense advice intended to help LGBTQ+ travelers make informed and safe choices. Knowledge is a powerful thing and knowing how to stay out of trouble (or how to get out of it!) is important for everyone who travels.

Whether you're planning a trip, deepening your awareness, or simply trying to understand the state of LGBTQ+ rights around the world, this *Law of The Land LGBTQ+* book offers a thoughtful starting point for becoming a more informed, responsible, and compassionate global citizen.

Last, but not least, this book does NOT purport to offer legal advice. It does, however, provide the information you need to stay safe, follow the law and how to navigate potential legal difficulties.

How This Book is Organized

Part 1: LGBTQ+ Friendly Countries (High Safety).

This section highlights countries that generally offer robust legal protections, inclusive policies, and positive societal attitudes toward LGBTQ+ individuals. These are places where LGBTQ+ people can live, work, and travel with a strong sense of freedom and safety. Anti-discrimination laws are enforced, same-sex relationships are recognized or even celebrated, and public events like Pride are openly supported. Support networks and LGBTQ+ services are widely available, and public acceptance is high.

Countries in this section include: **Spain, Thailand, Portugal, France, Malta, Greece, Iceland, New Zealand, Canada,** and **Belgium.**

Part 2: LGBTQ+ Tolerant Countries (Moderate Safety).

In these countries, there are legal protections in place for LGBTQ+ individuals, but the social climate may vary. Larger cities and more progressive areas tend to be welcoming, while rural or conservative regions may still pose challenges. Same-sex relationships are typically legal, but social acceptance can be inconsistent, and discrimination or hate crimes may still occur. Travelers may want to exercise some caution, particularly regarding public displays of affection.

Countries in this section include: **Brazil, Argentina, Uruguay, Italy, Mexico, South Africa, Japan, Bolivia, India,** and **Israel.**

Part III: LGBTQ+ Hostile Countries (Low Safety)

This section addresses countries where LGBTQ+ individuals face serious legal, social, and cultural risks. Same-sex relationships may be criminalized, and expressing LGBTQ+ identity can lead to harassment, imprisonment, or worse. In these environments, public displays of affection and LGBTQ+ advocacy are often unsafe, and societal acceptance is extremely low. Travelers should exercise extreme caution and thoroughly research local laws and customs before visiting.

Countries in this section include: **United Arab Emirates, Saudi Arabia, Yemen, Qatar (Middle East); Malaysia** and **Afghanistan (Southeast Asia); Egypt, Uganda,** and **Nigeria (Africa);** and **Russia (Europe/ Asia).**

Each country profile includes the following sections:

- **Politics & LGBTQ+ Legislation:** An overview of the political climate and legal status of LGBTQ+ individuals, including same-sex relationship laws, gender identity recognition, and anti-discrimination protections.
- **LGBTQ+ Scene:** A glimpse into LGBTQ+ life on the ground— nightlife, events, community spaces, and general visibility.

- **LGBTQ+-Related Crime:** Insight into crime and discrimination targeting LGBTQ+ individuals, including trends and how law enforcement responds.

- **LGBTQ+ and Prostitution:** A look at how sex work intersects with LGBTQ+ issues in the country, including its legal and cultural context.

- **LGBTQ+ and the Jail/Prison System:** Information on the treatment of LGBTQ+ individuals within the legal and penal system.

- **Arrested:** What to expect if an LGBTQ+ traveler is arrested—legal risks, detainment practices, and local attitudes.

- **Bail:** An explanation of the local bail process, including whether bail is commonly granted, how it works, and any unique challenges LGBTQ+ individuals might face when trying to secure release.

- **Legal Representation:** Guidance on accessing legal support, including how to find a lawyer, whether LGBTQ+-friendly or culturally competent representation is available, and what legal aid resources exist.

- **Healthcare System and Medical Facilities:** An overview of the country's healthcare system, including the quality and accessibility of medical services. This section also considers how the system may affect LGBTQ+ individuals, especially in terms of safety, inclusivity, and available support.

- **Safety Precautions for LGBTQ+ Travelers:** Common-sense tips for navigating cultural norms and minimizing risks while traveling.

- **Emergency Contact Numbers:** Key contacts for embassies and emergency services.

While this book provides a snapshot of each country's current situation, LGBTQ+ laws and societal attitudes can evolve over time. For the most up-to-date information, travelers are encouraged to consult the **Law of The Land App** to stay informed about changing laws, safety tips, and real-time updates on LGBTQ+ issues around the world.

Glossary

Icons Used in this Book

What do those pictures throughout the book mean? See below:

 **LEGAL STATUS**: This icon points to LGBTQ+-related legislation (e.g., same-sex marriage, anti-discrimination, and criminalization).

 **LGBTQ+ SCENE**: This icon points to LGBTQ+ culture, key cities, pride events, and organizations that promote equality, visibility, and rights within the country.

 **LGBTQ+-RELATED CRIME**: This icon points to issues related to violence, discrimination, and legal challenges faced by LGBTQ+ individuals.

 **DISCRIMINATION / DANGER**: This icon points to areas where LGBTQ+ people face persecution, violence, or legal penalties.

 **INSIGHT / REFLECTION**: This icon points to things to think about.

 **EMERGENCY INFO**: This icon points to urgent safety guidelines, emergency contacts, or legal tips.

 **Disclaimer:** While the recommendations in this book primarily address U.S. citizens, the information is relevant and applicable to citizens of any country.

LGBTQ+ FRIENDLY COUNTRIES
(HIGH SAFETY)

LGBTQ+ FRIENDLY COUNTRIES

These countries generally offer robust legal protections, inclusive policies, and positive societal attitudes towards LGBTQ+ individuals. They are places where LGBTQ+ people can live, work, and travel freely without significant fear of discrimination or violence. LGBTQ+ rights are enshrined in law, and there are widespread support networks and services for the community. Public LGBTQ+ events are celebrated openly, and discrimination is actively challenged.

 **SPAIN**

Spain is a democratic constitutional monarchy with King Felipe VI as the head of state (as of 2024), operating under a parliamentary system. The country is culturally diverse, with a rich history shaped by various regional identities and traditions, while Roman Catholicism remains the dominant religion alongside others. Known for its **progressive stance on LGBTQ+ rights**, Spain has made significant advancements in promoting equality and inclusion in recent decades.

 ## Politics and LGBTQ+ Legislation

Spain's political landscape is characterized by a complex interplay of liberal and conservative ideologies, reflecting the country's historical, social, and economic influences. In recent years, Spain has been recognized for its progressive policies on social issues, including LGBTQ+ rights, gender equality, and environmental legislation, suggesting a liberal orientation in many areas of governance.

Same-sex marriage was legalized in Spain in July 2005, making it the third country globally to do so, after the Netherlands and Belgium. The law, signed by Prime Minister José Luis Rodríguez Zapatero, **also permits same-sex couples to adopt children**. Since then, openly gay individuals have held prominent political roles, including Jerónimo Saavedra, Ada Colau, and Manuela Trasobares. There are no legal penalties for being openly gay in Spain, with public displays of affection, same-sex marriage, and gender identity fully protected. The "Comprehensive Law" passed in 2022 further promotes equality, prevents discrimination, and ensures the dignity of LGBTQ+ individuals, expanding their rights in daily life and the workplace.[1]

 ## LGBTQ+ Scene

Spain has a vibrant and welcoming LGBTQ+ scene, with major cities offering a wide range of events, venues, and communities. Madrid and Barcelona are the most prominent hubs for LGBTQ+ culture.

Madrid: Known for its inclusive atmosphere, Madrid has one of the largest Pride celebrations in Europe. The Chueca neighborhood is the heart of LGBTQ+ culture, with numerous bars, clubs, and restaurants

---

1 https://www.garrigues.com/en_GB/new/spain-new-comprehensive-law-equal-treatment-and-nondiscrimination-also-applies-employment

catering to the community. Madrid also hosts the Madrid LGBTQ+ Film Festival and the Madrid Summit, which brings together activists and human rights leaders.

Barcelona: Famous for its lively nightlife and beach culture, Barcelona is also very LGBTQ+ friendly. The city's gay district, Gayxample, is full of gay-friendly bars, clubs, and shops. Barcelona also hosts its own Pride celebrations, attracting thousands of visitors from around the world.

Other Cities: Valencia, Sitges, and Gran Canaria are also known for their inclusive environments and LGBTQ+ friendly venues. Sitges, in particular, is famous for its beach resorts and as a popular destination for LGBTQ+ travelers.

Spain has made significant strides in LGBTQ+ rights, becoming one of the first countries to legalize same-sex marriage, and is widely regarded as a welcoming destination for LGBTQ+ travelers. Beyond its major cities, Spain supports its LGBTQ+ community through several key organizations, including **FELGTB**, the largest LGBTQ+ network in the country, **COGAM** in Madrid, and **Lambda** in Valencia. These organizations provide a range of services such as counseling, support groups, advocacy, and legal support, while promoting diversity, equality, and acceptance across the nation.

 **LGBTQ+-Related Crime**

Despite being one of the safer places to visit, Spain too is not entirely free of hate crimes as related to the LGBTQ+ community. Common incidents of LGBTQ+ discrimination include harassment by teenagers, hostility from local communities, workplace discrimination, and online hate speech. In 2021, 80 hate crimes against LGBTQ+ individuals were reported in Catalonia, though only 16% to 20% of these cases led to official reports, and very few resulted in convictions. As a result, LGBTQ+ travelers are advised to research destinations carefully, select safe and inclusive accommodations, and stay informed about local laws to ensure a secure experience.

LGBTQ+ and Prostitution

Spain recognizes legal sex work through OTRAZ (*Organización de Trabajadorxs Sexuales*), which gained legal status in 2021. The organization supports over 600 members, many of whom are part of the LGBTQ+ community, offering them opportunities for sustainable employment in a field with limited options for equality. However, sex work still carries a stigma in some areas of Spain, and it can sometimes be linked to negative perceptions, resulting in hate crimes and accusations against those who advocate for the rights of sex workers. Travelers should be aware of the situation and exercise caution when discussing such topics with strangers, to avoid drawing unwanted attention.

LGBTQ+ and Jail System

The jail system in Spain, overseen by the Spanish Ministry of the Interior, emphasizes rehabilitation and social reintegration of inmates rather than mere punishment Spanish prisons operate under a legal framework that prioritizes human rights, providing inmates access to education, vocational training, and healthcare, thus supporting their reintegration into society upon release. Despite this progressive approach, challenges such as overcrowding and varying conditions across facilities persist.[2]

In Spain, the distinction between jails (pre-trial detention) and prisons (long-term incarceration) is similar to many other countries. However, when it comes to LGBTQ+ individuals, both facilities are governed by laws ensuring equal rights. The "Comprehensive Law" guarantees that LGBTQ+ prisoners have the same rights and protections as others, including access to healthcare, safety, and respectful treatment.

While LGBTQ+ individuals in jails or prisons may face challenges, particularly in terms of discrimination or violence, Spain's legal framework—coupled with a commitment to equality—ensures that LGBTQ+ inmates are treated fairly. This is further supported by the upcoming

---

2 https://www.vaia.com/en-us/explanations/spanish/spanish-social-issues/ prison-system-spain

"Full and Effective Equality" bill, which will provide enhanced protections for LGBTQ+ people, including those in detention, regardless of their nationality.[3]

 ## Arrested in Spain

The arrest process for foreigners in Spain follows a structured legal framework designed to ensure the protection of their rights. Upon arrest, individuals must be informed of the reasons for their detention and the specific charges against them in a language they understand, ensuring compliance with the Miranda Doctrine. Foreigners have the right to consult with legal counsel, request the assistance of an interpreter, and notify their consulate or embassy of their situation. The police can detain individuals for up to **72 hours** without formally charging them, during which they must be processed at a police station where personal information is recorded, and relevant legal documents are prepared. After the 72-hour period, detainees must be presented before a judge, who will determine whether to release them or continue with legal proceedings, maintaining the individual's right to a fair trial throughout the process.[4]

Bail

In Spain, bail decisions for foreign nationals depend on the seriousness of the crime and the detainee's ties to the country. Judges may release someone without bail or set higher amounts if they're a flight risk. Bail can be paid in cash or through a surety company, and amounts are usually predetermined by law for each offense.

---

3   https://www.garrigues.com/en_GB/new/spain-new-comprehensive-law-equal-treatment-and-nondiscrimination-also-applies-employment

4   https://rodriguezbernal.com/foreigners-involved-in-criminal-proceedings-in-spain-some-valuable-tips/

If a detainee fails to appear in court, they face strict penalties, including losing the full bond and possible re-arrest. Insurance companies often serve as bail bondsmen in Spain, helping with the process. Detainees have the right to legal counsel and may contact their consulate for support.

It's highly recommended to seek legal advice—local lawyers and insurance companies can guide you through the bail process, and ensure all legal requirements are met. To find qualified bail bond agents in Spain, visit **https://lawzana.com/bail-bond-service-lawyers/madrid-madrid**.

Legal Representation

Foreigners are entitled to legal representation throughout this process, which is crucial for navigating the complexities of Spanish law and facilitating bail negotiations. Article 24 of the Spanish Constitution guarantees everyone the right to effective legal protection, which includes access to public defenders for those unable to afford private counsel. This legal aid is especially crucial in civil cases where lack of local knowledge can severely impact outcomes.

To access legal services, foreigners typically consult lawyers or law firms that specialize in their specific needs. Legal professionals in Spain are required to be registered with a Bar Association, ensuring adherence to professional standards. Organizations like the *Colegio de Abogados* provide resources to assist foreigners in finding appropriate legal representation, and many firms offer bilingual services to facilitate understanding of the legal process for non-Spanish speakers.

Besides your family, the first point of contact in case of an arrest should be your home country's embassy or consulate in Spain. They can provide you with important assistance, including:

- Ensuring that you are treated fairly and in accordance with local laws.
- Providing a list of local attorneys who speak your language.

- Helping to arrange communication with family or friends back home.
- Providing advice on your legal rights and obligations.

U.S. Embassy in Madrid

Calle de Serrano, 75
28006 Madrid, Spain
(+34) 91-587-2200

For a list of English-speaking attorneys in Spain, visit **https://es.usembassy.gov/legal-services/**.

Healthcare System and Medical Facilities

Spain is known for its excellent healthcare system, which is primarily public and provides nearly universal coverage to its residents. The country's medical facilities are well-equipped and staffed, with hospitals consistently delivering high standards of care. In the 2021 *Health Care Index*, Spain was ranked eighth out of 89 countries globally for healthcare quality and accessibility, reflecting its strong position among the top healthcare systems in Europe.[5]

Spain is home to several renowned hospitals that offer top-tier services for international patients. The **Hospital Universitario La Paz** in Madrid is known for its advanced medical technologies and wide range of specialties, attracting both local and foreign patients seeking specialized treatments. Another leading institution, the **Clínica Universidad de Navarra**, provides exceptional care with personalized treatment plans through its dedicated international patient services department, specializing in advanced procedures and complex medical cases. These hospitals exemplify Spain's commitment to high healthcare standards and cater to the needs of medical travelers.

---

5   https://www.expatica.com/es/healthcare/healthcare-basics/
     healthcare-in-spain-101467/

Access to Pre-Exposure Prophylaxis (PrEP) Treatment

PrEP is **legally available** in Spain through the public healthcare system. Oral PrEP (TDF/FTC) has been offered since 2019, while injectable PrEP (Apretude) was approved in 2023, it is still being rolled out publicly. It's dispensed only in hospital infectious disease or STI units, with access varying by region.

For eligible residents, PrEP is free under the National Health System, though non-residents face private costs of **€200–250/month (about $215-$270 USD)**. Access is stronger in cities, supported by NGOs, while pharmacies cannot dispense it. Telemedicine pilots are expanding access in rural areas.

Eligibility prioritizes men who have sex with men and transgender women with multiple risk factors. Users must complete HIV testing and regular medical check-ups to continue treatment.

 ## Safety Precautions for LGBTQ+ Travelers

While Spain is generally regarded as one of the safest countries, it's still wise to stay cautious and do your research. Look for LGBTQ+-friendly cities, venues, hotels, and activities to minimize the risk of discrimination. It's also important to stay informed by following the news for any uptick in homophobic incidents, particularly in more conservative regions. Consider joining *Law Of The Land* as a member for reliable updates!

Emergency Contact Numbers

- **Police:** 112 or 092 (local police)
- **Ambulance:** 112
- **Fire Department:** 112
- **U.S. Embassy in Madrid:** (+34) 91 587 2200

Useful Emergency Phrases in Spanish

HELP! – ¡Ayuda! *(ah-YOO-dah)*

CALL AN AMBULANCE! – ¡Llame a una ambulancia! *(YAH-meh ah oo-nah am-boo-LAHN-thyah)*

I NEED A DOCTOR – Necesito un médico *(neh-seh-SEE-toh oon MEH-dee-koh)*

POLICE – Policía *(poh-lee-SEE-ah)*

I'M LOST – Estoy perdido/a *(ehs-TOY pehr-DEE-doh/dah)*

IT'S AN EMERGENCY – Es una emergencia *(ehs oo-nah eh-mehr-HEN-thee-ah)*

THAILAND

Thailand is a democratic constitutional monarchy with a history of political instability marked by coups and military rule. The country is predominantly Buddhist, with Theravada Buddhism shaping much of Thai culture, values, and daily life, while Thai society emphasizes tradition, hierarchy, and communal harmony. Thailand is seen as **largely liberal regarding LGBTQ+ rights**, especially in cities like Bangkok, though there remain both legal progress and societal challenges.

 ## Politics and LGBTQ+ Legislation

Thailand's political landscape is marked by a tension between **liberal** movements, such as the growing influence of progressive parties, and **conservative** forces, particularly the military and royalist factions. This dynamic creates a conflict between aspirations for a more democratic society and the persistence of traditional power structures. While Thailand is considered largely liberal on LGBTQ+ rights, this stands in contrast to the historically conservative attitudes in Southeast Asia, with legal advancements and activism driving a complex, evolving journey toward equality.

In June 2024, **Thailand became the first Southeast Asian country to legalize same-sex marriage**, with the Senate passing the bill by a wide margin. The law grants same-sex couples full legal rights, **including adoption and inheritance**, and uses gender-neutral terms instead of "husband" and "wife." **Homosexuality is legal**, and there are no penalties for being LGBTQ+. While Thailand is considered one of the most LGBTQ+-friendly countries in Asia, social stigma may still exist, and LGBTQ+ individuals are advised to be discreet with public displays of affection.[6]

 ## LGBTQ+ Scene

Thailand is home to a vibrant and prominent drag scene, making it a popular destination for same-sex marriage celebrations and LGBTQ+ events. **Bangkok** is especially famous for its vibrant and energetic atmosphere, with **Silom 2**—known as the gay strip—being the main hub where all the excitement gathers.

While Bangkok is the heart of Thailand's LGBTQ+ scene, cities like **Chiang Mai, Pattaya**, and **Phuket** also have thriving gay communities, each offering a unique experience for visitors. These cities, like the capital, are known for their inclusivity and acceptance.

Thailand's Pride Month has become a vibrant celebration of LGBTQ+ rights and culture, with events throughout June promoting equality, visibility, and acceptance. Major events include the *Thailand PRIDE Festival* in the fall, Bangkok Pride in early summer, *Chiang Mai*

---

6   https://pridethailand.com/news/thailand2024

Colourful Pride Month, and regional festivals like *Pride Nation Samui* and *Discover Phuket Pride*. These celebrations are vital for fostering acceptance in Thai society and raising awareness about ongoing issues like discrimination, while marking progress toward the legalization of same-sex marriage and broader LGBTQ+ rights.

Beyond Pride Month, Thailand is home to several organizations that support the LGBTQ+ community, with one of the most accessible being the **Rainbow Sky Association of Thailand** (RSAT), based in Bangkok. RSAT offers assistance to LGBTQ+ individuals in areas such as healthcare, mental health support, and services for travelers.

 **LGBTQ+-Related Crime**

Despite growing support for the LGBTQ+ community in Thailand, many still face discrimination. LGBTQ+ individuals in Thailand often face significant discrimination and violence, with studies showing that 53% of LGBTQ+ respondents reported verbal harassment and 16% experienced sexual assault due to their sexual orientation or gender identity. Many LGBTQ+ people also feel pressured to hide their identities, with 42% admitting to pretending to be heterosexual in social or work settings. While urban areas are generally more accepting, hate crimes and abuse are more prevalent in conservative and rural regions, with reports indicating that 56% of LGBTQ+ individuals have faced bullying, including social exclusion, physical violence, and verbal harassment.[7]

LGBTQ+ travelers are advised to focus on more progressive cities like Bangkok and Chiang Mai, where they are more likely to experience acceptance and safety.

---

7   https://www.undp.org/thailand/press-releases/new-study-reveals-favour-able-attitudes-towards-lgbt-people-thailand-also-persistent-stigma-discrimination-violence-and

LGBTQ+ and Prostitution

While **prostitution remains illegal in Thailand**, it persists underground, leaving sex workers, especially transgender individuals, vulnerable to abuse, exploitation, and legal consequences. Transgender sex workers often face violence from clients but are treated as criminals under Thai law, making it difficult to seek justice. Many sex workers endure unsafe conditions and risk abuse without legal protections, particularly freelancers who work without agency support.

Organizations like *Service Workers in Group Foundation* (SWING) advocate for the decriminalization of sex work and provide essential support, including health services, shelter, and advocacy. Despite the challenges, there is growing demand for legal reform to protect sex workers' rights and improve their working conditions.[8]

LGBTQ+ and Jail System

Thailand's jail system is characterized by significant overcrowding and challenging living conditions, with prisons operating at more than double their official capacity, affecting the humane treatment of inmates. As of early 2020, the prison population had increased to over 374,000 inmates, a substantial number of whom are incarcerated for drug-related offenses, highlighting an ongoing struggle with narcotics issues.[9] Despite efforts to reform the system and introduce rehabilitation programs, the quality of food, healthcare, and overall treatment of prisoners remains inadequate, leading to numerous human rights concerns.

Even though Thailand has made significant progress in LGBTQ+ rights, legal recognition of gender identity remains limited, particularly concerning gender reassignment surgeries and their acknowledgment in prisons. As of 2016, around 4,448 LGBTQ+ individuals were incarcerated in Thailand, often facing discrimination and violence, especially those

---

8   https://prachataienglish.com/node/10268
9   https://en.wikipedia.org/wiki/Department_of_Corrections_(Thailand)

who do not conform to traditional gender norms.[10] Transgender prisoners face additional challenges, such as inadequate medical care and heightened risks of violence when housed with male inmates. Although policies have been introduced to improve safety, issues of discrimination and unsafe conditions continue.

 ## Arrested in Thailand

The arrest process for foreigners in Thailand follows the country's legal procedures, ensuring due process, with police having the authority to arrest with or without a warrant, depending on the circumstances. Upon arrest, foreign nationals must be informed of the charges and their rights, including the right to remain silent and the right to legal representation. They also have the right to contact their embassy or consulate for assistance, and family members can be notified of the arrest. Foreigners can be held for up to **48 hours** without formal charges, after which they must be brought before a judge.[11]

Bail

Bail in Thailand is regulated by the Criminal Procedure Code and is generally available for non-capital offenses, depending on crime severity, criminal history, and flight risk. Courts set the bail amount, and property can be used as collateral, sometimes with installment options. Foreigners may post bail but must surrender their passport or a certified copy. Bail is usually denied for serious crimes, like drug offenses, or when flight risk is high. Violating bail conditions can lead to revocation and re-arrest. Legal assistance from the Thai Bar Association or criminal law firms is recommended. You can find qualified bail bondsman service agents at **https://lawzana.com/bail-bond-service-lawyers/thailand**.

---

10 https://thaicriminology.com/transgender-prisoners-in-thailand-keep-growing.html

11 https://travel.gc.ca/travelling/advisories/overview-of-the-criminal-law-system-in-thailand

Legal Representation

Being arrested while visiting Thailand can be a stressful and disorienting experience, particularly for tourists and foreign nationals unfamiliar with the local legal system. Legal representation is crucial as the local legal system can be complex and challenging, especially with language barriers and cultural differences. Engaging a qualified local lawyer ensures that a foreign national's rights are protected, particularly in criminal cases, civil disputes, and immigration matters. Embassies and consulates can assist by providing a list of trusted attorneys in the area and facilitating communication with family members. In addition to legal counsel, family and friends can offer support, while non-governmental organizations (NGOs) can provide further help. Two of the most notable NGOs in this regard are **Asylum Access Thailand** (AAT) and the **Thailand Institute of Justice** (TIJ).

> ### U.S. Embassy Bangkok
> 95 Wireless Road
> Bangkok 10330, Thailand
> Tel: +66-2-205-4000

A list of English-speaking attorneys in Thailand can be found through the U.S. State Department at **https://th.usembassy.gov/wp-content/uploads/sites/90/Attorney-List-Updated-Nov-4-2024.pdf**

Healthcare System and Medical Facilities

Thailand's medical facilities are renowned for their high quality and affordability, making the country a premier destination for medical tourism in Southeast Asia. The healthcare system features a robust mixture of public and private hospitals, with many private institutions catering effectively to expatriates and international patients due to their advanced technology, multilingual staff, and shorter wait times. Notable hospitals, such as **Bumrungrad International Hospital** and **Bangkok Hospital** in Bangkok, as well as **Samitivej Hospital**, offer comprehensive services and are accredited by international bodies, ensuring high standards of care. Additionally, **Phuket International Hospital** and **Chiang Mai Ram Hospital** have established themselves as reputable healthcare providers, catering to the needs of both locals and foreign patients. The affordability of treatments—often significantly lower than in Western countries—coupled with the Thai government's efforts to promote medical tourism, has further solidified the nation's reputation for quality healthcare services.

Access to Pre-Exposure Prophylaxis (PrEP) Treatment

PrEP access in Thailand was added to the Universal Health Coverage Scheme (UCS) in 2019, making oral PrEP free for eligible Thai citizens at public hospitals and designated clinics. Injectable PrEP became available in early 2025 at select urban clinics but is not yet part of the nationwide public system.

For foreigners and those outside UCS, oral PrEP costs around THB 495–1,090 ($14–$30 USD) per month, with initial lab tests around THB 900 ($26 USD). Injectable PrEP is available privately at THB 14,900–15,900 ($420–$450 USD) per dose.

Access points include public hospitals, NGOs, and key population-led clinics, though 2023 regulations restricted prescribing and dispensing to government doctors and pharmacies, reducing community distribution. Urban areas (Bangkok, Chiang Mai, Pattaya) have the best access; rural access is limited. Some private clinics offer telemedicine and home delivery.

Eligibility requires behavioral risk factors, confirmed HIV-negative status, STI screening, and regular follow-up tests every three months.

 ## Safety Precautions for LGBTQ+ Travelers

Thailand is part of a broader region with deeply rooted traditions, where many East Asian countries face challenges when it comes to embracing change and progressive thinking. However, Thailand stands out for its openness and progressiveness, creating many opportunities for people, both during Pride Month and throughout the year, to celebrate their identities. While it's safe for travelers to be open about their sexuality and be with their partners, it's still important to approach the culture with respect and courtesy. As long as travelers are considerate, they can expect to feel welcomed and experience little to no issues.

Emergency Contact Numbers

- **Police:** 191
- **Ambulance:** 1669
- **Fire Department:** 199
- **U.S. Embassy in Bangkok:** +66-2-205-4000

Useful Emergency Phrases in Thai

HELP! – ช่วยด้วย! (Chuai duai!)

CALL AN AMBULANCE! – เรียกรถพยาบาล! (Rîak rót phá-yaa-baan!)

I NEED A DOCTOR – ฉันต้องการหมอ (Chăn tông-gaan mŏr)

POLICE – ตำรวจ (Tam-rùat)

I'M LOST – ฉันหลงทาง (Chăn lŏng thaang)

IT'S AN EMERGENCY – นี่คือเหตุฉุกเฉิน (Nîi kheu hèet chùk-chĕrn)

 # PORTUGAL

Portugal is a parliamentary democracy marked by a stable political system, regular elections, and a firm commitment to civil liberties, although it faces some challenges relating to corruption and social inequality. The majority of the population identifies as Roman Catholic; however, many are non-practicing, and Portugal ensures religious freedom. Additionally, Portugal is recognized as one of the most liberal nations in Europe concerning LGBTQ+ rights, having made significant progress in promoting equality and acceptance for LGBTQ+ individuals over recent decades.

 ## Politics and LGBTQ+ Legislation

Portugal is generally considered politically liberal, characterized by progressive policies and a strong commitment to civil liberties, including LGBTQ+ rights and social justice. The dominant political parties, such as the Socialist Party, promote social democracy and pro-European Union sentiments, reflecting a tendency towards liberal ideals. Despite facing challenges such as corruption and social inequality, the overall political landscape remains focused on promoting inclusivity and protection of individual rights.

Portugal has made significant strides in LGBTQ+ rights, with key milestones including the **decriminalization of homosexuality in 1982, the legalization of same-sex marriage in 2010, adoption rights for same-sex couples in 2016, and the 2018 law allowing gender identity changes without surgery**. The country has strong anti-discrimination protections, including constitutional and employment-based laws. While Portugal is considered LGBTQ+-friendly, some societal prejudice remains, highlighting the need for continued awareness and acceptance efforts.

 ## LGBTQ+ Scene

Portugal is considered one of the safest countries for LGBTQ+ individuals, thanks to its progressive attitude and strong commitment to equality. Public support for LGBTQ+ rights has steadily grown over the years, with a significant majority of Portuguese people now in favor of same-sex marriage and viewing same-sex relationships as completely acceptable.

Lisbon and Porto are home to Portugal's two largest LGBTQ+ scenes. In Lisbon, Rua Barroca is the heart of the gay scene, though LGBTQ+ establishments are scattered throughout the city. **Lisbon** is renowned as one of the best destinations for LGBTQ+ travelers, with lively gay bars, a vibrant underground drag scene, and a welcoming atmosphere. **Porto**, similarly, offers a mix of gay-friendly bars, clubs, and parties, along with unique spots like the gay-run Sauna Camoes. Beyond the cities, the **Algarve region** has long been a safe haven for LGBTQ+ immigrants and retirees. Known for its tourist-friendly vibe, the Algarve features a mix of luxury and affordable restaurants, fantastic hotels, gay nightclubs, and gay-owned businesses, making it a top getaway for LGBTQ+ travelers.

Lisbon's *Gay Pride* goes beyond celebration, focusing on raising awareness of the issues facing the LGBTQ+ community, which gives it a deeper, more meaningful vibe. While Lisbon's gay scene may not be as large as some other European cities, hosting *Eurovision 2023* helped solidify its status as a top destination for gay travelers. With late-night parties, sunny weather, gay-friendly nude beaches, affordable alcohol, and the warm hospitality of the Portuguese people, Lisbon truly offers something special for LGBTQ+ visitors.[12]

Beyond Pride Month, two prominent organizations that support the LGBTQ+ community are the **Youth Pride Association** (YPA) and **the Lisbon Gay and Lesbian Centre** (CGL). The YPA focuses on enhancing social inclusion and quality of life for LGBTQ+ individuals and their families, while combating discrimination and promoting human rights. Meanwhile, the CGL serves as a national non-profit dedicated to fostering acceptance in educational settings, providing valuable resources and support both locally and internationally

---

12 https://www.beportugal.com/lisbon-gay-pride/

 ## LGBTQ+-Related Crime

While Portugal has made significant strides in LGBTQ+ rights, discrimination remains, particularly against the transgender community. A 2020 EU survey found that 40% of LGBTQ+ respondents in Portugal faced discrimination, with 30% experiencing harassment and 20% workplace discrimination. One in five transgender individuals had been attacked in the past five years, and nearly 15% reported violence by police. Given these challenges, LGBTQ+ tourists should be cautious and discreet about their identity, especially in less inclusive environments.[13]

LGBTQ+ and Prostitution

While prostitution itself is legal, organized prostitution—where a third party, such as a brothel or strip club, profits from the sex work—is not. This means that while individuals can legally offer sexual services, businesses cannot profit from managing or organizing such activities.

Statistics specifically detailing the LGBTQ+ population in prostitution in Portugal are limited; however, studies indicate that a notable percentage, particularly transgender individuals, engage in sex work due to socio-economic pressures exacerbated by discrimination in the labor market. For instance, approximately 19.8% of apartment sex workers identified as transgender, reflecting significant representation within the industry. LGBTQ+ sex workers often face increased vulnerabilities, including violence and discrimination, which hinder their access to healthcare and support services.[14]

---

13 https://journals.sagepub.com/doi/10.1177/13634607231197059?icid=int.sj-abstract.citing-articles.3

14 https://fra.europa.eu/sites/default/files/fra_uploads/lgbti-survey-country-data_portugal.pdf

LGBTQ+ and Jail System

Portugal's jail system consists of 49 prisons, which include central, regional, and military institutions, accommodating a diverse inmate population.[15] As of recent reports, the prison occupancy rate is over 90%, indicating significant overcrowding. The Portuguese penal system prioritizes rehabilitation and social reintegration of offenders, reflected in various programs focusing on vocational training and support services.[16]

There is limited data on the number of LGBTQ+ individuals in Portuguese prisons, but studies show they face significant challenges, especially transgender prisoners, who are at higher risk of discrimination and violence. The stigma and invisibility of LGBTQ+ identities worsen their vulnerabilities, making it harder to seek help. LGBTQ+ prisoners often face violence from fellow inmates, particularly transgender individuals housed according to their assigned sex at birth. They also struggle with inadequate healthcare, including lack of access to mental health services and hormone therapy, affecting their overall well-being.[17]

 ## Arrested in Portugal

Foreigners can be arrested in Portugal for various reasons, including criminal activities such as drug offenses, theft, assault, public disorder violations, or breaches of immigration laws, such as overstaying a visa.[18]

In Portugal, individuals who are detained by law enforcement must be brought before a magistrate within **48 hours** of their arrest. This is in

15 https://photius.com/countries/portugal/national_security/portugal_national_security_penal_system.html

16 https://www.tandfonline.com/doi/full/10.1080/10509674.2024.2353568

17 https://journals.sagepub.com/doi/10.1177/13634607231197059?icid=int.sj-abstract.citing-articles.3

18 https://ocindex.net/country/portugal#:~:text=An%20assessment%20of%20the%20value%2C%20prevalence%20and%20non%2Dmonetary)

line with the constitutional principle that limits the duration of pretrial detention to ensure the individual's right to a fair and speedy trial. The 48-hour period begins from the moment of arrest, and during this time, the detainee must be informed of the charges and given the opportunity to challenge their detention. If the magistrate determines that there is sufficient evidence to justify continued detention, the individual may remain in custody, though they will still have the right to appeal the decision. Alternatively, the magistrate may order release or other measures, such as bail or judicial supervision, depending on the circumstances.

Upon arrest, they are entitled to several rights, including being informed of the charges against them and their rights in a language they understand. They have the right to contact their consulate or embassy for assistance, access legal representation, and receive necessary medical care. The Portuguese legal system ensures that arrested foreigners are treated with dignity, protected from inhumane treatment, and allowed to remain silent until they have consulted a lawyer, which reinforces the country's commitment to international human rights standards.

Bail

In Portugal, bail is regulated by the Penal Code and related legal procedures. There are two main approaches: conditional liberty, which allows release under court-imposed conditions (e.g., movement restrictions, regular reporting), and preventive detention, used when there are high risks of flight or evidence tampering, leading to denial of bail.

Bail amounts are set by judges based on case severity and risk, with no fixed limits—ranging from a few hundred euros for minor offenses to several thousand for serious crimes.

For bail assistance, it's important to hire a qualified lawyer specializing in criminal law, understand their fee structures, and maintain communication with them. Additional resources include the Portuguese Bar Association and the Directorate-General for Justice Policy. You can also research reputable bail bondsman agents in Portugal at **https://lawzana.com/bail-bond-service-lawyers/lisbon-lisbon.**

Legal Representation

Navigating legal matters in a foreign country can be daunting for visitors, particularly since language and cultural barriers may complicate the process. For foreign visitors needing legal assistance, it is essential to seek representation from professionals knowledgeable about Portuguese law and capable of communicating in the visitor's native language. Specialized law firms, such as **Urban Thier & Federer, P.A.**, provide services that cater specifically to Americans residing in or visiting Portugal, ensuring legal needs are met across various areas like immigration, business, and civil law.[19] Additionally, resources exist for those facing financial constraints, including access to state-funded legal aid through Segurança Social, which can help cover attorney fees for eligible individuals.[20]

The Portuguese Bar Association[21] plays a crucial role in appointing lawyers to those who cannot afford legal representation, thereby ensuring that justice is accessible to all, regardless of their financial situation. Visitors should also leverage their embassy or consulate services, which can provide lists of local attorneys and general support in navigating the legal landscape.

U.S. Embassy in Lisbon

Avenida das Forças Armadas

1600-081 Lisboa

Phone: 351-21-727-3300

Email: conslisbon@state.gov.

You can access the list of English-speaking attorneys in Portugal at **https://common.usembassy.gov/wp-content/uploads/sites/157/2024/03/Attorneys-list-2022-portugal.pdf**.

---

19 https://www.urbanthier.com/blog/2024/07/legal-team-for-americans-living-in-or-visiting-portugal

20 https://withportugal.com/en/blog/apoio-judiciario-2024

21 https://portal.oa.pt/ordem/organization

Healthcare System and Medical Facilities

Portugal offers an accessible and well-structured healthcare system for travelers, ensuring that both residents and visitors can receive necessary medical attention. International travelers are advised to carry travel insurance that covers health expenses, as tourists are not covered by the public healthcare system, the Serviço Nacional de Saúde (SNS). In emergencies, travelers can call **112** for immediate medical assistance, which connects them to ambulance services, police, and fire departments. Many hospitals, particularly in urban areas, are equipped to handle a range of medical issues and often have English-speaking staff to help facilitate care for non-Portuguese speakers.

Portugal has several hospitals and healthcare facilities specifically geared toward foreign visitors, particularly in major cities and tourist destinations. Many hospitals, such as **Hospital da Luz** and **CUF hospitals**, are known for their high-quality care and have multilingual staff who can assist international patients. These facilities are often equipped to accept international health insurance plans, making it easier for travelers to access necessary medical services without facing substantial out-of-pocket costs. In addition, they provide a range of services tailored to expatriates and tourists, including emergency care, general consultations, and specialized treatments, ensuring that foreign visitors can receive effective and timely healthcare during their stay in Portugal.

Access to Pre-Exposure Prophylaxis (PrEP) Treatment

PrEP has been part of Portugal's public health system (SNS) since 2018, dispensed mainly at hospital infectious disease clinics. It is free for eligible residents (including migrants with 90+ days in Portugal), covering medication, consultations, and lab tests. However, non-residents and tourists are not eligible for free PrEP and must rely on limited private options, costing around €210/month (about $225 USD).

Access is concentrated in Lisbon and northern regions, with rural areas facing major barriers. Uptake remains low (~1,600 users), hindered by stigma, long hospital wait times, and lack of awareness.

43

Community-based pilot services (e.g., Checkpoint LX, GAT Intendente) launched in 2023 aim to expand access but are not yet fully funded.

Eligibility follows national guidelines (Norma 025/2017, updated 2018) for people at high HIV risk (e.g., recent condomless sex, HIV-positive partners without viral suppression, STIs, drug injection, chemsex, serodiscordant couples planning pregnancy). Clinical protocols require HIV-negative status, STI screening, kidney/liver tests, and 3-month follow-ups.

Portugal's criteria are among the most sensitive in Europe, but studies suggest they may still miss up to 40% of future HIV cases.

 ## Safety Precautions for LGBTQ+ Travelers

Portugal is considered one of the safest countries for the LGBTQ+ community, with a history of low violence and high levels of acceptance. However, outside of Pride Month and in smaller, less urban areas, it's advisable for travelers to exercise caution and be discreet about their sexuality. While the country is largely welcoming, being conservative and mindful of local norms in certain areas is still a smart approach.

Emergency Contact Numbers

- **Police:** 112 /117
- **Ambulance:** 112
- **Fire Department:** 112
- **U.S. Embassy in Lisbon:** +351 21 770 2122

Useful Emergency Phrases in Portuguese

HELP! – Socorro! *(so-KOH-hoo)*

CALL AN AMBULANCE! – Chame uma ambulância! *(SHAH-mee OO-mah ahm-boo-LAN-syah)*

I NEED A DOCTOR – Preciso de um médico *(preh-SEE-zoo jee oong MEH-jee-koo)*

POLICE – Polícia *(poo-LEE-syah)*

I'M LOST – Estou perdido/a *(es-TOH pehr-DEE-doo for males, pehr-DEE-dah for females)*

IT'S AN EMERGENCY – É uma emergência *(EH OO-mah eh-mehr-ZHEN-syah)*

FRANCE

France is a diverse and influential country located in Western Europe, known for its rich history, culture, and global impact. As a democratic republic with a semi-presidential system, France has a long tradition of republican values, secularism, and human rights. Its landscape is varied, from the rolling vineyards of Bordeaux to the Alps and Mediterranean coastline. France is a global leader in art, fashion, and cuisine, while also being a key player in international diplomacy, the European Union, and global organizations like the United Nations. With a population of over 67 million, it is home to diverse regional cultures and traditions, while maintaining a strong sense of national identity rooted in its revolutionary past.

Politics and LGBTQ+ Legislation

France is considered a primarily **liberal** country, particularly in terms of social policies, such as strong protections for individual rights, progressive stances on issues like same-sex marriage, and a commitment to secularism. France has developed one of the most comprehensive legal frameworks for LGBTQ+ rights in the world. **Key legislation includes the decriminalization of homosexuality in 1791, the equalization of the age of consent in 1982, and the legalization of same-sex marriage and adoption in 2013.** Anti-discrimination laws protecting sexual orientation and gender identity have been in place since 1985, with further enforcement in 2012. Transgender individuals gained the right to change their legal gender without surgery in 2016. France also has laws targeting hate crimes and hate speech against LGBTQ+ individuals, while actively advocating for LGBTQ+ rights internationally.

While there are currently no punishable crimes associated with the LGBTQ+ community in France, the ongoing political unrest within the French government raises concerns that this could change in the future. As such, it's crucial for LGBTQ+ travelers to stay informed and up to date on any legal developments that may affect their rights. A Law of The Land membership would provide critical updates.

 ## LGBTQ+ Scene

Paris, particularly the Le Marais district, is home to one of the most vibrant gay scenes in Europe, rivaled only by Madrid and London. **Nice**, known for its summer allure, offers not one, but four gay beaches, adding to France's appeal as an LGBTQ+ destination. The country boasts a wealth of Pride events, bars, clubs, and a sex-positive culture, with even lesbian-focused spaces contributing to its status as a favorite spot for LGBTQ+ travelers worldwide. **Bordeaux**, though lacking a designated gay district, also offers a lively LGBTQ+ scene. Visitors can enjoy a range of gay bars, nightclubs, and LGBTQ+-friendly hotels that welcome all guests. **Montpellier** is also a top destination for LGBTQ+ travelers, known for its artistic, food, and shopping scenes, where gay people are embraced as a natural part of the city's culture.

France has a long history of LGBTQ+ activism, with the first Pride march in Paris in 1977, evolving into one of Europe's largest celebrations. Pride

Month not only celebrates LGBTQ+ culture but also highlights the ongoing fight for equality. Key events include *Paris Pride* (Marche des Fiertés), held on the last Saturday of June, and regional celebrations like *Lyon Pride* and *Nice Pride*, showcasing local LGBTQ+ culture. While progress, such as the legalization of same-sex marriage in 2013, has been made, Pride Month also raises awareness about ongoing issues like discrimination and healthcare access. Local businesses and organizations engage by hosting events and creating safe spaces, fostering a sense of community and support.

Beyond Pride Month, the LGBTQ+ scene in France thrives year-round. In addition to Paris Pride, held in late June, notable events include Lou *Queernava* in Nice, coinciding with the city's Carnival in February, and the *Festival des Cultures LGBT* in Paris each January, which showcases gay cinema from around the world. These events, along with other community initiatives, contribute to a rich cultural calendar that supports LGBTQ+ visibility and inclusion throughout the year.

 ## LGBTQ+-Related Crime

While same-sex marriage is legal in France, hate crimes against the LGBTQ+ community have been on the rise. In 2023, violent crimes and threats increased by 19%, and fines for insulting LGBTQ+ individuals, issued by French police and the Gendarmerie, rose by 4%, following a 9% decline in 2022. Despite this, victims remain hesitant to report incidents, according to the country's statistical service.[22]

SOS Homophobie has raised concerns over growing anti-LGBTQ+ sentiment, with early 2024 data confirming the troubling trend. Most attacks are perpetrated by individuals in their 30s and older, so it's recommended for LGBTQ+ travelers to remain discreet about their sexuality, especially in unfamiliar or less accepting areas.

---

[22] https://www.reuters.com/world/europe/
france-anti-lgbt-offences-rose-13-2023-2024-05-16/

LGBTQ+ and Prostitution

Since Law No. 2016-444, **buying sex has been illegal in France, while selling sex remains legal**, following the Nordic model that criminalizes demand but aims to support sex workers. LGBTQ+ individuals, particularly male sex workers, represent a significant but marginalized group within the industry, facing unique challenges. They often experience discrimination, violence, and rejection from social services, and are disproportionately targeted by law enforcement. Advocacy groups like *STRASS* are pushing for decriminalization and better protections for LGBTQ+ sex workers, as violence has increased since the law's implementation.

LGBTQ+ and Jail System

Historically, LGBTQ+ individuals have been disproportionately represented in the criminal justice system. For example, while specific statistics on the current LGBTQ+ population in French prisons are difficult to quantify, historical patterns suggest a significant over-representation of LGBTQ+ individuals in incarceration rates, particularly among marginalized groups. Trans women are often incarcerated in men's facilities, leading to potential victimization and abuse. Though exact numbers are not typically reported, the experiences of LGBTQ+ people in prisons often include higher rates of isolation, stigma, and abuse compared to their heterosexual counterparts. Studies indicate that LGBTQ+ detainees experience unique mental health challenges exacerbated by the environment of incarceration.

 **Arrested in France**

The arrest process for foreign visitors in France initiates as soon as the authorities identify the individual as needing to be detained due to alleged wrongdoing. Initially, the police will conduct an identification check, during which they may ask for the visitor's passport and other identifying documents. If arrested, the individual will be informed of the reasons for the arrest and their rights, including the right to remain silent and the right to contact their consulate or embassy for assistance.[23] During this time, it is crucial for the detainee to remain calm and cooperate, as any resistance could lead to further complications.

Following the initial arrest, the foreign visitor may be taken to a police station for questioning. According to French law, detainees, including foreign nationals, must be brought before a magistrate within **48 hours** of their arrest, who will then determine whether there is sufficient evidence to continue the legal process or to release the individual.[24] Throughout this process, detainees have the right to legal counsel, and if they cannot afford one, a government-appointed lawyer will be provided. Importantly, foreign visitors are also entitled to have their consulate notified, ensuring they receive necessary support and guidance during legal proceedings.

Bail

France has a restrictive bail system, where release on judicial supervision may be granted based on factors such as offense severity, flight risk, and community ties. Foreign visitors often face extra scrutiny due to residency and absconding concerns. If bail is approved, conditions may include regular reporting or surrendering a passport.

Bail bond service laws differ by region, so consulting a local lawyer is essential to understand rights and obligations. Assistance can also be sought through the French Bar Association, legal aid organizations, or licensed bail bondsmen. A lisst of bail bond service agents in France can be accessed at **https://lawzana.com/bail-bond-service-lawyers/ france.**

Legal Representation

In France, legal representation for foreign detainees is a critical aspect of ensuring that their rights are upheld within the legal system. Under

---

23   https://www.aclu.org/know-your-rights/immigrants-rights

24   https://www.sba-avocats.com/criminal-defense-attorney-paris-france-police-custody.html

French law, all individuals, including foreigners, have the right to legal counsel when detained. This right is specifically enshrined in the *Code of Entry and Residence of Foreigners* and of the *Right of Asylum*, which mandates that detainees be informed of their legal rights, including the provision for legal assistance. Foreign detainees can secure free legal representation through public defense systems if they cannot afford to hire an attorney, ensuring that economic status does not impede access to justice.[25]

Moreover, various non-governmental organizations (NGOs) in France play a vital role in assisting foreign detainees. These organizations provide legal advice and representation tailored to the complex needs of foreigners, including issues related to immigration and detention procedures. For instance, NGOs such as *La Cimade* and France *Terre d'Asile* actively engage with detainees in administrative detention centers, offering support in understanding legal processes and helping to navigate appeals against detention. This collaborative effort between public defense mechanisms and NGOs helps to bolster the legal framework protecting foreign detainees, ensuring their rights are safeguarded throughout their interactions with the French legal system.

Most importantly, you should always contact your home embassy as soon as possible; they can provide essential assistance in navigating the local legal system. While embassies cannot provide direct legal counsel, they can offer a list of local lawyers who specialize in the area of law you need, ensuring you find someone qualified to represent your interests. For a list of English-speaking attorneys in France, provided by the U.S. State Department, please visit **https://fr.usembassy.gov/english-speaking-attorneys-in-france/**.

U.S. Embassy in France

2 avenue Gabriel

75008 Paris, France

---

25 https://asylumineurope.org/reports/country/france/
    detention-asylum-seekers/procedural-safeguards/
    legal-assistance-review-detention/

Healthcare System and Medical Facilities

France's healthcare system is renowned for its excellence and universal coverage, primarily structured around a statutory health insurance (SHI) model that ensures nearly all residents have access to comprehensive medical services.[26] Funded mainly through payroll taxes and a national income tax, the system allocates resources to both public and private healthcare providers, allowing for a mix of services that cater to diverse patient needs. Patients typically enjoy low out-of-pocket costs, benefited further by supplementary insurance that covers additional services not included under SHI, such as dental and vision care -reaching accessibility, contributing to high patient satisfaction and health outcomes.

France offers a range of hospitals specifically tailored to meet the needs of international travelers, particularly in major cities like Paris, Nice, and Lyon. Notable facilities include the **American Hospital of Paris** and the **Institut Hospitalier Franco-Britannique**, both of which provide high-quality medical care and feature multilingual staff to facilitate communication for expatriates and tourists. These hospitals accommodate patients from diverse backgrounds, ensuring a comfortable experience while addressing various health concerns. Additional centers, such as the **Institut Curie**, specialize in specific fields like oncology, welcoming foreign patients and providing dedicated support throughout their treatment. Overall, France's healthcare system proves to be accessible and accommodating for international visitors seeking medical assistance.

Pre-Exposure Prophylaxis (PrEP) Treatment

PrEP has been legally available and reimbursed in France since 2016 (fully authorized in 2017). Oral PrEP is widely available, while injectable PrEP (cabotegravir) is offered at select centers but not yet nationwide. All costs—including consultations, lab tests, and medication—are covered under national health insurance, though first-time users may pay a

---

26 https://www.commonwealthfund.org/international-health-policy-center/
countries/france

€91 co-payment (about $100 USD). With complementary insurance or low-income status, PrEP can be accessed free.

Non-residents and tourists are excluded from free coverage and must pay privately, typically €150–€210 ($165–$230 USD) monthly.

Access is primarily through hospital infectious disease units, free sexual health centers (CeGIDDs), and since 2021, general practitioners, which expanded reach but still leaves rural areas underserved. Community organizations play a role in awareness and linkage.

Eligibility is based on behavioral and clinical risk factors (e.g., condomless sex, recent STIs, multiple PEP uses, HIV-unknown partners). Before starting, candidates must test HIV-negative and undergo health screening; follow-ups with blood and STI testing occur every three months.

Despite an estimated 100,000 MSM being eligible, uptake remains limited, with about 42,000 users by mid-2021.

 ## Safety Precautions for LGBTQ+ Travelers

Staying informed is essential for LGBTQ+ travelers in France, especially given the political instability and shifting government dynamics. While LGBTQ+ rights remain legal and protected for now, concerns have emerged within the community due to political changes that could lead to a weakening of protections and a rise in homophobic sentiment. As a result, travelers should exercise caution, particularly in rural areas. While public expressions of LGBTQ+ identity are generally safe in larger cities, it's wise to keep a low profile and minimize public displays of affection to avoid drawing unwanted attention. By staying aware and practicing discretion, LGBTQ+ travelers can enjoy a safe and fulfilling visit to France.[27]

27 https://www.france24.com/en/europe/20240619-rights-safety-lgbtq-people-danger-risk-far-right-win-french-parliamentary-elections-bardella-le-pen-macron

Emergency Contact Numbers

- **Police:** 17
- **Ambulance:** 15
- **Fire Department:** 18
- **U.S. Embassy in Paris:** +33 1 43 12 22 22

Useful Emergency Phrases in French

HELP! – Au secours! (*oh skoor*)

CALL AN AMBULANCE! – Appelez une ambulance ! (*ah-pleh oon ahm-byoo-lahns*)

I NEED A DOCTOR – J'ai besoin d'un médecin (*zhay buh-zwan dun med-sanh*)

POLICE – Police (*poh-leess*)

I'M LOST – Je suis perdu(e) (*zhuh swee pair-doo for males, pair-due for females*)

IT'S AN EMERGENCY – C'est une urgence (*seh oon ur-zhahns*)

MALTA

Malta is a small island nation located in the Mediterranean Sea, south of Italy, known for its rich history, strategic location, and vibrant cultural heritage. It is a republic with a parliamentary system and a member of the European Union. Malta's history spans thousands of years, with significant influences from the Phoenicians, Romans, Arabs, and the Knights of St. John, whose legacy is evident in the island's impressive fortifications and Baroque architecture. Malta's culture is a blend of Mediterranean and British influences, with a strong emphasis on tradition, family, and religious values, as Roman Catholicism plays a central role in society. Socially, the country has seen increasing modernization, with progressive policies on LGBTQ+ rights and a growing emphasis on education and social welfare.

 ## Politics and LGBTQ+ Legislation

Dominated by two major parties—the Labour Party (center-left) and the Nationalist Party (center-right)—the country exhibits a blend of **progressive** social policies and traditional **conservatism**. Despite its strong Roman Catholic roots—divorce was only legalized in 2011, and abortion remains illegal—the country underwent a remarkable transformation after Marie Louise Coleiro Preca was elected president in 2014. She introduced groundbreaking pro-LGBTQ+ legislation, even criminalizing conversion therapy. Helena Dalli, the Civil Liberties Minister at the time, played a key role in advancing progressive trans rights laws. In a striking reversal, support for same-sex marriage jumped from just 18% in a 2006 Eurobarometer poll to 67% by 2019—the largest increase of any country.[28]

 ## LGBTQ+ Scene

The population of this island nation is about half a million people, and correspondingly the LGBTQ+ scene is relatively small. Nevertheless, Malta offers a variety of LGBTQ+-friendly bars, restaurants, and hotels, and Malta Pride, held in September, is considered one of the best late-summer Pride events in Europe.

---

28 https://outadventures.com/gay-travel-blog/
the-worlds-10-greatest-lgbt-friendly-countries-for-travellers/

At the forefront of the LGBTQ+ community is *Allied Rainbow Communities* (ARC), a group made up of LGBTQ+ individuals dedicated to promoting pride and supporting their community. ARC organized the 2024 celebrations, which included parades, concerts, and a variety of activities that offered days of enjoyment for everyone. The group uses this platform to raise global awareness about LGBTQ+ issues, and is also involved in hosting summits and discussions, which are broadcast on TV for a wider audience to watch and engage with.

As of 2023, Malta continues to hold the number one position on the *Rainbow Europe ILGA* index with a score of 89%, an index designed to assess and illustrate the legal and policy situation of LGBTI people across Europe, with annual updates reflecting progress or regression.[29] **Senglea**, and **Cospicua** are major cities in Malta that are great choices for gay travelers. These cities are known for being more open and welcoming, with a high volume of tourists, making them more inclusive and LGBTQ+ friendly.

 **LGBTQ+-Related Crime**

Besides being one of only five countries in the world to grant LGBT people equal constitutional rights, Malta has the second-lowest LGBTQ+-related crime statistics, with about 8% of the LGBTQ+ community reporting violent or sexual crimes linked to their sexual orientation.[30]

Malta being one of the safest places for the LGBTQ+ community, the numbers related to crime have historically been low. However, this doesn't mean such incidents don't occur. It is always advisable that tourists keep their sexuality private when around strangers or in unfamiliar areas, as a precaution.

---

29 https://www.ilga-europe.org/report/rainbow-europe-2023/

30 https://www.independent.com.mt/articles/2024-05-14/local-news/8-of-LGBTIQ-in-Malta-were-victims-of-physical-or-sexual-attacks-due-to-their-sexual-orientation-6736261092

LGBTQ+ and Prostitution

While **prostitution in Malta is legal**, other activities associated with it are not. It is illegal to run or own a brothel, or to profit from the prostitution of others in Malta, with some offenses punishable by up to 2 years in prison. Therefore, it's important for individuals to remain aware of their surroundings and avoid situations that may be linked to prostitution, particularly for those who may be targeted because of their LGBTQ+ identity.

LGBTQ+ and Jail System

The situation of LGBTQ+ individuals in prisons in Malta reflects broader issues of discrimination, violence, and the need for systemic reforms. While Malta is recognized for its advancements in LGBTQ+ rights, the conditions and treatment of LGBTQ+ prisoners remain a concern.

Accurate statistics regarding the population of LGBTQ+ individuals in Maltese prisons are not readily available, as specific data on sexual orientation or gender identity among inmates tends to be underreported. However, indications suggest that LGBTQ+ individuals, especially transgender and non-binary people, may face higher rates of incarceration and victimization compared to their heterosexual counterparts. Like elsewhere, LGBTQ+ inmates experience issues related to equitable healthcare and to mental health care.

However, Malta is more progressive in implementing policies to ensure that the rights of transgender, gender variant, and intersex inmates are recognized and respected. This policy mandates that inmates be housed in accordance with their gender identity. In addition, the Constitution of Malta prohibits discrimination on the basis of sexual orientation, and various legal avenues exist for prisoners to report mistreatment, although the effectiveness of these measures often hinges on implementation and the willingness of authorities to address violations.

 ## Arrested in Malta

The arrest process for foreign visitors in Malta begins when law enforcement authorities, typically the Malta Police, identify an individual as needing to be detained due to suspected involvement in criminal activity or violation of immigration laws. Upon arrest, the individual is informed of the reasons for their detention and has their rights explained, including the right to remain silent and the right to legal representation. Foreign visitors are entitled to contact their consulate for assistance during this process, which is crucial for ensuring that they receive appropriate support in a foreign legal environment.[31]

Once arrested, the individual is taken to a police station for questioning. Under Maltese law, they must be brought before a court within **48 hours** of their arrest, where a magistrate will decide whether to continue detention or grant bail. During this period, foreign nationals have the right to legal representation, which can be arranged through private counsel or, in cases of financial hardship, by the state. The involvement of legal counsel is especially vital for foreign visitors, as they may face complexities relating to both criminal and immigration laws, ensuring their rights are protected throughout the legal proceedings.

True Story

A recent case in Malta saw two men, charged with murder, granted bail after spending seven months under preventive arrest. Despite the serious charges, the magistrate found no legal grounds to deny bail, noting that the accused had already been detained for an extended period. The court granted bail with conditions, requiring a deposit of €30,000 (about $32,870 USD), a €20,000 (about $21,910 USD) personal guarantee, and daily signing of the bail book. This decision highlights the

---

31 https://asylumineurope.org/reports/country/malta/
     detention-asylum-seekers/legal-framework-detention/grounds-detention

legal principle that suspects, even in serious cases, are entitled to bail unless there are specific legal reasons to withhold it.[32]

Bail

Malta's bail system operates on the presumption of innocence, with detention considered the exception. Anyone accused of a crime, including serious offenses like murder, may apply for bail under Article 581 of the Criminal Code. Magistrates make bail decisions based on offense severity, flight risk, and ties to Malta.

Foreign visitors are eligible but face extra scrutiny regarding residency and the likelihood of remaining for proceedings. Bail may require sureties and conditions such as regular reporting or surrendering travel documents. To find a reputable bail bondsman in Malta, visit **https://lawzana. com/bail-bond-service-lawyers/malta**, or a similar site, where you can browse by specific city.

Legal Representation

In Malta, foreign visitors have a right to legal representation if they are arrested or detained. This right is governed by both national law and the European Convention on Human Rights, ensuring that all individuals, regardless of nationality, can access adequate legal counsel to protect their rights during legal proceedings.[33] Upon arrest, detainees must be informed of their right to legal assistance, and they are entitled to contact a lawyer to represent them. If a foreign visitor cannot afford a private attorney, Malta provides access to legal aid services, which can assign a public defender to assist with their case, ensuring that financial constraints do not impede access to justice.

---

32 https://timesofmalta.com/article/
    why-murder-suspects-are-eligible-for-bail.756517

33 https://euaa.europa.eu/
    asylum-report-2024/393-legal-aid-borders-or-detention

Moreover, the Maltese judicial system actively involves various non-governmental organizations (NGOs) in providing legal support and advice to foreign detainees. NGOs such as the *Jesuit Refugee Service* (JRS) Malta and the *Malta Refugee Council* work to assist individuals in navigating legal processes related to immigration and asylum, ensuring that visitors understand their rights and responsibilities throughout their engagement with the legal system.

Foreign visitors to Malta can hire local legal representation to handle issues such as disputes, criminal cases, immigration matters, or contractual issues. Maltese lawyers, often fluent in English, help navigate the country's legal system, ensuring the visitor's rights are protected and compliance with local laws. Legal assistance is particularly important for complex matters like visas, work permits, or serious charges, where local expertise is essential for a fair process. A list of local English-speaking attorneys can be accessed at
https://www.welcome-center-malta.com/post/
top-english-speaking-immigration-lawyers-in-malta.

As always, it is a good idea to contact your home embassy or consulate for assistance navigating local legal system and explaining your rights under the local legal system.

U.S. Embassy in Attard

Ta' Qali National Park
Attard, ATD 4000
Phone: +356 2561 4000
Email: usembmalta@state.gov

Healthcare System and Medical Facilities

Malta's healthcare system provides foreign visitors with access to medical services, though the extent of coverage depends on their specific situation. Visitors from the European Union (EU) or European Economic Area (EEA) countries can use their European Health Insurance Card

(EHIC) to receive necessary medical care at reduced costs or for free, depending on the nature of the treatment. Non-EU visitors are typically required to pay for healthcare services, either through travel insurance or out-of-pocket.

Emergency services in Malta are generally free for all visitors, and public hospitals and clinics are available for urgent care. However, for non-urgent services, foreign visitors are advised to have private health insurance, as this can cover the costs of treatment and prescriptions.

Malta offers a robust healthcare system that accommodates both residents and international visitors, including access to both public and private hospitals. Notable facilities like **Mater Dei Hospital** provide state-of-the-art medical care in English, making it convenient for foreign patients seeking treatment. Additionally, private hospitals such as **St. James Hospital** and **St. Thomas Hospital** are well-regarded for their specialized services and shorter wait times, often catering specifically to expatriates and tourists. The country's growing medical tourism sector further emphasizes its appeal, with numerous specialized clinics offering cosmetic, dental, and rehabilitation services implemented with the latest medical technology.

Pre-Exposure Prophylaxis (PrEP) Treatment

In Malta, PrEP is not yet part of the national healthcare formulary, though the government has committed to future public rollout. Since 2019, generic oral PrEP (TDF/FTC) has been available privately from pharmacies with a prescription, costing about €57 ($61 USD) per month. Non-residents and tourists can also access it, but only through private purchase.

Follow-up care—HIV/STI testing and kidney/liver monitoring every three months—is required but not always fully covered, creating financial barriers, especially for youth, migrants, and those without supplemental insurance.

Access is highly centralized, limited to prescriptions from GU or infectious disease specialists (mainly at Mater Dei Hospital). There are no nationwide eligibility programs or outreach, and awareness is mostly NGO-driven. Rural and marginalized groups face particular challenges.

Until PrEP is integrated into the public health system, access remains limited and inequitable despite growing demand.

 ## Safety Precautions for LGBTQ+ Travelers

In response to an increase in violence against the LGBTQ+ community, Malta saw a rise in activists fighting for stronger protections, making the streets safer for LGBTQ+ travelers. However, it's still wise to exercise caution, as public displays of affection or excessive expression could potentially lead to a hate crime. By doing research and choosing LGBTQ+-friendly accommodations, travelers can enhance their safety and enjoy a fun trip. Always stay informed about local laws by keeping resources like *Law Of The Land* close at hand!

Emergency Contact Numbers

- **Police:** 112 or 2132 0202
- **Ambulance:** 112 or 2545 0000
- **Fire Department:** 112 or 2132 0202
- **U.S. Embassy in Attard:** +356 2561-4000

Useful Emergency Phrases in Maltese

HELP! – Għajnuna! *(ah-YAY-noo-nah)*

CALL AN AMBULANCE! – Ikkuntattja ambulanza! *(ee-koon-TAH-tyah am-boo-LAHN-tsah)*

I NEED A DOCTOR – Għandi bżonn tabib *(AHN-dee b-ZOHN tah-BEEB)*

POLICE – Pulizija *(poo-LEE-tzee-yah)*

I'M LOST – Jien mitluf/a *(yeen mee-TLOOF/ah)*

IT'S AN EMERGENCY – Huwa emerġenza *(HOH-wah eh-mehr-JEN-tsah)*

GREECE

Greece is a democratic republic with a president as the head of state and a parliamentary system of government. The country has a rich cultural heritage, deeply influenced by its ancient history, and is known for its diverse regional traditions and strong national identity. Greek Orthodox Christianity is the dominant religion, although other faiths are practiced. Greece has made strides in modernizing its society, with growing attention to issues like gender equality and LGBTQ+ rights in recent years. Despite economic challenges, it remains a key player in European and global affairs, blending its ancient roots with contemporary values.

 ## Politics and LGBTQ+ Legislation

Although Greece has traditionally been a bit more conservative on social issues, influenced by its Orthodox Christian heritage, there has been significant progress in recent years, especially in LGBTQ+ rights through several key legislative reforms. **Same-sex marriage was legalized on February 15, 2024**, making Greece the first Orthodox Christian-majority country to recognize such unions, with full adoption rights also granted to same-sex couples.

The country has strong anti-discrimination laws, including comprehensive hate crime legislation and workplace protections against discrimination based on sexual orientation and gender identity. **Since 2017,**

Greece has allowed transgender individuals to legally change their gender without surgery, and minors over 15 can access legal gender recognition, though advocacy continues to improve access for younger individuals.

Nevertheless, non-binary individuals and those who identify with a gender different from their assigned birth sex still face legal challenges, as their gender is not legally recognized, and they are identified by their birth sex in official documents. However, it is not a criminal offense to identify as a gender different from the one assigned at birth.[34]

True Story

While same-sex marriage was legalized, Greek organizations such as Athens Colour Youth reported that homophobic violence is increasing. The Greek Orthodox Church, immensely influential in Greek politics, continues to condemn homosexuality. Likewise, the Greek public remains prejudiced; according to Eurobarometer 2019 "Discrimination in the European Union" survey, only 64% of Greeks think that LGBTQ+ people should have the same rights as heterosexual people, way below the European average of 76%.

 **LGBTQ+ Scene**

The *Athens Pride Parade*, held annually in mid-June, is the major LGBTQ+ event in Greece, attracting thousands of participants with colorful floats, performances, and speeches. Since its debut in 2005, it has grown significantly, with the 2023 edition featuring a focus on transgender rights. The parade winds through central Athens, celebrating unity and raising awareness of LGBTQ+ issues.

---

34 https://en.wikipedia.org/wiki/LGBTQ+_rights_in_Greece

Other cities in Greece, such as **Thessaloniki**, also host Pride events, including parades, performances, and speeches, promoting LGBTQ+ rights across the country. Smaller gatherings, like film screenings and art exhibitions, take place in cities like **Patras** and **Chania**, further fostering community engagement and dialogue.[35]

Beyond Pride Month, the LGBTQ+ community in Greece remains active and engaged throughout the year, with numerous events, support networks, and advocacy efforts. Organizations like the *Athens Lesbian Group, Colour Youth*, and *Faros* work continuously to provide resources, promote visibility, and support individuals facing discrimination and violence. Culturally, Greece hosts events such as the *Athens Queer Festival* and the *"Outview" LGBTQ+ Film Festival*, which celebrate gay art, cinema, and performances, fostering a space for creative expression and raising awareness of LGBTQ+ issues. These ongoing activities help strengthen the community and advocate for LGBTQ+ rights beyond Pride Month.

 LGBTQ+-Related Crime

Recent statistics reveal a troubling surge in violence against the LGBTQ+ community in Greece, underscored by data from the Racist Violence Recording Network (RVRN) which recorded 61 attacks in 2023, an increase from the previous year.[36] Discrimination, harassment, and violence against LGBTQ+ individuals, particularly transgender people, continue to be issues, though the legal framework has improved. Hate crimes based on sexual orientation or gender identity are reported irregularly and societal acceptance can vary, especially in more rural or conservative areas. However, Greece has made progress in addressing these issues, with legal protections for LGBTQ+ people. Activism and visibility have increased, particularly in urban areas like Athens, but challenges

35 https://www.misterbandb.com/gay-events/greece/gay-pride

36 https://www.reuters.com/world/europe/
    racist-violence-surges-greece-report-finds-2024-04-23

remain in ensuring full equality and safety for the LGBTQ+ community across the country.

LGBTQ+ and Prostitution

Prostitution is legal in Greece, but it is regulated by strict laws. Sex workers must adhere to specific guidelines, and failure to comply with these regulations can result in their activities being deemed illegal.

Sex workers can legally work only in licensed brothels and must undergo regular medical examinations, carrying an updated medical card that is checked every two weeks. Despite these regulations, some individuals still engage in illegal, underground prostitution. Tourists considering visiting Greece's red-light districts should be cautious, stay aware of their surroundings, and keep up to date with the local laws surrounding prostitution. LGBTQ+ travelers may be at greater risk of being targeted or scammed due to their sexual orientation. If an LGBTQ+ tourist gets caught up in illegal prostitution activities, they may face harsher treatment in the legal system.

LGBTQ+ and Jail System

While exact statistics on the LGBTQ+ population within the prison system are difficult to ascertain, it is recognized that sexual minorities, particularly transgender and non-binary individuals, face heightened risks of incarceration, discrimination, and victimization compared to their heterosexual counterparts.

LGBTQ+ individuals in Greek prisons face discrimination, violence, and inadequate healthcare, particularly transgender prisoners placed in facilities that do not align with their gender identity. Social isolation is common, and prison policies often fail to address their specific needs, leaving them vulnerable to abuse and neglect. These challenges highlight the need for reforms to protect the rights and safety of LGBTQ+ inmates.

 ## Arrested in Greece

When a foreign individual is arrested, they are typically informed of the charges against them and their rights, which include the right to legal representation and the right to contact their consulate for assistance. It is crucial for arrested individuals to request an attorney immediately, as the presence of legal counsel can significantly impact their treatment and understanding of the proceedings. Following an arrest, the individual will usually be detained at a police station for a period not exceeding **24 hours**, after which they must be presented before a prosecutor.[37] During this initial phase, individuals also have the right to remain silent and should be provided with information about their rights in a language they comprehend. Moreover, it is important to remember that if legal representation is not arranged, foreign individuals face heightened risks during their detention, potentially leading to protracted custody without adequate support or information regarding their case.

Bail

Foreign nationals in Greece are eligible for bail under the same legal framework as citizens but face closer scrutiny regarding flight risk. Courts consider factors such as residency, social or family ties, legal status, and criminal history. Additional conditions may apply, including travel bans, mandatory reporting, or sureties.

Not all crimes qualify for bail—serious offenses like those carrying life imprisonment or posing high flight risk are excluded. Bail bonds are regulated by the Greek Code of Criminal Procedure and Civil Code, and in Athens can be secured through registered bail bond agents or specialized insurance companies. You can research bail bonds agents in Greece at **https://lawzana.com/bail-bond-service-lawyers/athens-attica**. For further assistance related to bail bond issues, you can contact: Greek Ministry of Justice: **www.justice.gov.gr**; Athens Bar Association: **www. dsa.gr**; or Hellenic Association of Bail Bond Agents: **www.habb.gr**.

---

37 https://www.fairtrials.org/app/uploads/2022/01/Greece-advice-note.pdf

Legal Representation

As a foreigner in Greece, you have the right to legal representation, which is guaranteed by both Greek law and the European Convention on Human Rights. Upon arrest or detention, you should be informed of this right and can request an attorney. If you cannot afford a private lawyer, Greece provides a legal aid system with public defenders who can represent you at no cost.

One of the first steps you should take is to contact your country's consulate or embassy. They can assist you in finding a local attorney, help with language barriers, and provide guidance on navigating the Greek legal system. The consulate can also offer general support and ensure your rights are upheld during legal proceedings.

U.S. Embassy in Athens
91 Vasilisis Sophias Ave
10160 Athens, Greece
Phone: 30-210-721-2951

You can seek legal assistance by reaching out to local law firms. The U.S. Embassy in Greece, for example, provides a list of English-speaking attorneys who are familiar with the needs of foreign nationals; many other embassies and consulates offer similar resources.

**https://gr.usembassy.gov/wp-content/uploads/
sites/206/ATTORNEY-LIST-April-2018.pdf** or
https://greece.embassy.gov.au/athn/lawyers_gr.html.

If you're unable to afford a lawyer, Greece has a legal aid system that provides public defenders at no charge. These defenders can help with a variety of legal issues, from criminal cases to immigration matters, ensuring that financial limitations do not prevent you from accessing justice. Additionally, non-governmental organizations) such as the *International Rescue Committee (IRC)* and others can provide legal assistance, particularly in complex situations. NGOs often offer free legal advice, advocacy, and help navigating legal procedures, particularly for those who may face language or cultural barriers.

Healthcare System and Medical Facilities

The healthcare system in Greece provides a comprehensive framework for foreign visitors, allowing access to both public and private medical services. All citizens, residents, and visitors, including expatriates and individuals holding a European Health Insurance Card (EHIC), generally have access to emergency medical care. However, most foreign visitors are not eligible for Greece's public healthcare system, which means they may need to pay for medical services out of pocket or rely on private health insurance for non-emergency situations.[38]

Private healthcare in Greece is known for its high quality and relatively low costs compared to many Western countries, making it a popular choice for medical tourists. Facilities often cater specifically to international patients, offering services in English and maintaining modern equipment. Visitors are highly encouraged to obtain travel health insurance to cover potential medical expenses during their stay, as out-of-pocket costs can be significant, particularly for specialized treatments or prolonged care.

Greece is home to several reputable medical facilities that cater specifically to tourists. Hospitals like **Mediterraneo, AHEPA University, Evgenidion, European Interbalkan Medical Center**, and **Babydust Clinic** provide advanced medical care, excellent service, and the comfort of English-speaking staff. These facilities not only stand out for their specialized medical treatments but also for their commitment to maintaining high-quality healthcare standards that appeal to visitors from around the world. As such, when planning a trip to Greece, tourists can feel reassured knowing that they have access to excellent medical care should the need arise.

Pre-Exposure Prophylaxis (PrEP) Treatment

PrEP became available free of charge through Greece's public healthcare system in **May 2025**, covering medication, lab tests, and consultations

---

38 https://www.visitorscoverage.com/travel-insurance-requirements/greece/

at 24 designated public hospitals. Oral PrEP (TDF/FTC) is included, while injectable PrEP is authorized at the EU level but not yet offered nationally.

Access is limited to **eligible Greek residents**; non-residents and tourists must rely on private options, costing about €150–200 ($165–220 USD) per month, with availability varying by provider.

Distribution is managed through public hospitals in major cities (Athens, Thessaloniki, Patras, Heraklion, Rhodes), with prescriptions issued via the national electronic health system and anonymity ensured through beneficiary codes. Monthly pickups and quarterly follow-ups (HIV/STI testing) are mandatory.

Despite progress, **rural and island areas** still face access gaps due to distance from authorized centers.

 ## Safety Precautions for LGBTQ+ Travelers

LGBTQ+ travelers to Greece should be aware that while cities like Athens and Thessaloniki are generally welcoming, rural areas may have more conservative views, and public displays of affection could be frowned upon. Recent incidents in Thessaloniki highlight ongoing risks, so it's important to remain vigilant. To stay safe, consider travel insurance that covers discrimination or hate crimes and keep emergency contacts for LGBTQ+ support groups handy. When booking accommodations, re-search LGBTQ+-friendly options with positive reviews and inclusivity policies to ensure a safe stay.[39]

Emergency Contact Numbers

- **Police:** 100

---

39 https://www.iglta.org/destinations/europe/greece/

- **Ambulance:** 166
- **Fire Department:** 199
- **U.S. Embassy in Athens:** 30-210-721-2951

Useful Emergency Phrases in Greek

HELP! – Βοήθεια! *(vo-EE-thee-ah)*

CALL AN AMBULANCE! – Καλέστε ασθενοφόρο! *(ka-LES-teh as-theh-no-FOH-roh)*

I NEED A DOCTOR – Χρειάζομαι γιατρό *(khree-AH-zoh-meh ya-TROH)*

POLICE – Αστυνομία *(as-tee-no-MEE-ah)*

I'M LOST – Είμαι χαμένος/η *(EE-meh kha-MEH-nohs/ee)*

IT'S AN EMERGENCY – Είναι επείγον *(EE-neh eh-PEE-gon)*

 # ICELAND

Iceland is a democratic republic with a parliamentary system, where the president serves as the ceremonial head of state and the prime minister is the head of government. Iceland has a stable multi-party system, with strong emphasis on social welfare, environmental sustainability, and gender equality. Iceland is known for its rich Viking heritage, literary traditions, and modern artistic expressions, with Icelandic sagas playing a central role in its identity. Icelanders enjoy a high standard of living, universal healthcare, and education, supported by a robust welfare system. The majority of Icelanders identify as Lutheran, with the Evangelical Lutheran Church being the state church, though the country is increasingly secular, with a strong tradition of inclusivity and progressive social values.

 ## Politics and LGBTQ+ Legislation

Iceland is generally considered a **liberal** country, particularly in terms of its political and social policies. The country has progressive values on many issues, including human rights, gender equality, LGBTQ+ rights, and environmental sustainability.

Iceland repealed its law criminalizing homosexual acts in 1940. Since then, they have consistently implemented laws aimed at preventing discrimination, ensuring fair adoption practices, and establishing equal age of consent. Same-sex marriage was legalized in 2010, and Iceland's Parliament even unanimously amended the law to define marriage as a union between two "individuals" rather than "a man and a woman." According to the *2023 LGBT Equality Index*, Iceland ranks #1 for LGBTQ+ rights!"[40]

 ## LGBTQ+ Scene

Iceland has earned excellent reviews as a gay friendly destination, consistently appearing on various top ten lists. *Pride* is a key event in Iceland's LGBTQ+ calendar, reflecting the country's progressive stance on sexual and gender diversity. First held in 1999, it has grown significantly, with over 100,000 participants in recent years. The celebration, typically held in August, includes a parade, concerts, art exhibitions, and panel discussions.[41] Beyond its festive nature, *Reykjavik Pride* serves as a platform for promoting LGBTQ+ rights, raising awareness, and fostering pride within the community. The event plays a major role in de-stigmatizing LGBTQ+ identities in Iceland.

---

40   https://outadventures.com/gay-travel-blog/
      the-worlds-10-greatest-lgbt-friendly-countries-for-travellers/

41   https://hinsegindagar.is/en/about-us

Beyond Pride Month, the country has been a leader in LGBTQ+ rights; public support LGBTQ+ rights is strong, with 87% of Icelanders backing same-sex marriage.[42] **Reykjavik**, while lacking a designated gay district, offers several LGBTQ+-friendly venues like *Kiki Queer Bar* and *Gaukurinn*, which host drag shows, live music, and other regular gay events that contribute to a vibrant social scene.

The country has a strong record of gender equality, highlighted by Jóhanna Sigurðardóttir becoming the world's first openly LGBTQ+ head of state in 2009.[43] Iceland also celebrates feminist and LGBTQ+-owned businesses, such as *Pink Iceland*, a gay-owned travel agency offering LGBTQ+ tours and events. For those exploring the country's gay culture, the Culture Walk app provides a self-guided LGBTQ+ history tour.

 ## LGBTQ+-Related Crime

While Iceland is considered one of the safest places in the world, they still struggle with discrimination and prejudice against the LGBTQ+ community.

Much of this stems from a lack of protections for the LGBTQ+ community, an issue often overlooked because of the country's reputation as a safe and welcoming place. Incidents of hate crimes targeting LGBTQ+ individuals have risen in recent years, with 15 reported in 2021 and 18 in the first half of 2022. Although the numbers are still relatively low, the increase highlights a troubling trend.[44]

Harassment, particularly "barking" incidents in public, has raised concerns within the community. While Iceland's legal framework includes anti-discrimination protections for sexual orientation and gender

---

42   https://en.wikipedia.org/wiki/LGBTQ+_rights_in_Iceland

43   https://www.britannica.com/biography/Johanna-Sigurdardottir

44   https://www.politico.eu/article/violence-lgbtq-rights-rise-europe-report

identity, there is no specific hate crime legislation addressing bias-motivated violence. Advocates are calling for stronger laws to better protect LGBTQ+ individuals from hate crimes.[45]

True Story

LGBTQ+ teens in Iceland are experiencing increasing harassment, including being barked at, stoned, and chased, driven by a harmful TikTok trend that dehumanizes LGBTQ+ individuals. The bullying has made the teens feel unsafe, leading to severe emotional distress. Tragically, the group lost a close friend to suicide due to the ongoing harassment. Parents are urging the bullies to understand the devastating impact their actions have on these young people.

LGBTQ+ and Prostitution

Prostitution is legal in Iceland, but with strict restrictions. It is illegal for third parties to profit from prostitution, though it remains legal to buy and sell sexual services. Unfortunately, this has led to an increase in human trafficking and sex trafficking, exacerbated by a rise in tourism, which has driven demand for sex workers.

The LGBTQ+ community, like in many countries, is often targeted by traffickers and scammers. As such, it's important for LGBTQ+ travelers to stay vigilant and avoid any involvement in this side of the industry during their visit.

LGBTQ+ and Jail System

LGBTQ+ individuals in Iceland enjoy equal legal rights, including access to support and resources while in custody. Iceland's prison system,

---

45   https://grapevine.is/news/2022/05/27/
     lgbtq-teens-face-daily-harassment/

known for being among the most humane ones in the world, offers more autonomy and amenities compared to many other countries. The country has low incarceration rates, with approximately 141 people in prison as of early 2023.[46] While LGBTQ+ individuals are known to be part of the prison population, there is limited data on their numbers due to the lack of systematic tracking of sexual orientation or gender identity within the system. Though general anti-discrimination laws protect LGBTQ+ inmates, there are no specific provisions addressing hate crimes or harassment in prisons. Prison authorities are said to implement individualized treatment plans for all inmates, but details regarding how these plans address the needs of LGBTQ+ individuals are scarce.

 ## Arrested in Iceland

If you're arrested as a tourist in Iceland, you must adhere to local laws and could face serious consequences, such as fines, imprisonment, or even being banned from the Schengen area, depending on the nature of the offense. To avoid legal trouble, familiarize yourself with Iceland's laws and regulations. In Iceland, individuals who are detained must be brought before a judge within **24 hours** of their arrest. The judge will assess whether the detention is justified and can decide whether to extend it, impose conditions like bail, or release the individual. If detention is extended beyond 24 hours, it requires court approval. This ensures that detainees are not held without judicial oversight for too long, protecting their right to a fair process.

Key Points to Remember:

- **Local Laws Apply:** As a visitor, you are expected to follow all Icelandic laws, even if they differ from those in your home country. Ignorance of the law is not considered an excuse.
- **Common Offenses:** Some common reasons tourists may be arrested in Iceland include:

---

46 https://www.prisonstudies.org/country/iceland

- Possessing or using illegal drugs (even small amounts)
- Public intoxication
- Vandalism or property damage
- Driving under the influence (DUI)
- Violating wildlife protection laws

- **Contacting Your Embassy:** If you are arrested, you should immediately ask the authorities to contact your country's embassy or consulate. This is crucial, as the embassy can provide assistance and ensure your rights are respected. For U.S. citizens, the Department of State offers support in line with international law, including:

  - Providing a list of English-speaking local attorneys[47]
  - Contacting family, friends, or employers with your consent
  - Ensuring appropriate medical care and regular visits
  - Offering general guidance on the local criminal justice process
  - Helping ensure visits from clergy, if desired

Legal Representation

As a foreign visitor in Iceland, you have the right to legal representation and assistance from your embassy or consulate. If you are arrested, immediately ask for consular notification and seek a local lawyer through your embassy.

U.S. Embassy in Reykjavík
Engjateigur 7
105 Reykjavik
Iceland
Phone: (354) 595 2200

---

47 https://is.usembassy.gov/wp-content/uploads/sites/173/2024/08/List-of-attorneys.-May-2022-1.pdf

The embassy can also assist with language support and understanding the legal process. Be proactive in contacting your embassy, as they can provide essential resources and guidance to ensure fair treatment during your legal proceedings.

Foreign visitors in Iceland who cannot afford a lawyer are indeed eligible for legal aid outlined in Article 126 of the Act on Civil Procedure nr. 91/1991. This provision ensures that all individuals involved in judicial proceedings, regardless of their nationality, can access legal representation. To qualify, applicants must meet specific income criteria, and the legal aid assessment considers individual financial circumstances, allowing for some discretion. The process requires that foreign nationals file applications with the Ministry of Justice detailing their financial situation and the nature of their legal matter.

Bail

In Iceland, tourists and foreign nationals can be eligible for bail under certain conditions. Arrested individuals must be brought before a judge without delay, who decides on detention or bail. Eligibility depends on the severity of charges and community ties, with courts assessing flight risk. Bail is granted at the judge's discretion, evaluated on a case-by-case basis. You can find bail bonds agents in Iceland at **https://lawzana. com/ bail-bond-service-lawyers/iceland**.

Healthcare System and Medical Facilities

Tourists and foreign nationals do have access to healthcare services in Iceland, although the extent of this access largely depends on their insurance situation. While Icelandic residents benefit from a comprehensive national health insurance system, visitors are typically required to cover their medical expenses out-of-pocket unless they possess travel medical insurance or hold a European Health Insurance Card (EHIC). Those from EEA member states are entitled to necessary medical care during their temporary stay in Iceland, provided they present their EHIC, which allows them to access healthcare services at the same fees charged to locals.[48] Conversely, non-EEA visitors who do not have proper insurance must pay the full cost of healthcare services upfront, although they can seek reimbursement from their private insurance providers according to their policy terms.

Iceland offers a variety of healthcare facilities equipped to cater to international visitors. The main healthcare provider, **Landspítali University Hospital**, is well-prepared to assist both locals and tourists alike, offering comprehensive medical services, including emergency care and specialized treatments. Additionally, several health clinics across major towns provide general medical assistance and can accommodate patients from abroad, ensuring they receive necessary care without language barriers; interpreters can be arranged at these facilities when needed. Furthermore, private health clinics also operate within the country where foreigners can seek medical attention, particularly when immediate care is required.

Access to Pre-Exposure Prophylaxis (PrEP) Treatment

In Iceland, PrEP is available through the public healthcare system, mainly via regional health centers and sexual health clinics. It is generally subsidized for residents, with eligibility based on behavioral and clinical risk factors, including HIV testing and basic health screenings before prescription.

Non-residents and tourists must pay full costs, often through private providers, making access more expensive and limited. Distribution is concentrated in urban centers, and follow-up care (HIV/STI testing) is recommended for all users. Tourists are advised to plan ahead, bringing prescriptions or arranging access before travel.

---

48 https://visitreykjavik.is/medical-assistance

 ## Safety Precautions for LGBTQ+ Travelers

Iceland remains one of the safest places for the LGBTQ+ community in the world. Iceland's low overall crime rate means that crimes against the LGBTQ+ community are exceptionally rare, allowing gay couples to walk around confidently and securely. LGBTQ+ travelers can feel safe while visiting Iceland, as long as they remain respectful toward the locals. In general, there should be no issues for those vacationing in the country.

Emergency Contact Numbers

- **Police:** 100
- **Ambulance:** 166
- **Fire Department:** 199
- **U.S. Embassy in Reykjavik:** (354) 595 2200

Useful Emergency Phrases in Icelandic

HELP! – Hjálp! *(hyawl-p)*

CALL AN AMBULANCE! – Hringdu á sjúkrabíl! *(hring-thoo ow shoo-krah-beel)*

I NEED A DOCTOR – Ég þarf lækni *(yeh thahrf layk-nee)*

POLICE – Lögregla *(luhr-greh-glah)*

I'M LOST – Ég er týndur/týnd *(yeh er teend-ur/teend)*

IT'S AN EMERGENCY – Þetta er neyðarlegt *(theht-tah er ney-thar-legt)*

NEW ZEALAND

New Zealand is a democratic parliamentary system with a head of government, the Prime Minister, and a ceremonial head of state, the British monarch, represented by the Governor-General. It is known for its progressive policies, including strong environmental protections, social welfare programs, and a focus on indigenous rights, particularly for the Māori population. Culturally, New Zealand is famous for its Māori heritage, vibrant arts scene, and outdoor lifestyle, with a strong focus on sports like rugby. New Zealand boasts a high standard of living, universal healthcare, and education. The country is largely secular, though Christianity remains the dominant religion, and it is recognized globally for its inclusive and tolerant society, with active efforts toward LGBTQ+ rights and gender equality.

 ## Politics and LGBTQ+ Legislation

New Zealand is considered a liberal country, with progressive policies on social issues such as LGBTQ+ rights, gender equality, and environmental protection. It also has a strong commitment to human rights and is known for its inclusive political environment and progressive social welfare system.

New Zealand is a leader in LGBTQ+ rights, with significant legal protections. Same-sex marriage has been legal since 2013, granting same-sex couples equal rights in areas like inheritance and adoption. The *Human Rights Act 1993* protects against discrimination based on sexual orientation and gender identity in employment, housing, and services. Transgender individuals can change their legal gender on official documents without surgery and hate crimes targeting LGBTQ+ individuals are specifically addressed in the legal system. Additionally, access to gender-affirming healthcare is ensured, based on informed consent rather than psychiatric evaluations, making New Zealand one of the most LGBTQ+-friendly countries globally.[49]

In 1995, Georgina Beyer made history as the world's first transgender mayor when she was elected in the town of Carleton. A few years later, in 1999, she became the world's first transgender member of parliament.

 ## LGBTQ+ Scene

New Zealand's LGBTQ+ scene is vibrant and diverse, with key cities like Auckland, Wellington, and Christchurch serving as cultural hubs for the community.

Auckland, the largest city, is home to a thriving LGBTQ+ scene, particularly in neighborhoods like Karangahape Road and Ponsonby. It offers numerous LGBTQ+-friendly venues such as the Eagle Bar and hosts the major Auckland Pride event in February, attracting thousands of participants. **Wellington**, known for its cultural richness, also hosts a strong LGBTQ+ community, with events like the *Wellington Pride Festival* and venues like *The Beehive and Ivy Bar*. **Christchurch**, though smaller, has a growing LGBTQ+ scene, with events like Christchurch Pride helping foster visibility and support.

New Zealand's LGBTQ+ events include *Auckland* and Wellington Pride festivals, featuring parades, parties, and cultural activities. Additionally, *Winter Pride Queenstown*, the largest winter LGBTQ+ festival in the Southern Hemisphere, offers a unique chance for community gathering during the winter months.

The nightlife scene in New Zealand is an integral part of the LGBTQ+ culture, with many bars and clubs offering inclusive spaces. In Auckland, venues like *Caluzzi* and *The Glasshouse* are popular for their drag

---

49 https://en.wikipedia.org/wiki/LGBTQ+_rights_in_New_Zealand

shows, while Wellington's *White House* and *The Fringe Bar* host regular LGBTQ+ events. Drag performances are an important part of New Zealand's LGBTQ+ culture, showcasing artistic talent and providing a platform for community expression.

Beyond Pride Month, the LGBTQ+ scene in New Zealand thrives year-round, supported by organizations like *RainbowYOUTH*, *InsideOUT*, and *OutLine*, which provide resources, mental health support, and advocacy for the community. These groups work to promote safety in schools, reduce bullying, and empower youth. Cultural representation is also strong, with LGBTQ+ films, art exhibitions, and educational programs that foster inclusivity and understanding. Cities like Auckland, Dunedin, and Hamilton offer particularly welcoming environments, with Dunedin's tight-knit gay community and Hamilton's lively student culture providing gay-friendly spaces for both locals and travelers. New Zealand's commitment to LGBTQ+ rights and visibility creates a vibrant, inclusive atmosphere for people of all identities.

 **LGBTQ+-Related Crime**

Despite New Zealand's progressive stance on LGBTQ+ rights, hate crimes targeting the LGBTQ+ community are on the rise. In 2023, incidents of hate crimes against transgender individuals increased by 42%, highlighting growing safety concerns. A survey of 32,000 New Zealanders revealed that 46% of LGBTQ+ individuals had been victims of at least one crime in the past year, with 22% facing repeated victimization, a higher rate than non-LGBTQ+ individuals. Recent high-profile attacks, like the assault of a gay man in Auckland, have raised alarm, alongside incidents of vandalism, such as the defacing of rainbow pedestrian crossings. These cases reflect a wider issue of persistent anti-LGBTQ+ sentiment and violence in New Zealand.[50]

---

50 https://www.rnz.co.nz/news/national/514532/reports-of-hate-crimes-against-trans-people-jump-42-percent-spike-month-of-posie-parker-visit

True Story

"The sexual violence against the bisexual community is pretty terrible - over the course of their lifetimes, about two-thirds experience sexual violence at some stage," Tim Hampton, deputy secretary at the Ministry of Justice, told Newshub.

LGBTQ+ and Prostitution

New Zealand's *Prostitution Reform Act of 2003* decriminalized sex work, making it the first country to fully decriminalize the industry. The law distinguishes between voluntary and involuntary prostitution, aiming to protect sex workers' rights and improve health and safety. LGBTQ+ individuals are notably present in New Zealand's sex work sector, often entering the industry due to economic necessity and discrimination in other job markets. Many transgender and non-binary individuals are more visible in the industry, as sex work can be a survival strategy for those facing social and economic marginalization.

LGBTQ+ and Jail System

The LGBTQ+ population in New Zealand's prisons is small but significant, with specific challenges faced by individuals, particularly transgender prisoners. In 2020, 35 transgender individuals were reported in custody, highlighting their unique vulnerabilities.[51] Trans prisoners often experience higher rates of harm and mental health issues, requiring special protections. LGBTQ+ prisoners also face discrimination, bullying, and harassment from both fellow inmates and staff, compromising their safety and well-being. Additionally, access to adequate healthcare, especially gender-affirming care for transgender inmates, remains a significant concern.

---

51 https://pmc.ncbi.nlm.nih.gov/articles/PMC10756016/

 **Arrested in New Zealand**

If you're arrested as a tourist in New Zealand, it's crucial to know your rights and how to navigate the situation. Upon arrest, you have the right to contact a lawyer, and you should ask for one immediately. You also have the right to have your embassy or consulate notified, so make sure to request this as soon as possible. Consular staff can assist in finding a lawyer, helping with communication, and ensuring your fair treatment, but they cannot intervene directly in the legal process.

Once you're in custody, the police are required to bring you before a court within **24 hours**. Your first appearance will typically involve a judge deciding whether you'll be granted bail or remain in detention. During this time, having legal representation is crucial, as a lawyer will guide you through the process and explain your options. If you're not fluent in English, the police will provide an interpreter, ensuring you understand the proceedings. Additionally, if you're unable to afford a lawyer, you may be eligible for legal aid. Your embassy can help you find a lawyer and provide further guidance but remember that they cannot pay for your legal fees.

While being arrested can be stressful, staying calm, cooperating with authorities, and documenting the events will help. It's also important to remain silent until you've consulted with a lawyer. To avoid legal trouble in the first place, make sure you respect New Zealand's laws, particularly regarding drug use, public intoxication, DUI, and any behavior that could disrupt public order.

Bail

In New Zealand, tourists and foreign nationals are generally eligible for bail under the same legal framework as residents, subject to a District Court judge's discretion. Factors considered include the nature of the charges, flight risk, potential reoffending, and community ties. Certain cases, such as immigration offenses under section 128, may have restricted bail eligibility.

New Zealand does not use private bail bondsmen. Instead, courts set bail conditions directly, and the Department of Corrections provides Bail Support Services to help individuals comply (e.g., arranging sureties, counseling, or rehabilitation programs). Legal guidance from a lawyer is recommended for navigating the process and advocating for favorable terms.

For more information on Bail Support Service and District Courts locations, please visit **https://www.corrections.govt.nz/our_work/ courts_and_pre-sentencing/bail_support_services.**

Legal Representation

As a foreign visitor in New Zealand, you have the right to legal representation if arrested. You should be informed of this right and can request a lawyer immediately. If you cannot afford a lawyer, you may be eligible for legal aid, especially in criminal cases. You also have the right to contact your embassy, which can help find an English-speaking lawyer and ensure fair treatment. If you don't speak English, an interpreter must be provided for legal proceedings.

Additionally, you have the right to remain silent, which can protect you from self-incrimination. It's recommended to exercise this right until consulting a lawyer. The U.S. Embassy in Wellington can assist with legal resources:

U.S. Embassy in Wellington

29 Fitzherbert Terrace
Thorndon, Wellington 6011, New Zealand
Phone: +64 4 462 6000

Legal aid is available for those facing criminal charges, and the New Zealand Law Society provides a directory of criminal lawyers, including those experienced with foreign nationals. Visit Law Society at **https:// www.lawsociety.org.nz/for-the-public/find-a-lawyer/.**

If you're unsure where to start, your embassy can also provide a list of lawyers, accessible at **https://nz.usembassy.gov/services/attorneys-list/#list**. Remember that police are required to inform you of your rights and help connect you with legal support.

Healthcare System and Medical Facilities

Tourists and foreign nationals do have access to healthcare services in New Zealand, although the level of coverage largely depends on their **residency** status and insurance arrangements. New Zealand residents benefit from a **publicly funded healthcare system**, which provides heavily subsidized or free medical services. However, **visitors** are **generally not covered** under this public system and are expected to pay for any medical treatment unless they have valid travel insurance or are covered under specific reciprocal healthcare agreements.

New Zealand has healthcare agreements with a limited number of countries, including Australia and the United Kingdom. Citizens of these countries may be eligible for some publicly funded urgent medical treatment during their temporary stay, though they are still strongly advised to have comprehensive travel insurance. Visitors from countries without such agreements must pay the full cost of medical services out-of-pocket, although reimbursement may be possible through their private travel insurance depending on the terms of their policy.

New Zealand provides a wide range of healthcare facilities suitable for both residents and international visitors. Public hospitals, such as **Auckland City Hospital**, **Wellington Regional Hospital**, and **Christchurch Hospital**, are well-equipped to handle emergency care and specialized treatment for foreign nationals. Additionally, general practitioners (GPs) and urgent care clinics operate across all major towns and cities, offering accessible medical assistance for non-emergency situations. These facilities are generally well-versed in accommodating international patients, and interpreters can be arranged to assist with communication when necessary. Private healthcare services are also available throughout the country and may offer faster access to consultations and treatments. Many tourists and non-residents opt for private clinics for convenience and to ensure prompt medical attention. Regardless of the facility used, all visitors are encouraged to carry proof of insurance and identification to streamline the treatment process.

Pre-Exposure Prophylaxis (PrEP) Treatment

In New Zealand, oral PrEP has been publicly funded for eligible residents since 2018. Injectable PrEP (long-acting cabotegravir) is not yet available through the public system. Prescriptions can be issued or renewed by GPs, nurse practitioners, or sexual health clinics, including via telehealth.

For eligible residents, medication costs about NZD $5 ($3 USD) for a three-month supply, with standard fees for consultations and lab tests (HIV, STI, kidney function). Non-residents, tourists, and international students must pay out-of-pocket, typically NZD $30 ($18 USD) per month plus consultation and test fees. Some community programs offer limited free PrEP for low-income individuals or students.

Eligibility requires HIV-negative status and elevated risk of HIV exposure (MSM, transgender/non-binary networks, HIV-positive partners, recent condomless sex, multiple partners, or injection drug use). Since 2022, clinicians can grant access based on professional judgment without strict behavioral thresholds.

 ## Safety Precautions for LGBTQ+ Travelers

Before traveling to New Zealand, it's important to research the areas you plan to visit. Major cities are generally LGBTQ+-friendly, but rural areas may hold more conservative views. Look for LGBTQ+-friendly accommodations, nightlife, and events to ensure a safe and comfortable experience. While New Zealand is largely open-minded, it's advisable to be discreet with public displays of affection in more conservative or rural areas to avoid negative reactions.

Emergency Contact Numbers

- **Police/Ambulance/Fire Department:** 111
- **U.S. Embassy in Wellington:** 64 4 462 6000

Useful Emergency Phrases in Māori

While English is the most widely spoken language and the primary language for everyday communication, education, and business, the official language taught in schools and used in cultural and governmental contexts is Māori.

HELP! – Āwhina! *(ah-fee-nah)*

CALL AN AMBULANCE! – Karangahia he tāmihi rongoā! *(kah-rahng-ah-hee-ah heh tah-mee-hee roh-ngoh-ah)*

I NEED A DOCTOR – Kei te hiahia au i te taakuta *(kay teh hee-hee-ah ow ee teh tah-ah-koo-tah)*

POLICE – Pirihimana *(pee-ree-hee-mah-nah)*

I'M LOST – Kua ngaro au *(koo-ah nah-roh ow)*

IT'S AN EMERGENCY – He ohorere tēnei *(heh oh-hoh-reh-reh teh-neh)*

 # CANADA

Canada is a constitutional monarchy and parliamentary democracy, with the British monarch as head of state, represented by the Governor General. It has a federal system, sharing power between the national government and ten provinces. Canada is known for its stable democracy, commitment to human rights, and the rule of law, known as vastly diverse and multicultural, with over 200 ethnic groups and both English and French as official languages. The country embraces progressive policies on LGBTQ+ rights, gender equality, and environmental sustainability, and offers a robust social welfare system. Religiously, Canada is pluralistic, with Christianity as the largest religion, but also significant communities of Muslims, Sikhs, Hindus, Buddhists, and others, reflecting the country's respect for religious freedom.

 ## Politics and LGBTQ+ Legislation

Canada is generally considered a liberal country, particularly in terms of its political and social policies. Canada's LGBTQ+ rights are supported by key legislation. The *Canadian Human Rights Act* (1977, amended in 1996) prohibits discrimination based on sexual orientation, ensuring protection in employment and services. The *Civil Marriage Act* (2005) legalized same-sex marriage, granting same-sex couples equal legal rights. Finally, *Bill C-16* (2017) extended protections to gender identity and expression, also enhancing safeguards against hate crimes targeting transgender individuals.[52]

 ## LGBTQ+ Scene

Canada is known for its vibrant LGBTQ+ communities, with major cities and festivals offering inclusive environments and diverse celebrations. Toronto, Montreal, Vancouver, and Ottawa are key LGBTQ+ hubs, each with thriving communities and events. **Toronto's** Church-Wellesley Village is a focal point for LGBTQ+ culture and activism, while **Montreal's** Gay Village offers a rich cultural scene. **Vancouver's** Davie Village is a hub for LGBTQ+ activities, and **Ottawa's** Bank Street features community organizations and bars.

---

52 https://queerintheworld.com/lgbt-rights-in-canada/

Prominent LGBTQ+ festivals include *Toronto Pride*, one of the largest globally, *Montreal Pride* in August, *Vancouver Pride*, *Calgary Pride* in September, and *Halifax Pride* in July, each celebrating LGBTQ+ visibility, rights, and diversity. These cities and events foster a sense of community and offer important platforms for advocacy and celebration.

Beyond Pride Month, Canada is known for its LGBTQ+-friendly atmosphere, with major cities hosting inclusive events year-round. Toronto features festivals like the *Inside Out* and Toronto *Queer Film Festivals*, while Montreal celebrates with *Fierté Montréal* and other cultural events. Vancouver hosts the Vancouver Queer Film Festival and gay art exhibitions. Smaller communities, like Warkworth, also contribute with local festivals. These events promote LGBTQ+ visibility and rights, making Canada an attractive destination for gay travelers throughout the year.

 ## LGBTQ+-Related Crime

While Canada is considered one of the safest places for the LGBTQ+ community, it is not completely devoid of discrimination. Recent data from *Statistics Canada* shows a sharp rise in hate crimes related to sexual orientation (which range from verbal abuse to physical violence), with a 69% increase in 2023 alone and a 388% rise since 2016.[53] Canada has laws to address hate crimes, including provisions in the Criminal Code that increase penalties for crimes motivated by hate. Additionally, many police departments have developed specific protocols and training to better handle hate crimes and support LGBTQ+ victims.

LGBTQ+ and Prostitution

In Canada, **selling sexual services is legal, but purchasing them is not**, under the *Protection of Communities and Exploited Persons Act*

---

53   https://egale.ca/egale-in-action/2023-hate-crimes-july29/

(PCEPA) enacted in 2014. LGBTQ+ individuals, especially transgender and non-binary people, face unique challenges in sex work, often driven by economic necessity due to limited job opportunities and discrimination. Many report safety risks, with transgender sex workers particularly vulnerable to violence from clients and law enforcement. The stigma around sex work can lead to mental health issues, substance abuse, and social isolation, further complicating their ability to seek support.

LGBTQ+ and Jail System

LGBTQ+ individuals, particularly transgender and gender non-conforming people, are overrepresented in Canada's criminal justice system, often due to factors like family rejection and discrimination. In correctional facilities, they face significant discrimination and higher rates of victimization, especially transgender inmates who experience violence from both fellow prisoners and staff. Systemic barriers, such as inadequate healthcare and lack of access to mental health or hormone treatments, further compound their difficulties. Additionally, the discrimination and isolation they face discourage seeking help, perpetuating a cycle of abuse and distress.[54]

 **Arrested in Canada**

The legal foundation for the arrest and detention of foreign nationals in Canada is predominantly anchored in the Immigration and Refugee Protection Act (IRPA). Under this act, officers have the authority to arrest and detain foreign nationals without a warrant under certain conditions. These include situations where the officer suspects that the individual poses a danger to the public or is unlikely to appear for required proceedings.[55] The IRPA specifies that all arrests must adhere to the *Canadian Charter of Rights and Freedoms*, which mandates the informed consent of the arrested individual regarding their rights, including the right to legal representation.

---

54 https://www.prisonpolicy.org/blog/2021/03/02/lgbtq/

55 https://laws.justice.gc.ca/eng/acts/i-2.5/section-55.html

When a foreign national is detained in Canada, their case must be reviewed by the Immigration Division of the *Canada Border Services Agency* (CBSA). The first review must occur within **48 hours** of detention to assess the legitimacy of the detention and determine if it should continue.

After the initial 48-hour review, the Immigration Division must conduct periodic reviews: at least once within seven days of the first review, and then every 30 days thereafter. This ensures ongoing oversight and prevents unjust prolonged detention.

For foreign nationals aged 16 or older, there are special provisions requiring a review within 14 days of detention, followed by the same periodic reviews as other detainees. This emphasizes the importance of timely judicial oversight, especially for individuals with potentially more complex immigration cases.[56]

Bail

In Canada, all individuals, including foreign detainees, have a constitutional right to bail under section 11(e) of the Canadian Charter. Foreign nationals may face additional challenges due to immigration status, visa history, public safety concerns, language barriers, and unfamiliarity with the legal system. Courts assess charges, flight risk, and public safety when granting bail. Serious offenses may involve a "reverse onus," increasing the burden on defendants.

Canada does not allow commercial bail bonds; bail is granted through cash deposits or personal recognizance. Foreign detainees are advised to consult criminal lawyers or legal aid services for guidance. Professional organizations like the Surety Association of Canada provide resources but do not act as bail bondsmen. For more information, visit:

https://suretycanada.com/ and
https://lawzana.com/bail-bond-service-lawyers/ottawa-ontario.

---

56 https://laws.justice.gc.ca/eng/acts/i-2.5/page-8.html

Legal Representation

Under Canadian law, foreign travelers are entitled to legal representation, a right guaranteed by the *Canadian Charter of Rights and Freedoms*, which ensures all individuals, regardless of nationality, can access legal counsel.

Upon arrest, foreign nationals must be informed of their rights, including the right to contact a lawyer and request consular assistance. Travelers are also entitled to know their visa status and their rights under Canadian law. If they cannot afford a lawyer, Legal Aid may be available to assist with legal representation. In Canada, foreign visitors may be eligible for legal aid if they are facing serious criminal charges and cannot afford to hire a lawyer, though eligibility is primarily based on financial need and the severity of the case. Legal aid is generally more accessible for permanent residents and citizens, but some provinces may offer assistance for specific matters, such as immigration-related issues.

Visitors can also receive support through their embassy or consulate. These offices can provide vital support, including help with finding local attorneys and offering legal guidance. Consular officials can facilitate communication between the traveler and a local lawyer, provide lists of English-speaking attorneys, and explain the legal rights and procedures in Canada.

U.S. Embassy in Ottawa

490 Sussex Drive
Ottawa, Ontario, K1N 1G8, Canada
Phone: 613-688-5335

Healthcare System and Medical Facilities

Canada's healthcare system, Medicare, is publicly funded and primarily available to Canadian citizens and permanent residents, offering universal coverage for medically necessary services. However, foreign travelers typically face challenges in accessing these services, as they are generally required to pay for medical care. While emergency services are available to non-residents, they are billed at rates far higher than those covered by the public system. Some provinces may offer limited coverage, but the rules vary, so travelers need to be aware of the healthcare policies in the region they are visiting.[57]

Travelers are advised to purchase private health insurance to cover any medical expenses, including for outpatient services, as costs for services such as emergency room visits can be substantial. Challenges for visitors include high medical costs, potential language barriers, and the complexity of navigating the healthcare system.

Canada is home to various specialized medical facilities that cater specifically to international travelers seeking high-quality healthcare services. Notably, hospitals such as **Toronto General Hospital** and **Vancouver General Hospital** have garnered reputations for their advanced medical technology and experienced healthcare professionals. These institutions often provide a range of medical services, including elective surgeries, specialized treatments, and comprehensive health assessments tailored to the needs of foreign patients. In addition, some facilities offer concierge-style services that assist international travelers with everything from arranging appointments to providing translation services, ensuring a seamless experience during their visit.[58]

Access to Pre-Exposure Prophylaxis (PrEP) Treatment

In Canada, PrEP is available nationwide, though access, funding, and distribution vary by province. Oral PrEP has been approved since 2016; injectable PrEP was approved in 2024 but is limited and not widely covered by public drug plans. Access points include sexual health clinics, family doctors, HIV specialty clinics, telemedicine, and some pharmacies. Routine lab tests (HIV, STI, kidney function) are required every three months.

---

57 https://www.hostalky.com/blog/
    understanding-the-costs-of-health-care-in-canada-for-non-residents

58 https://www.internationalinsurance.com/hospitals/canada

Costs depend on provincial coverage: in provinces like BC, Ontario, Quebec, and Alberta, eligible individuals may receive PrEP free or with low co-payments. Elsewhere, brand-name PrEP can cost CAD $200–250/month ($150–$190 USD), and generics CAD $60–80/month ($45–$60 USD). Community organizations may provide assistance for uninsured or underinsured patients.

Eligibility requires HIV-negative status and elevated risk of HIV exposure, with clinicians in some provinces authorized to prescribe based on professional judgment. National guidelines promote a client-centered approach to reduce stigma and barriers.

 ## Safety Precautions for LGBTQ+ Travelers

Canada is one of the safest places for the LGBTQ+ community, but there is still some backlash in smaller, more rural areas of the country where LGBTQ+ individuals may encounter more conservative attitudes. LGBTQ+ travelers are still advised to research LGBTQ+-friendly areas before visiting, especially in more rural regions, to avoid potential conflict.

Emergency Contact Numbers

- **Police/Ambulance/Fire Department:** 911
- **U.S. Embassy in Ottawa:** 613-688-5335

Useful Emergency Phrases in French

Canada is officially bilingual, meaning that both English and French are recognized at the federal level for government and legal purposes. While **English** is the most widely spoken language, used for daily communication, business, and government in most regions of Canada, **French** is predominantly spoken in the province of Quebec and some other regions. It is also used in certain areas of New Brunswick and other parts of Canada with significant French-speaking communities.

HELP! – À l'aide! *(ah led)*

CALL AN AMBULANCE! – Appelez une ambulance! *(ah-pleh oon am-boo-lahnss)*

I NEED A DOCTOR – J'ai besoin d'un médecin *(zhay buh-zwah duh meh-deh-sahn)*

POLICE – Police *(poh-leess)*

I'M LOST – Je suis perdu(e) *(zhuh swee pehr-doo/pehr-due)*

IT'S AN EMERGENCY – C'est une urgence *(seh oon oor-zhahns)*

BELGIUM

Belgium is a constitutional monarchy in Western Europe with a parliamentary democracy and a federal structure, divided into Flanders, Wallonia, and Brussels. The country has a strong economy, driven by manufacturing, services, and technology, and plays a key role in global diplomacy as the headquarters of the European Union and NATO. Belgium is known for its rich cultural heritage, including art, architecture, chocolate, waffles, and beer, as well as its linguistic diversity, with Dutch, French, and German as official languages. Socially progressive, Belgium offers a high standard of living, strong healthcare, and social welfare systems. The country is predominantly Christian, with Roman Catholicism as the largest religion, though secularism and religious diversity are on the rise.

 ## Politics and LGBTQ+ Legislation

Belgium is one of the most progressive countries globally when it comes to LGBTQ+ rights, with strong legal protections and recognition of LGBTQ+ relationships. **Same-sex sexual activity has been legal since 1795**, and in 1985, Belgium equalized the age of consent for all sexual orientations.

The country made history **in 2003 by legalizing same-sex marriage**, becoming the second nation to do so. In 2006, same-sex couples gained the right to adopt, ensuring equality in family rights. Belgium also has robust anti-discrimination laws, first passed in 2003 to protect against discrimination based on sexual orientation, gender identity, and gender expression. More recently, in 2023, Belgium enacted a law banning conversion therapy, which seeks to alter an individual's sexual orientation or gender identity.[59]

 ## LGBTQ+ Scene

Belgium is widely recognized as one of the most LGBTQ+ friendly countries in Europe, with strong public support for equal rights and a general atmosphere of inclusivity. Prominent political figures, such as openly gay former Prime Minister Elio Di Rupo, have played a key role in increasing visibility and acceptance. While challenges remain, Belgium is celebrated for its commitment to diversity and equality.

Several cities in Belgium are particularly known for their vibrant LGBTQ+ communities and events. **Brussels**, the capital, is one of Europe's most LGBTQ+-friendly cities, offering a lively scene, especially in areas like Saint Jacques. **Antwerp** is renowned for its open-mindedness and hosts **Antwerp Pride**, a major celebration of LGBTQ+ rights. **Ghent** blends historical charm with an inclusive atmosphere, while **Liège** adds to the country's LGBTQ+ culture with its lively bars, clubs, and events.

---

59   https://www.unia.be/en/discrimination-sexual-orientation

Belgium celebrates *Pride Month* with numerous events. *Brussels Pride*, held in May, is one of the largest, featuring a parade and cultural activities, with the 2025 event coinciding with the *International Day Against Homophobia, Biphobia, and Transphobia. Antwerp Pride* in August fills the streets with parades, drag shows, and festivities. The country also hosts LGBTQ+ film festivals, local street parties, drag performances, and educational events that promote LGBTQ+ rights and culture.

Even beyond Pride Month, Belgium celebrates LGBTQ+ diversity through various events, including the *Pink Screens Queer Film Festival*, LGBTQ+ sports activities, and monthly parties like *La Démence* in Brussels.The country also has LGBTQ+ friendly establishments, such as bars and clubs in Brussels and Antwerp, including *Macho Sauna* and *La Reserve*, as well as community spaces like the LGBTQ+ bookstore Darakan in Brussels.

 ## LGBTQ+-Related Crime

Despite having progressive laws and protections for LGBTQ+ individuals, there are concerns regarding rising statistics of hate crimes, and incidents of violence and discrimination continue to affect the community. Hate crimes against LGBTQ+ individuals in Belgium have seen a troubling rise in recent years. In 2021, 466 anti-LGBTQ+ hate crimes were reported, a significant increase from 277 in 2020. A report from *Unia*, the inter-federal equality center, revealed 54 such cases in 2022, with nearly half involving physical violence, marking the highest figures in five years. [60]

Additionally, underreporting of hate crimes is a major challenge in addressing LGBTQ+ violence. Many victims fear discrimination or believe their complaints won't be taken seriously. Studies show that around half of LGBTQ+ individuals in Belgium who experience violence do not report it, making it harder to fully understand the extent of the issue.[61]

---

60 https://www.brusselstimes.com/508568/
    lgbti-community-facing-increased-violence-despite-legal-advances

61 https://www.brusselstimes.com/225516/unacceptable-violence-belgium-t
    o-crack-down-on-crimes-against-lgbtq-community

LGBTQ+ and Prostitution

In Belgium, LGBTQ+ sex workers face both progress and challenges. In December 2024, Belgium became the first European country to grant sex workers formal labor rights, including access to health insurance and retirement benefits.[62] However, LGBTQ+ sex workers still face significant stigma and discrimination, both within the LGBTQ+ community and society, leading to increased vulnerability. These workers often experience worse mental health outcomes, police harassment, and limited access to essential services and support. Despite legal advancements, societal attitudes continue to pose significant challenges to their safety and well-being.

True Story

In 2024, Belgium passed a new law allowing sex workers to work under employment contracts, providing access to social protections like health insurance and paid leave. The law also ensures autonomy and safety for sex workers. However, UTSOPI warns that local regulations could still restrict sex work and harm vulnerable workers, urging continued vigilance to ensure the law benefits all sex workers.[63]

LGBTQ+ and Jail System

The lack of comprehensive data on sexual orientation and gender identity in Belgium's prison system hinders a full understanding of LGBTQ+ representation and their specific needs. Advocates call for better data collection, including questions on sexual orientation in intake forms and health assessments, to improve support and interventions. Despite progress in recognizing LGBTQ+ rights, including decriminalizing

---

62 https://www.npr.org/2024/12/01/nx-s1-5212435/
    belgium-sex-workers-labor-protections-rights-first

63 https://www.nswp.org/news/
    belgian-parliament-approves-labour-law-sex-work

homosexuality and anti-discrimination laws, LGBTQ+ prisoners still face significant challenges. They experience higher rates of abuse, including sexual violence, and report systemic discrimination, harassment, and neglect of their healthcare, especially mental health needs, within the Belgium's prison system.

 ## Arrested in Belgium

If a foreign visitor is arrested in Belgium, the process and rights during detention are guided by Belgian law, EU regulations, and international treaties which ensure that the rights of individuals are upheld while allowing law enforcement to address potential legal violations. Upon arrest, the police are required to inform the individual of the grounds for their detention, which must be done promptly and clearly. Foreign visitors have the right to remain silent, seek legal counsel before answering any questions, and to contact their embassy or consulate.

In terms of detention duration, Belgian law stipulates that the maximum period of detention on the territory is generally six months, while detention at the border must not exceed five months.[64] After an arrest, if criminal charges are involved, the individual must be presented before a judge within **24 hours** to determine whether they should remain in custody or be released. The legal process after an arrest involves a hearing where the charges are evaluated, and if necessary, the judicial authority will review evidence and circumstances to decide on pre-trial detention. Throughout their detention, foreign visitors are entitled to respect for their human rights, which is reinforced by international agreements that Belgium adheres to.

One peculiarity of Belgian arrest law is the prohibition of nighttime police raids. According to Belgian law, police officers are barred from conducting raids between 9 PM and 5 AM unless specific circumstances

---

64 https://asylumineurope.org/reports/country/belgium/
detention-asylum-seekers/legal-framework-detention/duration-detention

arise that justify such actions.[65] This law was initially enacted to protect citizen privacy and ensures that arrests or searches are conducted during daylight hours, providing a measure of safety for individuals, including foreign visitors.

Bail

In Belgium, foreign visitors can apply for bail but face additional scrutiny compared to citizens. Courts consider proof of identity, financial stability, and local residency or arrangements, mainly to mitigate flight risk.

Belgium does not use commercial bail bondsmen; bail is granted via financial guarantees (cash deposits or pledges) to the court. For those unable to pay, alternatives like judicial supervision or conditional release are available.

Legal assistance from a qualified criminal lawyer is recommended to navigate the bail process and represent applicants in court. You can search for qualified lawyers at: **https://lawzana.com/bail-bond-service-lawyers/ brussels-brussels-capital.**

Legal Representation

In Belgium, visitors and foreign nationals have the right to legal representation, ensuring their rights are protected in cases involving immigration, criminal charges, or civil disputes. Legal assistance is essential, particularly for those seeking international protection, as it can influence the outcome of their applications. Private lawyers, many specializing in immigration and refugee law, provide primary legal representation, while pro bono services are available for those who cannot afford legal fees. These services are offered by NGOs, legal aid offices, and organizations like *NANSEN* and the *Jesuit Refugee Service*, helping individuals understand legal processes and navigate challenges like asylum applications and court appearances.

---

65 https://www.expatica.com/be/living/gov-law-admin/
    unbelievable-laws-belgium-774171/

For those needing financial assistance, the *Bureau for Legal Aid* can help secure a pro bono lawyer. However, accessing legal aid can be hindered by challenges such as language barriers and bureaucratic complexities. Additionally, while organizations like the UNHCR support legal aid systems, they do not provide direct representation, relying on partnerships with local entities.

Despite the availability of legal resources, foreign nationals may still face obstacles due to inconsistent quality of services and high demand, making it difficult for some to receive timely or adequate support. As always, embassies and consulates are a good initial source of information, connecting their citizen to local legal professionals.

U.S. Embassy in Brussels

Regentlaan 27 Boulevard du Régent,
B-1000 BRUSSELS
Phone: (32-2) 811-4000

List of English-speaking attorneys in Belgium, provided by the U.S. State Department, can be accessed at **https://uploads.mwp.mprod.getusinfo. com/uploads/sites/69/2023/02/Lawyer-list-February-02212023. pdf**

Healthcare System and Medical Facilities

Tourists and foreign nationals can access healthcare services in Belgium, though the cost depends on their insurance status and country of origin. Citizens from EEA countries and Switzerland can receive necessary medical treatment at the same rates as Belgian residents by presenting a valid European Health Insurance Card (EHIC). Visitors from non-EEA countries must cover healthcare expenses in full unless they have comprehensive travel insurance, which is strongly recommended to avoid high out-of-pocket costs.

Belgium has a well-developed healthcare system with modern public and private medical facilities. Major hospitals such as UZ Leuven and CHU

Saint-Pierre in Brussels provide emergency and specialized care, while general practitioners and pharmacies are widely available for non-urgent needs. English is commonly spoken by medical staff, and interpreter services can be arranged to assist foreign patients when necessary.

Emergency medical assistance is accessible by dialing **112**, the European emergency number. Non-emergency medical services typically require payment at the time of treatment, with receipts available for insurance reimbursement. Whether visiting for a short trip or an extended stay, travelers are advised to carry valid ID, proof of insurance, and any necessary health documentation to ensure smooth access to medical care.

Pre-Exposure Prophylaxis (PrEP) Treatment

In Belgium, PrEP has been available since 2017 and is approved by the FAMHP. Oral PrEP is widely accessible and fully reimbursed for eligible residents through the national health insurance system, with small co-payments (€5–15 per consultation, or $5.50-$16.50 USD). Injectable PrEP (cabotegravir) is approved at the EU level but remains limited and not broadly reimbursed.

Non-residents or uninsured individuals can access PrEP privately, at higher costs (€60–80/month or $65–87 USD). Distribution is mainly through sexual health clinics, infectious disease specialists, and trained general practitioners, concentrated in major cities (Brussels, Antwerp, Ghent) with improving rural access. Community organizations support outreach and education for key populations.

Eligibility requires HIV-negative status and elevated risk of HIV infection, including recent condomless sex, STIs, multiple PEP uses, or partners of unknown HIV status. Follow-up includes lab monitoring every three months.

 # Safety Precautions for LGBTQ+ Travelers

Belgium is a welcoming destination for LGBTQ+ travelers, with strong legal protections and a vibrant LGBTQ+ scene, especially in cities like Brussels and Antwerp. However, travelers should stay aware of local laws and attitudes, as views can vary, particularly in rural areas. It's advisable to exercise caution in unfamiliar neighborhoods, especially at night, and avoid public displays of affection where negative reactions may occur. Utilizing resources like *RainbowHouse Brussels* can provide valuable support and information on LGBTQ+ events and safe spaces.

Emergency Contact Numbers

- **Police/Ambulance/Fire Department:** 112
- **U.S. Embassy in Brussels:** +32 2 811-4000

Useful Emergency Phrases in Dutch, French, and German

Belgium has three official languages:

- **Dutch** (Flemish) is spoken primarily in the northern region of Flanders. It is the most widely spoken language in Belgium.
- **French** is spoken in the southern region of Wallonia and in the Brussels-Capital region. French is widely used in administration, education, and media.
- **German** is spoken by a small minority in the eastern part of Belgium, in the region near the German border.

Dutch (Flemish):

HELP! – Help! *(help)*

CALL AN AMBULANCE! – Bel een ambulance! *(bel een am-boo-LAHN-tseh)*

I NEED A DOCTOR – Ik heb een dokter nodig *(ik heb een dok-ter NOH-dig)*

POLICE – Politie *(po-LEE-tsie)*

I'M LOST – Ik ben verloren *(ik ben vehr-LOH-ren)*

IT'S AN EMERGENCY – Het is een noodgeval *(het is een NOOT-je-VAHL)*

French:

HELP! – À l'aide! *(ah led)*

CALL AN AMBULANCE! – Appelez une ambulance! *(ah-pleh oon am-boo-lahnss)*

I NEED A DOCTOR – J'ai besoin d'un médecin *(zhay buh-zwah duh meh-deh-sahn)*

POLICE – Police *(poh-leess)*

I'M LOST – Je suis perdu(e) *(zhuh swee pehr-doo/pehr-due)*

IT'S AN EMERGENCY – C'est une urgence *(seh oon oor-zhahns)*

German:

HELP! – Hilfe! *(HIL-feh)*

CALL AN AMBULANCE! – Rufen Sie einen Krankenwagen! *(ROO-fen zee EYE-nen KRAHN-ken-vah-gen)*

I NEED A DOCTOR – Ich brauche einen Arzt *(ikh BROW-khe EYE-nen ARTST)*

POLICE – Polizei *(poh-lee-TSAI)*

I'M LOST – Ich bin verloren *(ikh bin fer-LOH-ren)*

IT'S AN EMERGENCY – Es ist ein Notfall *(es ist ayn NOHT-fahl)*

PART 2

LGBTQ+ TOLERANT COUNTRIES

(Moderate Safety)

IN THIS CHAPTER

- Brazil
- Argentina
- Uruguay
- Italy
- Mexico

- South Africa
- Japan
- Bolivia
- India
- Israel

105

LGBTQ+ TOLERANT COUNTRIES

These countries have legal protections for LGBTQ+ individuals, though societal attitudes may still vary widely. In larger cities or more progressive regions, LGBTQ+ individuals may find a welcoming environment, but there could still be significant challenges in rural or conservative areas. While same-sex relationships might be legal, social acceptance can lag, and incidents of discrimination or hate crimes may still occur. Additionally, public displays of affection may attract unwanted attention in some regions.

 **BRAZIL**

Brazil is a federal republic, with a history of military rule followed by a transition to democracy in the 1980s. The political landscape is complex, characterized by frequent shifts between left-wing and right-wing leadership, as well as ongoing struggles with corruption, inequality, and environmental issues, particularly in the Amazon. Its society is marked by racial and cultural diversity, with significant African, Indigenous, and European roots, reflected in its music, food, and festivals like Carnival. Religion plays a major role, with Roman Catholicism historically dominant, though Protestantism and Afro-Brazilian faiths also have strong followings.

 ## Politics and LGBTQ+ Legislation

Brazil's political landscape is fluid, with both **liberal** and **conservative** factions, but in recent years, the country has seen a rise in conservative leadership, particularly under former President Jair Bolsonaro. Nevertheless, Brazil has made significant progress in LGBTQ+ rights through key legal reforms. In 2011, the Supreme Federal Court **recognized same-sex civil unions**, granting equal social and financial rights to same-sex couples. This was followed by the **legalization of same-sex marriage in 2013**, ensuring full equality, including adoption rights.

In 2018, Brazil allowed transgender individuals to change their legal gender without surgery or hormone therapy, and a year later the Supreme Court ruled that discrimination based on sexual orientation and gender identity is a crime, similar to racism. In 2022, the country banned conversion therapy, recognizing its harmful effects. These legal changes have expanded LGBTQ+ rights, though challenges remain in societal acceptance and enforcement.[66]

 ## LGBTQ+ Scene

Brazil is known for its vibrant LGBTQ+ events, with the São Paulo *Gay Pride Parade* standing out as the world's largest, attracting millions of attendees each year. In 2024, the parade drew over 3 million people celebrating diversity and advocating for LGBTQ+ rights amid a challenging political climate.[67] Carnival also plays a key role in LGBTQ+ visibility,

---

66 https://en.wikipedia.org/wiki/LGBTQ+_rights_in_Brazil

67 https://www.brazilreports.com/sao-paulo-brazils-lgbt-parade-draws-over-3-million-in-a-spectacle-of-pride-and-politics

with Rio de Janeiro hosting LGBTQ+-friendly celebrations, including themed parades and drag performances.

Several Brazilian neighborhoods are recognized for their LGBTQ+ inclusivity, such as **São Paulo**'s Vila Madalena and Avenida Paulista, **Rio de Janeiro**'s Ipanema and Copacabana, and **Salvador**'s Rio Vermelho, which are all known for their lively LGBTQ+ nightlife and cultural landmarks.

Beyond Pride Month, Brazil's LGBTQ+ scene is vibrant and resilient, with ongoing activism and community events throughout the year. Organizations like *Grupo Gay da Bahia* continue to address violence and discrimination, while grassroots groups focus on the needs of marginalized communities, particularly transgender people and immigrants. Brazilian cities, including São Paulo, Rio de Janeiro, and Salvador, host LGBTQ+ friendly spaces, bars, and cultural events, creating year-round visibility and fostering a sense of belonging. Despite facing significant challenges, the LGBTQ+ community in Brazil remains a powerful force for advocacy and change.

 **LGBTQ+-Related Crime**

Discrimination and violence against the LGBTQ+ community in Brazil is widespread; LGBTQ+ people are disproportionately harassed and victimized precisely because of who they are. One reason for ongoing discrimination in Brazil is the deep-rooted social conservatism in the country. Despite recent reports, the full extent of LGBTQ+ discrimination remains unclear, as many incidents go unreported due to fear of retaliation. While discriminatory violence against the LGBTQ+ community is criminalized, these laws have had limited impact in reducing violence or ensuring peace.[68]

---

68 https://www.opendemocracy.net/en/democraciaabierta/
    violencia-anti-lgbtq-brasil-en/

Despite legal advancements in LGBTQ+ rights, violence against the community remains prevalent. According to *Grupo Gay da Bahia*, at least 242 gay and trans people were violently killed in Brazil in 2022, which equates to one person every 34 hours.[69]

True Story

Consider the case of Julio Haag, a young schoolteacher, struck by a stone on his way home from teaching some years ago. His attacker claimed that Julio, who is gay, was looking at him suggestively. Years later, Julio considered running for the city council in Sarapiranga, a small municipality in Rio Grande do Sul. He withdrew his candidacy when his social media profiles were flooded with homophobic hate mail and threats. He worried that the next message coming his way could be a bullet.

LGBTQ+ and Prostitution

Sex workers in Brazil, particularly those who identify as LGBTQ+, face significant challenges despite the legal status of sex work. While **sex work itself is legal**, it remains unregulated, which often leads to complications and exploitation. The lack of regulation is exacerbated by the political climate under former President Jair Bolsonaro, who has encouraged criminalization and further marginalization of LGBTQ+ sex workers. This creates an environment where even legal practices are met with hostility and discrimination, putting vulnerable individuals at greater risk.[70]

---

69 https://xtramagazine.com/power/brazil-lgbtq-homicides-2022-244785

70 https://theconversation.com/jair-bolsonaros-administration-is-hurting-the-lives-of-lgbtq-sex-workers-in-brazil-173706

LGBTQ+ and Jail System

LGBTQ+ individuals in Brazilian prisons face significant physical, psychological, and sexual violence, with reports indicating widespread abuse across all prison units. Many prisoners also experience denial of basic rights, such as access to medical care and support services.[71]

While Brazil has implemented guidelines like *Resolution 348/2020* to improve the treatment of LGBTQ+ detainees, including allowing prisoners to identify with their chosen name and gender and ensuring access to healthcare, enforcement is inconsistent.[72] Discrimination, harassment, and fear of retaliation prevent many inmates from reporting abuse, while LGBTQ+ prisoners are often subjected to harsher sentences, further exacerbating their vulnerability.

 ## Arrested in Brazil

When a foreign national is arrested in Brazil, law enforcement officials are required to follow specific procedures. Upon arrest, individuals must be informed of the charges against them and their rights, including the right to legal counsel and to inform their consulate. The Constitution of Brazil mandates that any person detained must be brought before a judge within **24 hours** following their arrest.

After the arrest, the detained foreign national must be formally charged by the judiciary. The law stipulates that detainees must be charged within a stipulated time frame, which is typically set at 30 days for those arrested in the act (flagrante delicto) and up to 45 days for other defendants. If the authorities fail to file charges within these time frames, the individual may have grounds for release. Following the initial charge, the

---

71 https://www.apt.ch/news/
    placing-lgbti-persons-deprived-their-liberty-focus-brazil

72 https://www.apt.ch/news/
    brazil-landmark-report-ensures-lgbtiq-detainees-are-no-longer-invisible

pretrial detention situation is subject to a judicial review, where a judge assesses whether the detention should continue for the duration of the legal proceedings, considering factors such as the gravity of the crime, the potential for flight, and the risk of tampering with evidence.

Foreign visitors in Brazil have the right to consular assistance upon arrest. Under the Vienna Convention on Consular Relations, an arrested individual can request that local authorities notify their respective consulate, which is crucial for obtaining legal support.

U.S. Embassy in Brasília

SES - Av. das Nações, Quadra 801, Lote 03
70403-900 - Brasília, DF
Phone: (55-61) 3312-7000

Bail

In Brazil, bail is regulated by the Criminal Procedure Code, which distinguishes between bailable and non-bailable offenses. While bail is legally available for most crimes, it is not commonly granted and depends on factors like flight risk, public safety, crime severity, and the accused's background.

For minor offenses (sentences up to four years), police may set the bail amount; for more serious crimes, judges handle it. Bail requests require an attorney's petition highlighting community ties, clean record, and employment. If approved, conditions may include check-ins, travel restrictions, or court appearances.

Bail is typically secured through a judicial bond from an insurance company, with costs tied to crime severity and risk. Legal guidance from a qualified lawyer is strongly recommended to navigate this process.

To find a qualified lawyer, please visit **https://lawzana.com/ bail-bond-service-lawyers/brazil**

Legal Representation

Foreign visitors who encounter legal troubles or require assistance navigating Brazilian laws can find substantial support through various entities. For instance, the Public Defender's Office (Defensoria Pública) provides free legal aid to those who cannot afford it, including asylum seekers and vulnerable migrants. Furthermore, numerous non-governmental organizations operate within Brazil, offering essential legal support and advocacy for international migrant, including help with documentation and navigating Brazil's complex legal landscape.[73]

Brazil's legal framework facilitates the involvement of specialized lawyers who understand international and Brazilian laws, providing valuable guidance for foreign visitors facing legal issues such as immigration matters, criminal allegations, or civil disputes. This access to legal representation is vital in a country that welcomes numerous tourists and expatriates, ensuring that they can receive fair treatment under Brazilian law. Additionally, the Brazilian Constitution guarantees equal treatment of foreigners to Brazilians, reinforcing the commitment to upholding fundamental rights and facilitating legal recourse.[74]

As always, the best starting point is your home embassy that can provide you with a list of English-speaking attorneys, based on your specific location in Brazil. This list is available through the U.S. State Department at **https://br.usembassy.gov/u-s-citizen-services/attorneys/**

Healthcare System and Medical Facilities

Brazil's public healthcare system, the **Sistema Único de Saúde (SUS)**, provides free medical services—including primary care, emergency treatment, and specialty services—to both residents and foreign travelers, regardless of nationality. While SUS ensures universal access, foreigners may face challenges such as overcrowding and language barriers.

---

73 https://www.iom.int/news/legal-assistance-migrant-population-brazil

74 https://ilg2.org/2016/11/24/
the-rights-of-aliens-in-brazil-beyond-the-use-of-a-mistaken-term/

Many travelers instead choose **private healthcare**, which offers faster service and modern facilities but requires out-of-pocket payment or private insurance. Travel insurance is recommended to cover these costs. Brazil also has internationally accredited hospitals, such as **Hospital Israelita Albert Einstein** and **Hospital Sírio Libanês**, which provide high-quality care, multilingual support, and concierge services for international patients.

Access to Pre-Exposure Prophylaxis (PrEP) Treatment

In Brazil, **PrEP has been free through the public health system (SUS) since 2017**, covering both medication and required lab tests. Oral PrEP is widely available, while injectable PrEP, approved in 2023, is still limited in rollout. Access is strongest in major cities but is gradually expanding to smaller areas.

Most users obtain PrEP through SUS, but it is also available in **private clinics** at a cost of BRL 200–400 ($40–80 USD) per month. Nonresidents can access it privately, usually needing a passport or visa.

PrEP is provided at HIV/AIDS clinics, community health centers, and through some general practitioners since 2021. Eligibility targets HIV-negative individuals at higher risk, with **mandatory 3-month follow-ups and lab monitoring** to ensure safety and adherence.

 ## Safety Precautions for LGBTQ+ Travelers

As with many countries, LGBTQ+ travelers should exercise caution, especially in unfamiliar areas, as attitudes toward the community can vary. It's advisable to minimize public displays of affection and research destinations ahead of time to identify LGBTQ+-friendly places. Opting for LGBTQ+ friendly hotels, resorts, and activities is highly recommended for a safer experience. Additionally, it's best to be discreet about one's sexual orientation, avoiding outwardly expressing it or wearing identifiable symbols until in private spaces.[75]

Emergency Contact Numbers

- **Police:** 190
- **Ambulance:** 192
- **Fire Department:** 193
- **U.S. Embassy in Brasilia:** (55-61) 3312-7000

Useful Emergency Phrases in Portuguese

HELP! – Socorro! *(soh-KOH-hoo)*

CALL AN AMBULANCE! – Chame uma ambulância! *(SHAH-mee OO-mah am-boo-LAN-see-ah)*

I NEED A DOCTOR – Eu preciso de um médico *(eh-ooh preh-SEE-zoo jee oong MEH-jee-koo)*

POLICE – Polícia *(poo-LEE-syah)*

I'M LOST – Estou perdido/a *(ehs-TOH pehr-DEE-doo/dah)*

IT'S AN EMERGENCY – É uma emergência *(eh OO-mah eh-mehr-ZHEN-syah)*

---

75 https://queerintheworld.com/lgbt-rights-in-brazil

ARGENTINA

Argentina is a federal republic with a history marked by political instability, military dictatorship, and economic crises, but today it boasts a strong democratic tradition. The political landscape is polarized, with significant divisions between center-left and center-right parties. Socially, Argentina is progressive, having legalized same-sex marriage and abortion, but it still faces challenges such as inflation, poverty, and political polarization. The country is heavily influenced by its European roots, particularly Italian and Spanish, visible in its food, music, and dance, like the tango. While Roman Catholicism is the predominant religion, secularism is strong, and religious diversity is growing.

 ## Politics and LGBTQ+ Legislation

Argentina is generally considered considerably **liberal** country, particularly on social issues. It became the first country in Latin America to legalize same-sex marriage in 2010. Additionally, the *Gender Identity Law*, passed in 2012, allows individuals to change their legal gender without undergoing surgery or requiring a mental health diagnosis, making Argentina one of the most progressive countries regarding transgender rights.

 ## LGBTQ+ Scene

Argentina's LGBTQ+ community, especially in **Buenos Aires**, is active and diverse, with the city offering an inclusive nightlife scene, including numerous gay bars, clubs, and cultural hubs in neighborhoods like

Palermo and San Telmo. The annual *Buenos Aires Pride Parade*, or "Marcha del Orgullo," is a major event, attracting over a million participants to celebrate diversity and advocate for LGBTQ+ rights. The first Pride march in Argentina took place in 1992, with modest participation, but it has grown significantly, moving to November to coincide with the anniversary of the founding of Nuestro Mundo, Argentina's first LGBTQ+ organization. Today, the parade is one of the largest in the world, featuring vibrant celebrations and political statements on issues like discrimination and transgender rights.

Beyond Pride Month, Argentina hosts several LGBTQ+ friendly events, including the *Festival Internacional de Cine LGBTIQ+*, showcasing gay cinema, and *Día del Orgullo Trans*, which focus on transgender rights and visibility. The country also celebrates *La Diversidad en la Calle*, a community event with workshops and performances, and *Festejo por el Día de la Diversidad Sexual* in November, highlighting LGBTQ+ culture and rights. These events reflect Argentina's ongoing commitment to LGBTQ+ inclusion and advocacy.

True Story

Pierina Nochetti is a mother of three kids and the breadwinner of the family. She defines herself as a visible lesbian and an LGBTQ+ activist. For many years, she has participated on the committee organizing the Pride Parade in Necochea, a coastal town in the Buenos Aires Province. Though her activism, she has demonstrated a commitment to human rights, advocating for a world where people can freely and equally enjoy their human rights.

 ## LGBTQ+-Related Crime

While Argentina is generally accepting of LGBTQ+ individuals, especially in urban areas, challenges persist in smaller, more conservative rural regions where public expressions of sexuality can be discouraged, and incidents of violence still occur. Despite widespread support for LGBTQ+ rights, societal acceptance varies across the country and therefore it is highly advisable to research the area before traveling as part of LGBTQ+ community. In recent years, there has been a significant increase of hate-crimes targeting the LGBTQ+ community, with majority of crimes levied against the transgendered and non-binary communities.

In 2023, the *National Observatory of LGBT Hate Crimes* registered 133 incidents motivated by identity, gender expression or sexual orientation. Notably, 84% of these attacks were against transgender women. Of the total number of crimes, 40 were attacks against physical integrity, highlighting the severity and impact of violence faced by these vulnerable groups.[76]

LGBTQ+ and Prostitution

Although **prostitution is legal in Argentina**, there are legal ambiguities surrounding organized prostitution, such as brothel management and pimping, which remain illegal.

In Argentina, violence against sex workers, particularly transgender individuals, is a major issue, with reports showing that around 74% of trans people experience violence, often from law enforcement or in public spaces.[77] This is exacerbated by the intersectional discrimination they face as both transgender and sex workers, deepening their marginalization. A significant portion of the LGBTQ+ community, especially transgender women and transexuals, rely on sex work for survival, with about 70% engaging in prostitution due to limited job opportunities, social stigma, and discrimination. Many express a desire to leave sex work if alternative employment were available, but systemic barriers in education and the job market make this difficult. Transgender individuals also face high rates of family rejection and struggle with unstable housing,

---

76 https://www.amnesty.org.uk/urgent-actions/
argentina-ongoing-criminalisation-against-lgbt-activist

77 https://www.frontiersin.org/journals/sociology/articles/10.3389/
fsoc.2021.633699/full

particularly in Buenos Aires, pushing many into sex work from a young age.

LGBTQ+ and Jail System

The LGBTQ+ community in Argentina faces significant challenges within the prison system, despite the country's advancements in LGBTQ+ rights. Incarcerated individuals often experience systemic discrimination, violence, and inadequate healthcare, leading to heightened mental health issues, particularly among transgender individuals who are at greater risk of victimization.

Advocacy groups like *Yo No Fui* work to support LGBTQ+ inmates through artistic workshops and community initiatives, fostering resilience in a hostile environment. Despite legal progress, many LGBTQ+ individuals remain disproportionately incarcerated due to societal biases and systemic issues. Overall, comprehensive reform is essential to ensure the safety and dignity of LGBTQ+ prisoners in Argentina.

 **Arrested in Argentina**

In Argentina, the law provides robust procedural safeguards at the moment of arrest, requiring prompt judicial oversight of any deprivation of liberty. Under the Argentine Constitution and applicable criminal procedure laws, a person arrested without a warrant—such as in cases of *flagrante delicto*—must be brought before a competent judicial authority without delay. In practice, this obligation is interpreted strictly: detainees must be presented to judicial authorities within a very short timeframe, in some instances as quickly as six hours after arrest.[78] Additionally, Argentina's flagrancia procedures require that an initial judicial hearing occur within approximately 24 hours of detention, with only limited extensions permitted. At this stage, a judge reviews

---

78 https://www.hrw.org/news/2014/02/03/
    right-custody-hearing-under-international-law#

the legality of the arrest and determines whether continued detention is justified.

Despite these strong formal protections, practical concerns remain. Argentina has been criticized for its reliance on pretrial detention and delays in the resolution of criminal cases, which can result in individuals remaining in custody for extended periods after their initial judicial review.[79] For travelers, this means that while judicial oversight typically occurs quickly after arrest, release is not guaranteed, and detention may continue pending further proceedings.

Bail

Foreign visitors arrested in Argentina have the **right to bail**, though the process can be complex. Bail typically requires cash, property, or a judicial bond, with the amount set by a judge based on crime severity and flight risk. Unlike some countries, Argentina does not allow private bail bondsmen; bonds are arranged through the court or through an insurance company.

Foreign nationals may face added challenges, including delays in transferring funds, stricter scrutiny of immigration status, or being denied bail if seen as high flight risks. Inconsistent application of bail makes it vital to have a qualified lawyer to navigate procedures and advocate for detainees' rights. You can also check out a list of qualified lawyers offering assistance with bail at **https://lawzana.com/ bail-bond-service-lawyers/ buenos-aires-fd.**

Legal Representation

If you're a tourist arrested in Argentina, it's crucial to understand your rights and access to legal representation. To secure adequate legal representation, follow the following steps:

---

79 https://cidh.oas.org/annualrep/97eng/Argentina11205.htm

1. **Request Consular Assistance:** Contact your embassy or consulate immediately and inform them of your arrest. Under international law, you have the right to consular notification, and consular officials can provide you with a list of local lawyers who speak your language and can assist you in navigating the legal system.

> ### U.S. Embassy in Buenos Aires
> Av. Colombia
> 4300 (C1425GMN) Buenos Aires, Argentina
> Phone: (54-11) 5777-4533

2. **Ask for a Lawyer:** When arrested, you have the right to legal representation. If you don't have a lawyer, you can request one during your initial hearing or after being informed of the charges. The consulate can assist in facilitating this.

   List of local English-speaking attorney provided through the U.S. State Department can be accessed at **https://ar.usembassy.gov/list-of-attorneys/**.

3. **Ask for an Interpreter:** If you don't speak Spanish, you can request an interpreter during legal proceedings, and your consulate can help ensure one is provided.

4. **Contact a Local Lawyer:** If you're unable to reach your embassy immediately, you can seek out a local lawyer specializing in criminal law. It's advisable to work with a lawyer familiar with the Argentine legal system, as the procedures may differ from your home country.

Healthcare System and Medical Facilities

Argentina's healthcare system has **three sectors**—public, social security, and private. The **public** system provides free healthcare to everyone, including tourists, but may involve long waits and language barriers. The **private** sector offers faster, higher-quality care with multilingual staff, though at higher costs; foreign visitors are advised to carry international health insurance for coverage.

Argentina is also a **medical tourism hub**, with top hospitals in cities like Buenos Aires, Córdoba, and Mendoza (e.g., the British Hospital and Italian Hospital) known for international standards and English-speaking staff. These facilities provide emergency, routine, and advanced treatments—often at lower costs than in Western countries—while medical tourism agencies help coordinate care and logistics.

Access to Pre-Exposure Prophylaxis (PrEP) Treatment

In Argentina, **PrEP has been available free through the public health-care system since 2018**, mainly via the Ministry of Health's HIV/AIDS program. Oral PrEP is widely accessible in urban centers like Buenos Aires, Córdoba, and Rosario, while injectable PrEP was recently approved but is not yet broadly available.

Both residents and non-residents (including tourists and undocumented individuals) are legally entitled to public healthcare, though access can vary by province; some regions require non-residents to pay for non-emergency services. Public PrEP access includes free medication, consultations, and lab monitoring, while private clinics charge around ARS 7,000–10,000 ($35–50 USD) per month.

PrEP is provided through **specialized HIV clinics, sexual health centers, some trained general practitioners, and telemedicine services**, with eligibility based on HIV-negative status and elevated risk factors. Regular follow-ups and lab monitoring every three months are standard, and community organizations help navigate access and reduce barriers.

 Safety Precautions for LGBTQ+ Travelers

LGBTQ+ travelers in Argentina can enjoy a welcoming environment, especially in urban areas like Buenos Aires, known for its acceptance and vibrant culture. However, it's important to be aware that attitudes can vary, with rural regions often being more conservative. Understanding local laws and customs is crucial for a positive travel experience.

Emergency Contact Numbers

- **Police:** 911
- **Ambulance:** 911
- **Fire Department:** 100
- **U.S. Embassy in Buenos Aires:** (54-11) 5777-4533

Useful Emergency Phrases in Spanish

HELP! – ¡Ayuda! *(ah-ZHOO-dah)*

CALL AN AMBULANCE! – ¡Llamá a una ambulancia! *(zhah-MAH ah OO-nah am-boo-LAN-syah)*

> (NOTE: "Llamá" is the voseo form used in Argentina; in standard Spanish it would be "Llama")

I NEED A DOCTOR – Necesito un médico *(neh-seh-SEE-toh oon MEH-dee-koh)*

POLICE – Policía *(poh-lee-SEE-ah)*

I'M LOST – Estoy perdido/a *(ehs-TOY pehr-DEE-doh/dah)*

IT'S AN EMERGENCY – Es una emergencia *(ehs OO-nah eh-mehr-HEN-syah)*

URUGUAY

Uruguay is a stable, democratic republic known for its progressive political stance, **being one of the first countries in Latin America to legalize same-sex marriage**, abortion, and marijuana. The country boasts high standards of living, low corruption, and strong human rights protections. Culturally, it blends European influences, especially from Spain and Italy, reflected in its food, music (notably tango and candombe), and festivals. Most Uruguayans are secular, though Roman Catholicism is the largest religion, with religious diversity growing in recent years.

 ## Politics and LGBTQ+ Legislation

Uruguay is considered a **liberal** country, especially in terms of its social policies. The country has progressive labor laws and a strong focus on human rights and social equality. While traditionally more conservative in certain rural areas, Uruguay's political and social landscape has become increasingly liberal in recent decades, with a focus on individual freedoms and secularism.

Uruguay has been a pioneer in LGBTQ+ rights in Latin America. **Same-sex marriage has been legal since 2013**, although civil unions for same-sex couples were recognized in 2008, granting them many of the same rights as married couples. Uruguay also allows joint adoption by same-sex couples, making it the first in the region to do so. Comprehensive anti-discrimination laws protect LGBTQ+ individuals, including provisions against hate crimes. The country has also granted legal gender recognition to transgender individuals since 2009, without requiring surgery, and updated laws in 2018 removed medical or psychological requirements. LGBTQ+ individuals have been able to serve openly in the military since 2009.

 ## LGBTQ+ Scene

Uruguay has a vibrant, open LGBTQ+ scene, particularly in its capital, **Montevideo**, the cultural and political hub, and home to a thriving LGBTQ+ nightlife, with a variety of gay bars, clubs, and cultural events. The city's Pride Parade, known as *Marcha de la Diversidad*, is a significant annual event, attracting large crowds and celebrating the rights and visibility of the LGBTQ+ community. Other cities like **Punta del Este** and **Colonia** also host LGBTQ+ friendly venues, though the scene is smaller compared to Montevideo.

In addition to Pride celebrations, Uruguay has an active LGBTQ+ community involved in advocacy, with organizations working on issues such as HIV/AIDS prevention, transgender rights, and combating discrimination. The country's inclusive atmosphere and legal protections make it a popular destination for LGBTQ+ travelers seeking a safe and welcoming environment.

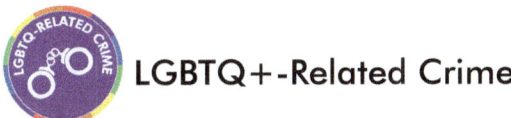 ## LGBTQ+-Related Crime

While there are few reported hate crimes against the LGBTQ+ community, it's unclear whether this is due to underreporting or an actual low incidence of such crimes. Uruguay's robust anti-discrimination laws are key in deterring hate crimes and protecting LGBTQ+ individuals from aggression. Since the early 2000s, the country has enacted laws that safeguard against discrimination based on sexual orientation and gender identity. Notably, *Article 149ter of the Penal Code* targets hate crimes, prescribing enhanced penalties for offenses motivated by prejudice, further strengthening protections for the LGBTQ+ community.

LGBTQ+ and Prostitution

Prostitution is legal in Uruguay, but it is regulated under *Law 17.515* of 2002, which established specific regulations for sex work. Under this law, sex workers must register with the government and undergo regular health checks to ensure their safety and well-being. However, activities such as pimping, operating brothels, or coercion into sex work remain illegal.

LGBTQ+ individuals, especially transgender people, are disproportionately represented in informal sex work, with many trans women facing high unemployment and discrimination. An estimated 67% of transgender women have engaged in sex work at some point in their lives.[80] These individuals face significant vulnerabilities, including physical violence, discrimination, and systemic exclusion from education and employment. Health risks, particularly high HIV rates among transgender sex workers, are a major concern.[81] While registered workers benefit from health checks, unregistered or street-based sex workers often lack access to essential health services, increasing their risks.

LGBTQ+ and Jail System

Uruguay has made significant strides in advancing LGBTQ+ rights, however, despite these advancements, serious concerns remain regarding the treatment of LGBTQ+ individuals within the prison system. The Uruguayan prison system historically has faced issues related to overcrowding, inadequate living conditions, and insufficient healthcare for inmates. LGBTQ+ individuals, particularly transgender prisoners, often encounter additional challenges.

In 2024, Uruguay announced plans to construct a new women's prison that will accommodate transgender inmates, marking an important step

---

80 https://ihrp.law.utoronto.ca/sites/default/files/media/Uruguay%20 Report-%20Final.pdf

81 https://www.worldbank.org/en/news/feature/2016/07/21/ uruguay-global-leader-lgbti-right

126

towards creating a safer and more inclusive environment for LGBTQ+ individuals in detention. This facility aims to provide a space that supports rehabilitation and allows inmates to choose whether they would prefer to be housed in a men's or women's facility, based on their gender identity.[82]

 ## Arrested in Uruguay

Understanding the legal system in Uruguay is crucial for any individual arrested while visiting the country. Uruguay operates under a civil law legal system, deeply influenced by Spanish law, characterized by its comprehensive codes that form the backbone of legal procedures.[83]

Individuals arrested in Uruguay are afforded several rights under the country's constitution. Among the key rights is the presumption of innocence, which is foundational to the judicial process. This means that individuals remain innocent until proven guilty in a court of law. Additionally, the constitution guarantees a general right to legal counsel. Thus, detainees have the right to access a lawyer of their choice, or one provided by the state, ensuring they receive adequate legal representation during legal proceedings.

Legal representation is critical, as Uruguayan courts operate under different protocols and may require specific legal knowledge. It is essential to understand the differences in criminal procedures compared to those of other jurisdictions, such as the United States. Staying informed about one's legal rights is crucial. For instance, detainees should be aware that any confession made under duress or without the presence of a lawyer may not stand in court. Furthermore, there are protections to prevent harsh treatment during detention, as Uruguay's legal system recognizes

82 https://insightcrime.org/news/brief/
    uruguay-considers-deporting-foreign-prisoners

83 https://library.law.northwestern.edu/UruguayITP/foreign

the significance of humane conditions for detainees.[84] Should any potential violations of these rights occur, these can be challenged through proper judicial channels.

Finally, understanding the possible implications of the arrest is important. Different offenses can lead to varied outcomes, including fines, community service, or imprisonment depending on the severity of the crime. The duration of detention prior to trial may also differ significantly from one country to another; therefore, legal advice is indispensable in navigating these factors effectively.

In Uruguay, if you're arrested, the law generally ensures that you will see a judge relatively quickly. According to Uruguayan law, you should be brought before a judge within **24 hours** of your arrest. This is in line with international human rights standards, ensuring that individuals are not held in detention without being formally charged or having the opportunity to contest their detention before a judge.

Bail

In Uruguay, foreign nationals may be granted bail, but eligibility depends on factors such as the severity of the offense—serious crimes like drug trafficking or violent acts usually preclude bail. The process requires judicial review by an Examining Magistrate and consent from the Public Prosecutor, with guarantees provided as monetary deposits or property collateral.

Foreigners often face challenges meeting these financial requirements, especially without local contacts, and delays can occur due to court backlogs. Legal representation is highly recommended, and embassies can assist by connecting detainees with lawyers, though they cannot provide bail funds directly. While not required, having a lawyer can provide legal guidance and representation throughout the bail bond process. You can find a list of qualified lawyers practicing

---

84   https://www.state.gov/wp-content/uploads/2024/02/528267_
     URUGUAY-2023-HUMAN-RIGHTS-REPORT.pdf

in Uruguay at **https://lawzana.com/bail-bond service-lawyers/ montevideo-departamento-de-montevide**o.

Legal Representation

One of the significant aspects of legal representation for foreigners in Uruguay is the ability to choose their attorney. Foreigners may select local lawyers or request a list of attorneys provided by their embassy. Lawyers in Uruguay, including those specializing in criminal defense, are expected to provide adequate representation, speaking to the detainee's rights.[85] The availability of interpreters is also a notable consideration; if a foreign national does not speak Spanish proficiently, interpreters can be arranged to facilitate effective communication with their legal counsel and judicial authorities.

However, there are unique challenges faced by foreign nationals when seeking legal representation in Uruguay. One of these challenges is financial, as foreigners may not have immediate access to funds to hire an attorney. In such cases, it is crucial for foreign nationals to explore options for legal aid available through the local bar association or legal assistance programs that may extend services to individuals lacking financial resources. Some lawyers may accept reduced fees or offer pro bono assistance, particularly in cases with significant humanitarian considerations.

The judicial system in Uruguay can differ significantly from those in other countries, particularly concerning timeframes for legal proceedings and procedural norms. For instance, protracted detention before a trial may occur, which necessitates prompt and effective legal representation from the outset to advocate for the rights of the accused. Foreign nationals must understand that their legal counsel will be pivotal in navigating these complexities and focusing on securing a favorable outcome, whether it involves contesting the validity of charges or negotiating plea agreements.

---

85 https://www.nyulawglobal.org/globalex/uruguay.html

If you are a U.S. citizen, establish contact with the U.S. embassy as soon as possible.

U.S. Embassy in Montevideo
Lauro Müller 1776
Montevideo, Uruguay
Phone: (+598) 1770-2000
Email: gpadigitalsupport@state.gov

The list of local attorneys in Uruguay, provided by the U.S. State Department, is accessible at
https://uy.usembassy.gov/legal-assistance-attorney-list/.

Healthcare System and Medical Facilities

Uruguay offers both **public** and **private healthcare**. The public system, managed by ASSE, provides low-cost or free care to residents and some expatriates, but foreign visitors often prefer private facilities for higher quality, shorter wait times, and personalized services. **International health insurance** is recommended, and proof of coverage may be required for entry.

Private healthcare options include plans like **Mutualista** and hospitals such as the **British Hospital, Asociación Española**, and **Médica Uruguaya**, which offer multilingual staff and specialized care. Teaching hospitals like **Hospital de Clínicas** provide advanced treatments but may have longer waits. These institutions cater well to foreign visitors seeking timely, high-quality medical services.

Access to Pre-Exposure Prophylaxis (PrEP) Treatment

In Uruguay, **oral PrEP has been available through the public health system since 2022** and is offered **free of charge** to eligible individuals, including MSM, transgender women, people who inject drugs, and serodiscordant couples. Eligibility can also be extended at the provider's discretion based on individual risk factors.

Access requires initial HIV testing, kidney function screening, and follow-up visits every three months, primarily through government-run sexual health and HIV prevention clinics. PrEP is available to both residents and non-residents, and community organizations may provide additional support, though awareness and access can be more limited outside major cities. Injectable PrEP is not yet available.

 ## Safety Precautions for LGBTQ+ Travelers

Uruguay is widely regarded as one of the safest and most LGBTQ+-friendly countries in Latin America, especially in urban centers like Montevideo. While LGBTQ+ travelers can enjoy a vibrant scene of bars, clubs, and cultural venues in cities, it's important to remain mindful of local customs, particularly in more conservative rural areas. Public displays of affection may draw attention outside major cities, but overall, Uruguay offers a welcoming and supportive environment for LGBTQ+ visitors.

Emergency Contact Numbers

- **Police:** 911 or 109
- **Ambulance:** 105
- **Fire Department:** 104
- **U.S. Embassy in Montevideo:** (598) 1770-2000

Useful Emergency Phrases in Spanish

HELP! – ¡Ayuda! *(ah-ZHOO-dah)*

CALL AN AMBULANCE! – ¡Llamá a una ambulancia! *(zhah-MAH ah OO-nah am-boo-LAN-syah)*

(**NOTE**: "Llamá" is the voseo form used in Uruguay; in standard Spanish it would be "Llama")

I NEED A DOCTOR – Necesito un médico *(neh-seh-SEE-toh oon MEH-dee-koh)*

POLICE – Policía *(poh-lee-SEE-ah)*

I'M LOST – Estoy perdido/a *(ehs-TOY pehr-DEE-doh/dah)*

IT'S AN EMERGENCY – Es una emergencia *(ehs OO-nah eh-mehr-HEN-syah)*

ITALY

Italy, located in Southern Europe, is a parliamentary republic with a multi-party system. The President is the head of state, and the Prime Minister leads the government. The country faces regional disparities, with the north being more prosperous than the south. Italian society is family-oriented, but challenges like an aging population, immigration, and youth unemployment are growing. Culturally, Italy is renowned for its art, cuisine, fashion, and Renaissance history, with Milan being a global fashion hub. While Roman Catholicism is dominant, Italy is becoming more secular, especially among younger generations, though the Vatican in Rome remains a key religious center.

Politics and LGBTQ+ Legislation

Italy is generally considered socially **conservative**, with some liberal influences, especially in urban areas and among younger generations. Traditionally, Italian society has strong ties to Catholic values, which has influenced views on issues like marriage, family, and sexual orientation. However, Italy has become more liberal over time, particularly on issues like LGBTQ+ rights and women's rights, especially in major cities like Milan and Rome.

While Italy is generally accepting of the LGBTQ+ community, legal recognition of LGBTQ+ individuals remains limited. Same-sex relationships are legal and widely accepted, and civil unions have been recognized by law since 2016. However, **same-sex marriage is still not legalized**. While there are anti-discrimination laws in place for employment, formal protections against discrimination based on sexual orientation or gender identity are lacking in many other areas of life.

True Story[86]

In October 2024, Italy passed a law banning citizens from seeking surrogacy abroad, criminalizing the practice in countries where it's legal, like the U.S. and Canada. The law, backed by Prime Minister Giorgia Meloni's far-right party, imposed fines and jail time for offenders. Critics argue the law targets LGBTQ+ families, who are most affected, and ignores Italy's declining birth rate. Activists call it discriminatory, noting that while most surrogacy users in Italy are heterosexual, they often keep it private, making the law disproportionately impact same-sex couples.

---

86 www.usatoday.com/story/news/world/2024/10/16/
italy-bans-surrogacy-meloni/

 **LGBTQ+ Scene**

Italy is generally LGBTQ+-friendly, particularly in major cities like Milan, Venice, Florence, and Rome, which are known for their vibrant LGBTQ+ scenes. Northern cities, along with popular spots like Capri and Taormina, are especially welcoming. However, rural areas tend to be less tolerant, and open displays of affection may attract attention.

Italy's LGBTQ+ community is diverse and vibrant, with several prominent Pride events across the country. In **Rome**, areas like Trastevere and Gay Street are hubs of LGBTQ+ life, hosting annual events such as *Roma Pride* and *Gay Village*. **Milan**, a fashion capital, is home to a lively LGBTQ+ culture, especially in *Porta Venezia*, with *Milan Pride* being a major celebration. **Florence**, known for its art, hosts the *Florence Queer Festival*, celebrating LGBTQ+ cinema and arts, while **Bologna**, a university city, features *Bologna Pride* and the Cassero LGBT Center, a key venue for activism and events. LGBTQ+ representation in Italy is also seen in cinema, literature, and performance, while festivals and platforms like *Gay.it* play a significant role in advocating for gay visibility and advancing LGBTQ+ rights.

Beyond Pride events, Italy offers a vibrant range of LGBTQ+ activities and organizations focused on advocacy, culture, and support. LGBTQ+ film festivals like the Tuscany Queer Film Festival and Firenze Queer Festival showcase gay cinema, while performances and drag shows in cities like Milan and Rome provide both entertainment and activism. Italy also has several active LGBTQ+ organizations that play a crucial role in advocating for rights, support, and visibility. *Arcigay*, the largest LGBTQ+ group, focuses on legal reforms and anti-discrimination efforts; *Agedo* works to support LGBTQ+ individuals and their families, fostering acceptance and understanding, while *Famiglie Arcobaleno* advocates for the rights of LGBTQ+ parents, particularly around adoption and family recognition.

 # LGBTQ+-Related Crime

Hate crimes targeting LGBTQ+ individuals in Italy have been a growing concern. In 2022, there were 1,393 reported hate crimes, but specific data on LGBTQ+ violence remains scarce. Advocacy groups have highlighted the lack of comprehensive statistics on LGBTQ+ hate crimes since 2018.[87]

Legislative efforts to strengthen protections have also faced setbacks, with a bill to classify violence against LGBTQ+ people as hate crimes rejected by the Senate in 2021, due to opposition from conservative and far-right groups. This lack of legal recognition and insufficient protections contribute to a climate where many LGBTQ+ individuals hesitate to report incidents. A recent survey showed that the percentage of LGBTQ+ people experiencing hate-motivated violence rose from 11% in 2019 to 14% in 2023, signaling increasing concerns about safety within the community.[88]

LGBTQ+ and Prostitution

Prostitution itself is legal; however, many operations connected to sex work are regulated. The *Merlin Law* (Law 75/1958) prohibits the operation of brothels and criminalizes pimping, but it allows individuals to sell sexual services independently. This legal backdrop creates a challenging environment for sex workers, as they have to navigate laws that aim to control rather than fully recognize their rights. Sex workers are not required to register or undergo mandatory health checks, though health and safety are promoted by advocacy groups. Public solicitation is also prohibited in many areas, with local authorities imposing fines for violations of street prostitution laws.

---

87 https://hatecrime.osce.org/italy

88 https://www.politico.eu/article/violence-lgbtq-rights-rise-europe-report

While there is a lack of comprehensive data regarding LGBTQ+ individuals in Italy, qualitative studies and observations suggest that LGBTQ+ sex workers, especially transgender people, are overrepresented in sex work due to discrimination and limited job opportunities. Like elsewhere, these sex workers face high rates of violence, both physical and sexual, and struggle with barriers to healthcare and legal support, while fear of retaliation and social stigma contribute to the underreporting of these crimes.

LGBTQ+ and Jail System

Italy's prison system presents both challenges and progress for LGBTQ+ inmates, particularly transgender individuals facing higher risks of abuse, harassment, and sexual violence.

Despite legal advancements like civil unions, the lack of comprehensive protections for LGBTQ+ people in prisons contributes to an environment of fear and marginalization.

In response, Italy has introduced some specialized accommodations, such as a dedicated unit for transgender inmates at Raffaele Cinotti prison in Rome, aimed at providing safer conditions. However, these measures have been criticized for isolating inmates from rehabilitation programs and other support services.

 **Arrested in Italy**

The process of arresting a foreign visitor in Italy can occur with or without a warrant. In serious criminal cases, an arrest may take place based on the urgency of the situation, where law enforcement has reasonable grounds to detain the person. As in other countries, upon arrest, individuals must be informed of their rights, including the right to remain silent, the right to contact their consulate, and the right to a legal representative.

According to Italian law, you must see a judge within **48 hours** of being arrested; the public prosecutor must notify the judge within this time-frame, and the judge will then decide whether to validate the arrest and order further detention or release the person. During this hearing, the accused has the right to legal representation, and if they cannot afford a lawyer, one will be appointed.[89] It is essential for visitors to have access to competent legal advice to navigate the complexities of the Italian legal system.

Bail

In Italy, bail (*"libertà provvisoria"*) is not automatically available to all foreign detainees, especially those held under immigration laws or without charge. Eligibility depends on factors like the detainee's **risk of flight**, the nature of the charges, and their immigration status. Courts must review detention and bail conditions within **48 hours**, and release may include restrictions or financial guarantees. Unlike some countries, Italy does **not allow private bail bonds**; bail is granted at judicial discretion within the pre-trial detention framework rather than as a guaranteed right.

To find Italian bail bonds service lawyers, please visit **https://lawzana. com/bail-bond-service-lawyers/rome-rome**.

Legal Representation

If you are arrested in Italy, as soon as possible, you should request to speak with a lawyer. Under Italian law, you have the right to consult with a lawyer immediately after your arrest.[90] If you do not have the means to hire a lawyer, you can request legal aid, which may be granted if you can demonstrate a lack of financial resources. In Italy, legal aid is available to

---

89 https://www.thelocal.it/20220524/
    what-happens-when-a-foreign-national-gets-arrested-in-italy

90 https://www.giambronelaw.com/site/advice/criminal-law/ital-
    ian-criminal-law/rights-proceedings-italy/arrested-accused-italy/
    your-rights-after-arrested-in-italy

individuals who cannot afford the services of a private lawyer. According to Italian law, foreign detainees who demonstrate economic hardship may qualify for free legal assistance. The process for applying for legal aid involves a formal request, which is submitted to the relevant legal authority, typically at the time of initial detention or arrest.[91]

Remember that as a foreign detainee you have the right to:

- Be informed of the reasons for your arrest.
- Consult with a lawyer of your choice.
- Be treated fairly and humanely during the detention process.
- Receive medical care if needed.
- Contact your family or a trusted person to inform them of your situation and whereabouts.

Also, a foreign national, it is highly advisable to inform your embassy or consulate of your arrest. You can request to make a phone call to your embassy, which can provide assistance such as legal referrals, language Aservices, and additional know-how regarding your rights as a foreigner. While consular representatives cannot interfere directly with the legal proceedings, they can help you understand your situation and rights in the Italian legal system.

U.S. Embassy Rome
via Vittorio Veneto 121
00187 Roma
Phone: (+39) 06 46741

A list of English-speaking attorneys in Italy, provided by the U.S. State Department, can be accessed at
https://it.usembassy.gov/u-s-citizen-services/attorneys/.

---

91 https://www.giambronelaw.com/site/advice/criminal-law/italian-criminal-law/rights-proceedings-italy/arrested-accused-italy/your-rights-after-arrested-in-italy/

Healthcare System and Medical Facilities

Italy's healthcare system offers both **public and private services**. EU citizens can use the **EHIC** for access similar to residents, while non-EU visitors are generally responsible for medical costs and are advised to have travel health insurance. **Emergency care** is available to all tourists without prior payment.

Many visitors use private facilities for faster or specialized care, though at higher out-of-pocket costs. Top hospitals for international patients include **Policlinico Universitario A. Gemelli** in Rome, **Ospedale San Raffaele** in Milan, and **Humanitas Research Hospital** in Milan, all offering multilingual staff and services tailored to foreign visitors.

Access to Pre-Exposure Prophylaxis (PrEP) Treatment

PrEP is available in Italy and has been approved since 2017, primarily as the daily oral tablet (TDF/FTC). Long-acting injectable PrEP is not yet widely accessible. From April 2023, high-risk individuals registered with the **National Health Service (SSN)** can receive PrEP and associated testing free of charge, though coverage varies by region.

Access points include hospital infectious disease clinics and certified community health centers, mainly in cities like Rome, Milan, Bologna, Turin, and Palermo, with limited availability in rural areas. **Non-residents and tourists** are not covered by SSN and must use private healthcare, paying for consultations, tests, and medication—typically around €150 ($177 USD) for the initial visit plus €60 ($77 USD) per month for the drug.

 ## Safety Precautions for LGBTQ+ Travelers

When traveling through Italy, it's advisable to exercise discretion and keep public displays of affection to a minimum. While Italy is a romantic country, many locals prefer to keep expressions of love private, particularly when it comes to gay relationships. With its strong religious influences, some areas can be less accepting, and LGBTQ+ travelers may face unwanted scrutiny so it's advisable to be discreet. Staying informed about local laws, knowing your rights, and choosing LGBTQ+ friendly accommodations can enhance safety and comfort during your trip.

Emergency Contact Numbers

- **Police:** 113
- **Ambulance:** 118
- **Fire Department:** 115
- **U.S. Embassy in Rome:** +39 06 46741

Useful Emergency Phrases in Italian

HELP! – Aiuto! *(ah-YOO-toh)*

CALL AN AMBULANCE! – Chiama un'ambulanza! *(KYA-mah oon am-boo-LAN-tsah)*

I NEED A DOCTOR – Ho bisogno di un dottore *(oh bee-ZOH-nyoh dee oon doht-TOH-reh)*

POLICE – Polizia *(poh-LEE-tsee-ah)*

I'M LOST – Mi sono perso/a *(mee SOH-no PEHR-soh/sah)*

IT'S AN EMERGENCY – È un'emergenza *(eh oon eh-mehr-JEN-tsah)*

MEXICO

Mexico, the third-largest country in Latin America, characterized by a diverse geography, is a federal republic with a multi-party system, where the president serves as both head of state and government. The country has a rich cultural heritage, blending indigenous traditions and Spanish influences, and is renowned for its cuisine, art, music, and festivals like Día de los Muertos. Mexico's society is family-oriented, with a young population facing challenges like poverty, inequality, and drug violence, particularly in certain regions. While Roman Catholicism is dominant, religious practice has declined in recent years, and Protestantism is growing. Urban areas like Mexico City are thriving, but rural regions still experience slower development.

 ## Politics and LGBTQ+ Legislation

Mexico is generally considered considerably **liberal** in terms of social policies compared to many other countries in Latin America. Over the past two decades, Mexico has made significant strides in areas such as LGBTQ+ rights, women's reproductive rights, and decriminalizing certain drugs.

As of end of 2022, all states in Mexico have passed laws to legalize same sex marriage. Mexico has made progress in LGBTQ+ rights, with anti-discrimination laws for sexual orientation in the federal constitution since 2011, though enforcement varies by state. Transgender individuals can legally change their gender and name in Mexico City and 18 states through a simplified process. **Joint adoption by same-sex couples is legal in Mexico City and 21 states**, but adoption rights are not consistent nationwide.

True Story

A prominent activist and Mexico's first openly non-binary judge was found dead in a suspected murder that led to "an outpouring of grief" from the country's LGBTQ+ community. Jesús Ociel Baena, 39, was found at home "slain with a razor blade", reported Reuters. A person identified by local media as Baena's partner Dorian Nieves Herrera was also found dead. Candlelit vigils and demonstrations took place in several cities, where "many shed tears and speakers lashed out at the insults and acts of violence that remain a common occurrence for many gay, transgender and non-binary Mexicans."

 LGBTQ+ Scene

Mexico has a vibrant and evolving LGBTQ+ scene, rooted in rich cultural history but shaped by colonial influences that led to widespread discrimination. Major cities like **Mexico City**, **Guadalajara**, and **Monterrey** are LGBTQ+ cultural hubs, hosting large `Pride parades and events like the *Lesbian-Gay Cultural Week*, which celebrates art and community. *Pride Month*, celebrated every June, features colorful parades and cultural events, with the *Mexico City Pride Parade*—Latin America's largest—drawing hundreds of thousands of participants. This month-long celebration includes street fairs, concerts, and workshops that promote visibility and engage with critical issues like anti-discrimination laws and mental health. While Pride serves as a joyful celebration, it also highlights ongoing struggles for equality and justice, with activists pushing for systemic change. Cities such as Mexico City, Puerto Vallarta, and Guadalajara, especially neighborhoods like Zona Rosa, are recognized for their LGBTQ+-friendly environments, offering safe spaces for socializing and advocacy.

Beyond Pride Month, Mexico has a vibrant LGBTQ+ scene with year-round cultural events, advocacy, and community activities. LGBTQ+ film festivals like the *Muestra Internacional de Cine Queer* and *Festival Internacional de Cine de Guanajuato* spotlight gay cinema, while cities like Mexico City, Guadalajara, and Monterrey host gay art exhibitions, drag performances, and LGBTQ+ theater. Organizations like *CONAPRED* and *Letra S* advocate for LGBTQ+ rights, focusing on anti-discrimination and HIV/AIDS awareness, while groups such as the *Red de Juventud LGBT* support LGBTQ+ youth, and *Almas Cautivas* advocates for LGBTQ+ rights in prisons.

 ## LGBTQ+-Related Crime

Mexico has seen a troubling increase in hate crimes against the LGBTQ+ community, including physical violence, discrimination, and even murders, with transgender individuals, especially trans women, being the primary targets. The recent murder of non-binary judge Jesús Ociel Baena in November 2023 underscores the severity of the issue.[92] Since 2014, 453 anti-LGBTQ+ hate crimes have been reported, with a significant rise in 2021.[93] Despite existing laws, many feel they are inadequate, leaving LGBTQ+ people—both locals and tourists—vulnerable to harassment, unless they take precautions and seek safe spaces.

LGBTQ+ and Prostitution

Sex work is not fully legalized but is regulated in some areas, with significant legal variations across states. Since 2019, Mexico City has decriminalized sex work, offering some protections to sex workers, but most states continue to criminalize activities like pimping and trafficking. In cities like Mexico City, Tijuana, and Guadalajara, sex work is allowed within regulated zones, which require registration and health checks.[94] However, brothels and establishments profiting from sex work remain

---

92 https://theweek.com/crime/death-nonbinary-judge-mexico-lgbtq-rights

93 https://www.statista.com/statistics/1280644/
number-lgbtq-hate-crimes-mexico/

94 https://revista.drclas.harvard.edu/
sex-work-law-and-police-in-mexico-city

illegal. Outside these zones, sex workers, particularly LGBTQ+ individuals, face discrimination, violence, and lack of legal protections, including limited access to healthcare and labor rights. Transgender sex workers are particularly vulnerable to violence, abuse, and human trafficking, often perpetrated by clients or law enforcement, further discouraging reporting of incidents.

LGBTQ+ and Jail System

While some legal protections for LGBTQ+ individuals exist in Mexico, societal prejudice and insufficient law enforcement training contribute to their mistreatment. Transgender individuals and those involved in sex work are often arrested on charges such as "public indecency" or "moral offenses." High-profile cases, like the 2021 arrest of a gay couple in Tulum for kissing on the beach, highlight the ongoing discrimination faced by the LGBTQ+ community, sparking public outrage and calls for reform.[95] Arrests are also influenced by profiling and discriminatory attitudes, especially in conservative regions. Once incarcerated, LGBTQ+ inmates, particularly transgender individuals, face increased risks of violence and abuse, with legal protections remaining inadequate.

 Arrested in Mexico

Understanding the arrest and detention process can help mitigate the stress associated with encountering the police in Mexico. When arrested, individuals may be held for up to **72 hours** before a determination is made on whether charges will be filed. It is important to note that the Mexican legal system is primarily based on the inquisitorial process. The district attorney, *"Ministerio Público,"* conducts the investigation and decides on the prosecution. Consequently, there are no jury trials;

---

95 https://mexiconewsdaily.com/news/tulum-police-arrest-gay-couple-for-kissing-in-public-with-children-present/

hearings occur in closed court sessions where the defendant may not see the judge directly.[96]

In the case of federal crimes, the judicial jurisdiction is stricter; offenses related to organized crime, drug trafficking, and human trafficking are often handled by federal courts.[97] Being informed about whether the offense you are accused of falls under state or federal jurisdiction can prepare you for differences in treatment and potential penalties.

In the event of an arrest, visitors should follow specific guidelines to protect their rights and interests. First, it is advisable to remain calm and respectful, as aggression can escalate the situation. Do not resist arrest, as this can lead to additional charges. Ask for the reason for the arrest and assert your right to contact your country's consulate. The consulate can provide assistance and guidance throughout the legal process, though they cannot interfere with the local judicial system.

It is essential to document the event accurately, including the names of the arresting officers and any witnesses. If possible, obtain a receipt of any belongings taken during the arrest, as this will help mitigate any potential disputes regarding property management. Finally, avoid making any statements to the police without legal counsel present as that may hurt your defense later.

Bail

In **Mexico,** foreign detainees may be eligible for bail, but it depends on the crime's severity and case specifics—serious offenses like violent or organized crime often preclude bail. Judges decide on bail based on flight risk, community ties, and the nature of the offense, rather than a traditional cash bail system.

Bail conditions can include electronic monitoring, check-ins, or surrendering a passport. The process typically begins with a **hearing**

---

96 https://math.ucr.edu/~ftm/bajapages/Legal.html

97 https://travel.gc.ca/travelling/advisories/mexico/
mexican-criminal-law-system

within 48 hours, where a defense attorney presents arguments for release. Competent legal representation and access to an interpreter for non-Spanish speakers are crucial, and procedures may vary by jurisdiction.

For assistance with bail, you may want to retain services of a qualified lawyer skilled in the applicable area of law that can be found at **https:// lawzana.com/bail-bond-service-lawyers/mexico**.

Legal Representation

If you're a foreign visitor in Mexico and need legal representation, it's essential to seek out a lawyer who specializes in international law or a local law firm experienced in assisting foreigners. These professionals can help guide you through various legal matters you may encounter, such as real estate transactions, business disputes, criminal charges, or immigration concerns. A list of local attorneys can be provided by your home embassy or consulate.

Given that legal systems differ across countries, hiring a Mexican lawyer with expertise in local laws and procedures is crucial to ensure that your rights are protected and that you comply with the local legal framework.

If you're unable to be physically present in Mexico for legal matters like property transactions or contract signings, you can grant a Power of Attorney to a local lawyer to act on your behalf. This allows a trusted lawyer to handle legal proceedings for you while you're abroad. Many large international law firms also have offices in Mexico and offer legal services to foreign clients dealing with complex legal issues. Common areas where foreign visitors may need legal assistance include immigration matters like visa applications and residency permits, criminal defense in case of arrest or accusations, civil disputes such as contract or property issues, and business transactions like company formation and real estate purchases. To find a lawyer, you can use online directories that list legal professionals specializing in international law, contact the Mexican Bar Association for recommendations, or consult your country's consulate in Mexico, which may offer referrals to local attorneys.

U.S. Embassy in Mexico City
Paseo de la Reforma 305
Colonia Cuauhtémoc
06500 Mexico City
Phone: +55 5080 2000

Healthcare System and Medical Facilities

Foreign visitors to Mexico are **generally not eligible for public healthcare** and must secure private or travel medical insurance. Private healthcare is widely available, high quality, and often English-speaking, though patients pay out-of-pocket unless insured. General consultations typically cost $30–$60 USD.

Mexico is also a popular destination for medical tourism, with top private facilities including **Hospital Médica Sur**, **Centro Médico ABC**, **Hospital Galenia**, **Hospitales Ángeles**, and **Christus Muguerza**, all offering specialized care, advanced technologies, and multilingual support.

Access to Pre-Exposure Prophylaxis (PrEP) Treatment

PrEP has been available in Mexico since 2021 as part of the national HIV prevention strategy. Oral PrEP is free through public healthcare systems like INSABI and IMSS for HIV-negative adults in high-risk populations, with services including follow-up and lab testing. Injectable PrEP is not yet approved.

Non-residents and tourists cannot access free public PrEP but can obtain it privately in cities like Mexico City and Guadalajara. Private access involves a consultation (~$60 USD), lab tests, and a prescription, with a one-month supply costing around $100 USD. Pharmacies generally require a prescription; PrEP is not available over the counter.

 ## Safety Precautions for LGBTQ+ Travelers

When traveling in Mexico, it's important to understand local attitudes toward LGBTQ+ individuals. While cities like Mexico City, Cancun, and Puerto Vallarta are LGBTQ+-friendly, more conservative areas may still harbor homophobic sentiments. In conservative areas, practice discretion—simple acts of affection like kissing or holding hands may attract negative attention. It's a good idea to always research the specific regions you plan to visit! To stay safe, opt for accommodations in LGBTQ+-friendly neighborhoods, such as Zona Rosa in Mexico City or the Romantic Zone in Puerto Vallarta, where you'll find a supportive community.

Emergency Contact Numbers

- **Police/Ambulance/Fire Department:** 911
- **U.S. Embassy in Mexico City:** +55 5080 2000

Useful Emergency Phrases in Spanish

HELP! – ¡Ayuda! *(ah-YOO-dah)*

CALL AN AMBULANCE! – ¡Llame a una ambulancia! *(YAH-meh ah OO-nah am-boo-LAN-syah)*

I NEED A DOCTOR – Necesito un médico *(neh-seh-SEE-toh oon MEH-dee-koh)*

POLICE – Policía *(poh-lee-SEE-ah)*

I'M LOST – Estoy perdido/a *(ehs-TOY pehr-DEE-doh/dah)*

　(Use "perdido" if you're male, "perdida" if you're female)

IT'S AN EMERGENCY – Es una emergencia *(ehs OO-nah eh-mehr-HEN-syah)*

SOUTH AFRICA

South Africa is a democratic republic with a multi-party system, led by the African National Congress (ANC) since the end of apartheid in 1994. The country is known for its cultural diversity, with 11 official languages and a mix of Black, White, Coloured, and Indian/Asian communities. Despite the end of apartheid, social inequality and poverty remain persistent challenges. Culturally, South Africa excels in music, art, and literature, and figures like Nelson Mandela are central to its identity. Religiously, it is predominantly Christian, though there is significant diversity, including Muslim, Hindu, and traditional African faiths, with religious tolerance embedded in the constitution.

 ## Politics and LGBTQ+ Legislation

South Africa is generally considered more **liberal** on social issues compared to many other countries, especially within the African context, due to its progressive constitution and policies. Since the end of apartheid in 1994, South Africa has been a leader in promoting human rights, equality, and social justice. LGBTQ+ rights in South Africa are protected by the Constitution, which prohibits discrimination based on sexual orientation and ensures equality before the law. Same-sex marriage has been legal since 2006, and same-sex couples have the same adoption rights as heterosexual couples. Additional protections include the *Promotion of Equality Act* and the *Employment Equity Act*, which guard against discrimination in various areas.

LGBTQ+ Scene

South Africa's LGBTQ+ scene has grown significantly since the end of apartheid, with vibrant communities in cities like Cape Town, Johannesburg, and Durban. **Cape Town**, known as the "gay capital" of Africa, is home to numerous LGBTQ+-friendly venues and events. **Johannesburg** and **Durban** also host lively LGBTQ+ scenes, with events like *Johannesburg Pride* showcasing the community's diversity and activism.

Pride Month, celebrated in October, marks the anniversary of the first Pride event in Africa in 1990. While Pride events, such as Cape Town Pride, celebrate LGBTQ+ identities, they also highlight ongoing issues like discrimination and violence which remains a serious concern, particularly in more conservative areas.

The LGBTQ+ community in South Africa continues to push for recognition and equality through a variety of initiatives beyond Pride Month, with major events like the *Pink Loerie Mardi Gras* in Knysna, *Durban Pride*, and the *Mother City Queer Project* in Cape Town. These festivals, along with cultural initiatives like the *Out In Africa Film Festival* and *Queer Cinema Nights*, celebrate diversity and promote LGBTQ+ inclusion.

LGBTQ+-Related Crime

Despite significant legal advances, challenges remain regarding societal attitudes and the enforcement of these rights. Hate crimes against LGBTQ+ individuals in South Africa remain a serious concern, with many reporting experiences of violence, bullying, and discrimination. Surveys indicate widespread fear of becoming victims of such crimes, with severe incidents including physical assault, sexual violence, and even murder. Particularly alarming are cases of "corrective rape" targeting lesbian and transgender individuals, as well as other forms of violence rooted in societal prejudices against sexual orientation and gender identity.[98]

LGBTQ+ and Prostitution

In South Africa, all forms of sex work, including buying, selling, and brothel-keeping, are criminalized. This legal framework puts sex workers, especially those from the LGBTQ+ community, at significant risk of violence, abuse, and social stigma. While there are ongoing efforts to decriminalize sex work, the current laws make it difficult for sex workers to access legal protections and healthcare. LGBTQ+ sex workers face heightened challenges, including increased discrimination and violence from both clients and law enforcement. Many also struggle with limited access to healthcare, facing barriers due to stigma, which increases their vulnerability to health issues such as sexually transmitted infections.

LGBTQ+ and Jail System

LGBTQ+ individuals, especially transgender prisoners, face severe challenges within South Africa's prison system, including widespread discrimination, violence, and inadequate healthcare. While the country's Constitution protects against discrimination based on sexual orientation, these legal safeguards are often poorly enforced in correctional facilities. Transgender prisoners are particularly at risk, as they are often misclassified and placed in prisons that do not align with their gender identity, leading to increased abuse and violence from both inmates and staff. Additionally, LGBTQ+ prisoners frequently experience stigma and isolation, making it difficult to report mistreatment or seek support. Healthcare access is another critical issue, with many prisoners lacking access to necessary treatments, such as hormone therapy for transgender individuals.

---

98 https://saiia.org.za/youth-blogs/
    hate-crimes-against-members-of-the-lgbtqia-community-in-south-africa/

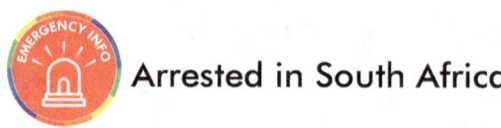 **Arrested in South Africa**

In South Africa, a visitor may be arrested for various reasons, including but not limited to committing a crime or failing to have valid immigration documents. For example, foreign nationals must possess valid documentation that supports their right to stay in South Africa legally; failure to provide such documentation may lead to arrest.[99]

In South Africa, individuals arrested have several rights under the law: they must be informed of the reasons for their arrest in a language they understand; they cannot be forced to provide self-incriminating information and have the right to remain silent; additionally, they must be brought before a court within **48 hours** of their arrest, or as soon as reasonably possible. You also have the right to contact a legal representative and may be eligible for legal aid if you cannot afford an attorney.[100]

The outcome of an arrest can varies based on several factors, including the nature of the alleged offense. If it involves minor charges, the individual might receive a fine or community service, while more serious offenses can lead to detention until trial. In cases where visitors are found to be undocumented immigrants, deportation may follow, and individuals may be banned from re-entering South Africa for a specified period after deportation, usually ranging from one to five years.[101]

Additionally, understanding the context and cultural nuances is essential. Local law enforcement may adhere to strict protocols and being respectful and cooperative can significantly influence how the situation unfolds, as aggressive behavior may lead to additional complications.

---

99 https://help.unhcr.org/southafrica/get-help/ arrest-detention-and-deportation/

100 https://www.saps.gov.za/faqdetail.php?fid=8

101 https://www.scalabrini.org.za/detentiondeportation/

Bail

In South Africa, bail is governed by the **Criminal Procedure Act 51 of 1977**. Foreign visitors can apply for bail, but their status may complicate the process, as courts assess the likelihood of them returning to court and the strength of evidence against them. First hearings occur within 48 hours of arrest, and bail conditions depend on the severity of the offense.[102]

For minor crimes, bail is generally granted with conditions like regular check-ins; for serious offenses, "exceptional circumstances" must be shown. Foreign nationals must demonstrate strong ties to South Africa to reduce flight risk. Bail can be paid in cash or via a bail agent, and failure to comply with conditions can result in forfeiture and re-arrest.[103] To find bail bond service lawyers in South Africa, visit **https://lawzana.com/bail-bond-service-lawyers/south-africa.**

Legal Representation

Traveling can be a wonderful experience, but unforeseen legal issues can arise, necessitating proper legal representation.

One of the most direct approaches to securing legal representation in South Africa is to reach out to local attorneys or law firms. Depending on your specific legal needs, you can use online directories such as the *Legal Practice Council* or platforms like *Attorneys.co.za*, where you can search for practitioners based on their location and area of expertise. Some law firms provide assistance specifically tailored to foreign travelers facing legal troubles, which can be an added advantage.

For travelers who may require assistance but cannot afford the costs associated with private legal representation, *Legal Aid South Africa* assists

---

102 https://www.hrw.org/legacy/reports98/sareport/App1a.htm#:~:text

103 https://mtramabala.co.za/how-to-secure-bail-fast-in-south-africa

individuals in need of legal support. They provide free legal advice and representation to those who qualify based on financial means.[104]

Travelers should not overlook the resources available through their respective consulates or embassies which maintain lists of local attorneys who are experienced in representing foreign nationals facing legal challenges. For example, the list of local attorneys provided by the U.S. Department of State can be accessed at **https://za.usembassy.gov/tag/legal-assistance/**.

If you are a U.S. citizen, the U.S. Embassy in Pretoria or one of the consulates in Johannesburg or Cape Town can be contacted for advice.

U.S. Embassy in South Africa

877 Pretorius St

Arcadia, Pretoria

Phone: +27-12-431-4000

Healthcare System and Medical Facilities

Foreign tourists in South Africa must pay for medical care, as public healthcare is reserved for citizens and permanent residents. The public system is extensive but can face overcrowding, underfunding, and staffing shortages, especially in rural areas.[105]

Many visitors prefer private healthcare, which offers higher quality, shorter wait times, and better-managed resources, though at higher costs. Key facilities for international patients include Chris Hani Baragwanath Hospital, the Netcare Hospital Group, Life Healthcare, Medi-Clinic, and clinics like Akasia Clinic, which provide multilingual

---

104 https://legal-aid.co.za/

105 https://www.internationalinsurance.com/health/systems/south-africa.php

support and specialized services. Travel insurance or sufficient funds are essential to access private care.[106]

Access to Pre-Exposure Prophylaxis (PrEP) Treatment

PrEP is available in South Africa in both oral and injectable forms. Oral PrEP has been publicly provided since 2016 and is free at public clinics, HIV centers, and NGO services, costing roughly R60–R90/month ($4–$6 USD) including monitoring. Injectable PrEP was approved in 2022 but is not yet included in public healthcare due to high costs.

Eligibility for public PrEP includes HIV-negative individuals at high risk, including refugees and asylum seekers. **Non-residents and tourists** must access PrEP privately, with consultations costing $30–$50 USD and oral PrEP $25–$60/month, while injectable PrEP remains very expensive in private settings.

 ## Safety Precautions for LGBTQ+ Travelers

Traveling as an LGBTQ+ individual in South Africa can be rewarding, but it's important to take precautions. Stay aware of your surroundings, especially in rural areas where conservative views may be more prevalent, and research LGBTQ+-friendly neighborhoods in cities like Cape Town and Johannesburg. In conservative areas, exercise discretion and use gender-neutral terms when discussing relationships. Engaging with local LGBTQ+ organizations can help identify safe spaces and potential risks. To stay safe, avoid high-risk areas, use trusted transportation options like rideshare services, and keep emergency contacts, including LGBTQ+ support groups and your embassy, readily available. Joining LGBTQ+-friendly tours can also enhance your safety and experience.

---

106 https://www.internationalinsurance.com/health/systems/south-africa.php

Emergency Contact Numbers

- **Police:** 10111
- **Ambulance:** 10177 or 112
- **Fire Department:** 10111 or 107
- **U.S. Embassy in Pretoria:** +27-12-431-4000

Useful Emergency Phrases in Afrikaners

South Africa is a linguistically diverse country with **11 official languages**, reflecting its rich cultural heritage. The two most commonly spoken home languages is **isiZulu**, spoken by about 23% of the population, and **isiXhosa**, spoken by around 16%. These Bantu languages are widely used in daily life, especially in provinces like KwaZulu-Natal and the Eastern Cape. While **Afrikaans** and **English** are also official languages and play important roles in education, government, and media, English is more commonly used as a second language and is the main language of business and official communication.

Zulu (isiZulu):

HELP! – Siza! *(SEE-zah)*

CALL AN AMBULANCE! – Biza i-ambulensi! *(BEE-zah ee-ahm-boo-LEHN-see)*

I NEED A DOCTOR – Ngidinga udokotela *(ngee-DEE-ngah oo-doh-koh-TEH-lah)*

POLICE – Amaphoyisa *(ah-mah-poh-YEE-sah)*

I'M LOST – Ngilahlekile *(ngee-lah-hleh-KEE-leh)*

IT'S AN EMERGENCY – Kuyiphuthumayo *(koo-yee-poo-too-MAH-yoh)*

Xhosa (isiXhosa):

HELP! – Nceda! *(N-click-EH-dah)*

　("NC" IS A CLICK – like the "tsk" sound)

CALL AN AMBULANCE! – Biza i-ambulensi! *(BEE-zah ee-ahm-boo-LEN-see)*

I NEED A DOCTOR – Ndifuna ugqirha *(n-dee-FOO-nah oo-GQ-ee-rhah)*

   ("gq" is a click with vibration)

POLICE – Amaphoyisa *(ah-mah-poh-YEE-sah)*

I'M LOST – Ndilahlekile *(n-dee-lah-hleh-KEE-leh)*

IT'S AN EMERGENCY – Limeko engxamisekileyo *(lee-MEH-koh en-gha-mee-seh-KEH-lee-yoh)*

Afrikaans:

HELP! – Help! *(HELP)*

CALL AN AMBULANCE! – Bel 'n ambulans! *(bel un ahm-boo-LAHNS)*

I NEED A DOCTOR – Ek het 'n dokter nodig *(ek het un DOK-ter NOH-dig)*

POLICE – Polisie *(po-LEE-see)*

I'M LOST – Ek is verlore *(ek is fer-LOH-ruh)*

IT'S AN EMERGENCY – Dis 'n noodgeval *(dis un NOHTCH-guh-fahl)*

JAPAN

Japan is a constitutional monarchy with a parliamentary government, where the emperor serves as a ceremonial figurehead and the Prime Minister holds executive power. Japan is known for its homogeneity, though it has seen increasing diversity due to immigration and globalization. The country faces challenges related to an aging population, low birth rates, and gender inequality. Japan blends deep traditional practices, such as tea ceremonies and calligraphy, with modern influences in technology, fashion, and pop culture, especially through anime and manga. Japan is primarily Shinto and Buddhist, with many people practicing a mix of both, though secularism is also widespread, and a growing interest in other faiths, including Christianity, is evident.

 ## Politics and LGBTQ+ Legislation

Japan's social landscape is characterized by a mix of **liberal** and **conservative** elements. While significant growth in liberal public sentiment concerning LGBTQ+ rights and gender equality is evident, the entrenched traditional values and political conservatism hinder substantial legislative changes. Key social issues, including reproductive rights, continue to reflect conservative barriers that limit women's autonomy.

While Japan's LGBTQ+ rights have evolved, they still face significant challenges. While same-sex sexual activity has been legal since the 1880s, same-sex marriage remains unrecognized nationally. Even though some municipalities offer partnership systems, they don't grant full marriage rights. The lack of comprehensive national anti-discrimination laws remains a challenge, although public support for LGBTQ+ rights is growing.

 ## LGBTQ+ Scene

Japan's LGBTQ+ scene has grown significantly, particularly in cities like **Tokyo** and **Osaka**, with Tokyo's Shinjuku Ni-chome district serving as a vibrant LGBTQ+ hub. Pride Month is celebrated with major events like *Tokyo Rainbow Pride*, the most prominent celebration, which attracts hundreds of thousands of participants. The 2024 event, celebrating its 30th anniversary, featured a parade, workshops, performances, and booths from LGBTQ+ supporters, highlighting both celebration and advocacy for LGBTQ+ rights in a country where same-sex marriage is not yet fully recognized. However, while acceptance is increasing, especially among younger generations, legal protections and full societal inclusion remain ongoing challenges.

Beyond Pride Month, Japan's LGBTQ+ community participates in various events throughout the year that promote advocacy, cultural expression, and community building. Key events include *Tokyo Rainbow Pride*, which features a vibrant parade and activities to raise awareness, and *Kansai Rainbow Festa in Osaka*, a celebration of LGBTQ+ culture. Additionally, film festivals like the *Tokyo Rainbow Film Festival* and *Yokohama Queer Film Festival* highlight LGBTQ+ stories, while the *Takarazuka Revue* offers performances exploring themes of love and gender fluidity. Throughout the year, cultural exhibitions, workshops, and talks further promote LGBTQ+ visibility and rights.

 **LGBTQ+-Related Crime**

LGBTQ+ individuals in Japan face significant issues of harassment, discrimination, and violence, with nearly 40% reporting sexual harassment or assault, particularly among transgender people.[107] Many victims fear reporting incidents due to inadequate law enforcement support. Workplace and school discrimination is also widespread, with around 50% of LGBTQ+ individuals experiencing discrimination at work and LGBTQ+ youth facing high rates of bullying.[108]

The problem of "outing" remains prevalent, with some municipalities attempting to address it, but these efforts lack strong legal enforcement and have led to severe emotional consequences, including suicide.

---

107 https://english.kyodonews.net/news/2020/12/2cfe9ff-
   21ca8-38-of-lgbt-people-sexually-harassed-or-assaulted-survey.html

108 https://www.robertwalters.co.jp/en/insights/news/blog/2024-05-30.html

LGBTQ+ and Prostitution

In Japan, the intersection of prostitution and LGBTQ+ rights is complex and often sensitive. While **prostitution itself is legal in certain contexts**, many aspects of the industry are wrapped in stigma, and LGBTQ+ individuals face unique challenges within this sphere.

The Anti-Prostitution Law of 1956 prohibits sexual intercourse for money, but other sexual services remain in a legal gray area. Many LGBTQ+ individuals, especially transgender and non-binary people, turn to sex work due to discrimination in housing and employment. LGBTQ+-friendly bars and clubs in cities like Tokyo and Osaka may employ sex workers, and advocacy groups offer support, including health resources and legal aid. However, LGBTQ+ sex workers face health risks, legal vulnerabilities, and discrimination, which often prevents them from seeking help or reporting abuse.

LGBTQ+ and Jail System

LGBTQ+ individuals in Japan's prison system face significant challenges, including legal gaps, discrimination, and inadequate protections. Although same-sex sexual activity is legal, the legal framework does not address the specific needs of LGBTQ+ prisoners, leading to systemic discrimination and inadequate care. Many LGBTQ+ inmates, particularly transgender individuals, experience higher rates of violence and sexual assault, with transgender prisoners often being housed according to their assigned sex at birth, increasing their risk of abuse. While advocacy groups like *Nijiiro Diversity* and *Stonewall Japan* work to raise awareness and improve conditions, access to healthcare, including hormone therapy for transgender inmates, remains insufficient, exacerbating health and mental health issues.

 ## Arrested in Japan

When traveling in Japan, it is crucial to understand the legal landscape, particularly regarding the potential for arrest. Japan has a unique legal system characterized by a high conviction rate, often exceeding 99%, which can lead to significant consequences for foreign travelers who find themselves in legal trouble.[109] The police in Japan have broad powers to detain individuals, and the process can be quite different from that in Western countries, which can be alarming for travelers unfamiliar with this system.

Additionally, cultural norms in Japan place a strong emphasis on social order and respect for authority, which can influence the likelihood of arrest in various situations, including public disturbances or perceived disrespect towards law enforcement. Travelers should also be aware that Japan has strict laws regarding drug possession, and even small amounts can lead to severe penalties, including arrest and deportation.

Upon arrest, the police in Japan may detain an individual for an initial period of up to **48 hours**. During this time, they are required to inform the suspect of the crime of which they are accused, their rights, and the nature of the investigation. Importantly, this initial detention is not yet under the jurisdiction of a judge; rather, it is conducted by the police. After the 48-hour period, if the police find sufficient grounds for further detention, they must seek authorization from a public prosecutor to detain the suspect longer.

If the prosecution agrees with the police findings, they can submit a request for an extended detention order to a judge. This initial request must be made within 24 hours after the first 48 hours of interrogation. If approved, the order allows for an additional detention period of up to ten days.[110] This means that individuals could potentially be in detention for a total of about ten days before any formal requirements for judicial review of their case are initiated.

Bail

In Japan, bail is not available during pre-indictment detention, which can last up to 23 days after arrest. Foreign detainees, like all suspects,

---

109 https://journals.sagepub.com/doi/10.1177/1057567716679232

110 https://www.moj.go.jp/EN/hisho/kouhou/20200120enQandA.html

may face extended detention before formal charges and often experience pressure to confess.[111]

After indictment, bail becomes possible but is rarely granted, especially for foreigners, due to concerns about flight risk or evidence tampering. Judges may also deny bail for defendants who refuse to confess. Legal representation is essential, and if bail is granted, it must be paid to the court, often requiring a guarantor.

Legal Representation

Japan's legal system is primarily based on civil law and matters often involve complex regulations that may differ significantly from those in a traveler's home country. Therefore, it is essential for foreign visitors to understand the structures of Japanese law, particularly regarding criminal procedures, as foreign travelers are subject to the same laws as Japanese citizens when they commit offenses within the country.

To secure effective legal representation in Japan, it is advisable for foreign travelers to reach out to their respective consulates upon arrival in Japan to obtain reliable information on lawyers who are experienced in working with foreign clients. If you are a U.S. citizen, the list of local English-speaking attorneys can be accessed at **https://jp.usembassy. gov/services/attorneys/**.

Japan Legal Support Center (Hoterasu) is another valuable resource, offering bilingual assistance and information on accessing legal services in multiple languages.[112] This center can help foreign travelers locate legal counsel suited to their individual needs.

As with most situations that arise while you are traveling abroad, the best initial resource is your home country that provide critical support

---

111 https://www.hrw.org/report/2023/05/25/japans-hostage-justice-system/
denial-bail-coerced-confessions-and-lack-access

112 https://www.japanlivingguide.com/expatinfo/lawsandlawyers/
free-consultations/

if you find yourself in trouble. Do not hesitate to establish a contact as soon as possible and seek assistance.

U.S. Embassy in Tokyo
1-10-5 Akasaka
Minato-ku, Tokyo 107-8420 Japan
Phone: +81-3-3224-5000

Healthcare System and Medical Facilities

Foreign visitors in Japan can access healthcare depending on their stay. Short-term tourists must have travel insurance, while those staying over three months can enroll in National Health Insurance (NHI) that caters to self employed individuals, students or the unemployed with premiums based on income,[113] or Social Health Insurance (SHI) which is shared between employers and employees. Public insurance covers about 70% of medical costs, but supplemental private insurance is recommended, especially to address language barriers.

Japan has high-quality hospitals catering to international patients, including St. Luke's International Hospital (Tokyo), Kameda Medical Center (Chiba), Nagoya University Hospital, and the Center Hospital of the National Center for Global Health and Medicine (Tokyo), all offering multilingual support and specialized services for foreign residents.[114]

Access to Pre-Exposure Prophylaxis (PrEP) Treatment

In Japan, PrEP is **not approved for HIV prevention** under the national health system and is only available through **private clinics**, mainly in Tokyo. Oral PrEP is approved for treatment, but injectable PrEP is not available. It is **not covered by National Health Insurance**, so all

---

113 https://wise.com/us/blog/healthcare-system-in-japan

114 https://www.internationalinsurance.com/health/systems/japan.php

costs—including consultations, lab tests, and medication—are paid out of pocket.

Private clinic costs range from about **¥11,000 ($80 USD)** for a starter month to **¥20,000 ($150 USD)** for ongoing three-month refills; imported PrEP purchased online can exceed ¥70,000 ($500 USD) per month. PrEP is not sold over the counter. Non-residents and tourists can access the same private services and may legally bring a **one-month personal supply** into Japan without a special permit; larger quantities require an import certificate (Yakkan Shoumei). Clinics typically require HIV-negative status and periodic testing for continued use.

 ## Safety Precautions for LGBTQ+ Travelers

Japan is a welcoming and hospitable country, but it has a strong cultural emphasis on manners and respect. This means that public displays of affection, overly expressive clothing, or gestures, and any form of disrespect are generally frowned upon by society. While this applies to all tourists, LGBTQ+ travelers may face extra scrutiny for behaviors like public displays of affection, which might not be as easily forgiven as they might be for heterosexual visitors. It's important for LGBTQ+ tourists to stay aware of their surroundings and to respect local customs and laws to ensure a positive experience.

Emergency Contact Numbers

- **Police:** 110
- **Ambulance/Fire Department:** 119
- **U.S. Embassy in Tokyo:** +81-3-3224-5000

Useful Emergency Phrases in Japanese

HELP! – 助けて! *(tas-KEH-teh!)*

CALL AN AMBULANCE! – 救急車を呼んでください! *(kyuu-kyuu-sha o yonde kudasai!)*

I NEED A DOCTOR – 医者が必要です *(isha ga hitsuyou desu)*

POLICE – 警察 *(keisatsu)*

I'M LOST – 道に迷いました *(michi ni mayoimashita)*

IT'S AN EMERGENCY – 緊急事態です *(kinkyuu jitai desu)*

BOLIVIA

Bolivia, a landlocked country located in the heart of South America, is known for its diverse landscapes that range from the towering Andes Mountains to the vast Amazon Basin. Bolivia is a democratic republic with a multi-party system, where the President serves as both the head of state and government. The country has a rich indigenous heritage and is one of the few nations in the world where indigenous people make up the majority of the population. The country places great importance on community, respect for nature, and its strong historical connection to the land. The nation has a unique approach to religion, with a majority practicing Roman Catholicism alongside indigenous spiritual beliefs. Bolivia's political landscape has been historically complex, shaped by social movements, indigenous rights activism, and a commitment to preserving its cultural identity. Today, the country is recognized for its focus on social justice, environmental preservation, and the fight for equality.

Politics and LGBTQ+ Legislation

Bolivia is considered largely **liberal**, especially under the leadership of figures like Evo Morales, who pushed for social and economic reforms focused on indigenous rights, wealth redistribution, and nationalization of industries. The country has strong progressive policies on social issues, though it also faces some political polarization between conservative and liberal factions. LGBTQ+ legislation in Bolivia has seen significant progress over the years, though challenges remain. Same-sex sexual activity has been legal since 1832, but the Constitution explicitly defines marriage as a union between a man and a woman, prohibiting same-sex marriage. However, a landmark ruling in March 2023 recognized same-sex civil unions, additionally granting them adoption rights. The Bolivian Constitution and the *Law Against Racism and All Forms of Discrimination*, enacted in 2010, offer protections against discrimination based on sexual orientation and gender identity. Additionally, the 2016 *Gender Identity Law* enables individuals to change their legal name and gender without needing surgery.[115]

True Story

The Altillo Benni Museum, the largest in the city of Santa Cruz de la Sierra, Bolivia, commemorated Pride Month for the first time on June 1, 2022. They opened an LGBTQ+ art exhibition called "Revolución Orgullo" or "Pride Revolution" led by La Pesada Subversiva. The collective's groundbreaking LGBTQ+ art exhibition faced vehement opposition. "We adorned the museum facade with trans and LGBTIQ+ flags," an organizer recounts, "but it lasted less than a day because a group of neighbors came to protest violently and aggressively." Despite this, the exhibition attracted over 400 visitors, demonstrating growing public support for their cause.

---

115 https://en.wikipedia.org/wiki/LGBTQ+_rights_in_Bolivia

 ## LGBTQ+ Scene

The LGBTQ+ scene in Bolivia is active and growing, with a strong network of organizations, working to promote visibility, rights, and support for the community. While rural areas may exhibit more conservative views, **La Paz** and **Santa Cruz de la Sierra** stand out as the most LGBTQ+ friendly regions in Bolivia, and cities like **Cochabamba** and **Potosí** making strides toward increasing acceptance as well.

The biggest Pride Month event in Bolivia is the *Cuir Festival* in La Paz. Held in June, this festival is the central celebration of LGBTQ+ pride in the country, marked by vibrant marches and events, advocating for equal rights and raising awareness about LGBTQ+ issues.

Beyond Pride, Bolivia's LGBTQ+ community continues to celebrate its culture and address important issues through art exhibitions, film festivals, and theater productions. These events offer platforms for gay expression, education, and dialogue on topics such as discrimination, violence, and mental health. Local support groups and advocacy campaigns also work year-round to strengthen connections within the community, providing crucial resources and raising awareness for LGBTQ+ rights and well-being.

 ## LGBTQ+-Related Crime

Despite the legal advancements, societal discrimination and violence against LGBTQ+ individuals persist, with the hate crimes often going unaddressed. In 2017, the Bolivian Ombudsman reported 64 murders of LGBTQ+ people, but only 14 were investigated, and none resulted in convictions, a trend that persist to today.[116]

---

116 https://en.wikipedia.org/wiki/LGBTQ+_rights_in_Bolivia

Societal attitudes, influenced by cultural and religious factors, often lead to violence and harassment, both in public and private. Many victims are hesitant to report crimes due to fear of discrimination, making it difficult to accurately gauge the extent of the issue. Activists are pushing for better law enforcement training and increased awareness to improve the safety and legal protection of LGBTQ+ individuals.

LGBTQ+ and Prostitution

Prostitution is legal and regulated, with registered sex workers required to undergo health checks every 20 days and operate in licensed brothels. However, sex work remains heavily stigmatized, leading to discrimination, particularly against LGBTQ+ workers.[117]

LGBTQ+ sex workers, especially transgender women, face heightened violence and discrimination, including street violence and harassment by law enforcement. Many do not report abuse due to fear of further victimization or mistrust of the authorities, resulting in underreported crimes. Economic hardship forces many LGBTQ+ individuals into sex work, perpetuating a cycle of poverty, marginalization, and violence.

LGBTQ+ and Jail System

The jail system in Bolivia presents significant challenges for the LGBTQ+ population, characterized by severe overcrowding and systemic discrimination. With prison facilities operating at over 250% capacity, issues include inadequate access to food, healthcare, and sanitation, creating dangerous environments for vulnerable groups, including LGBTQ+ individuals.[118]

LGBTQ+ inmates in Bolivia face systemic discrimination in prisons, often experiencing physical and sexual violence. Due to the stigma

---

117 https://onlinelibrary.wiley.com/doi/10.1111/lamp.12308

118 https://insightcrime.org/news/brief/
    report-highlights-overcrowding-other-problems-in-bolivia-prisons/

surrounding LGBTQ+ identities, they are frequently targeted for abuse by both fellow inmates and prison staff, worsened by the hypermasculine and heteronormative culture within prisons. Additionally, access to healthcare is severely limited, particularly when it comes to mental health support and gender-affirming care. There are also numerous documented cases of torture and inhumane treatment, reflecting wider human rights violations within the Bolivian prison system.[119]

 ## Arrested in Bolivia

Bolivia's laws prohibit arbitrary arrest and detention, affirming the right of individuals to challenge their detention. However, the application of these laws can vary, and reports indicate that the government does not always respect these legal protections.[120]

Under Bolivian law, police have the authority to detain any foreigner until they can prove their legal status within the country, be it in the form of a passport, visa, or residency card. Inability to provide such documentation may lead to prolonged detention, therefore it is essential for visitors to always carry relevant documents to avoid complications during law enforcement interactions.

Foreign visitors detained in Bolivia are entitled to specific rights, which, while outlined in law, may not consistently be upheld. Upon arrest, individuals are permitted to challenge the legality of their detention, and the law mandates that they should not be held without charge for an extended period. Moreover, Bolivian authorities are generally required to press official charges within **24 hours** of an arrest; if no formal charges are brought, detainees must be released within 48 hours.

---

119 https://pmc.ncbi.nlm.nih.gov/articles

120 https://www.state.gov/reports/2023-country-reports-on-human-rights-practices/bolivia/

However, investigative periods can extend indefinitely if investigations are prolonged.[121]

Importantly, foreign nationals must be informed of the charges against them, and they should have access to legal counsel which is fundamental to ensuring a fair trial and safeguarding the rights of the accused. The U.S. Embassy advises citizens detained in Bolivia to request a list of English-speaking attorneys from the embassy, which can also be accessed at **https://bo.usembassy.gov/wp-content/uploads/sites/16/2024/10/Attorneys-List-MASTER-LIST-English-September-2024.pdf**.

True Story

Alison Spedding, a British anthropologist, was sentenced to 10 years in 1998 for possessing 2kg of cannabis, which she claimed was for personal use. Her imprisonment, seen by some as politically motivated due to her opposition to Bolivia's coca crackdown, drew international protests. In 2021, reforms to Bolivia's penal code allowed her release on bail, though she must remain in La Paz until a final decision is made.[122]

Bail

In Bolivia, bail is **not always available**, particularly for drug-related offenses under **Law 1008**, which mandates imprisonment without bail. For less severe crimes, bail may be granted depending on factors like the offense, flight risk, and ability to provide a monetary guarantee ("surety"). Foreign visitors often face additional challenges, such as paying in local currency and adhering to conduct conditions while awaiting trial. Legal representation and advocacy can influence the approval of bail for eligible detainees.[123]

---

121 https://travel.state.gov/content/travel/en/international-travel/International-Travel-Country-Information-Pages/Bolivia.html

122 https://www.theguardian.com/uk/2000/oct/04/bolivia

123 https://www.refworld.org/reference/countryrep/hrw/1995/en/22256

Legal Representation

Your home embassy in Bolivia plays a critical supportive role by providing legal resources and ensuring that detainees understand their rights and responsibilities as they navigate the bail process. While the embassy cannot provide direct legal representation, it can assist visitors by offering a list of local attorneys, particularly those who are familiar with the concerns of foreign clients. The embassy also provides information on how to navigate the Bolivian legal system, including how to obtain legal representation, which is critical for those who might not speak Spanish fluently or understand local laws.

> ### U.S. Embassy in La Paz
> Avenida Arce 2780
> Casilla 425
> La Paz, Bolivia
> Phone: +591-2-216-8000

Legal aid organizations delineate another crucial component of support for foreign visitors in Bolivia. The Defensoría Publica, or Public Defense Office, offers free and accessible legal aid to individuals facing criminal charges, including those who are foreign nationals. The Defensoría is particularly important for those who may not have the resources to afford private legal counsel. Their services include providing legal representation in court, guidance on legal procedures, and assistance with documentation needed for legal proceedings. Additionally, the International Organization for Migration (IOM) also plays an essential role in assisting foreign visitors in legal challenges. This organization provides support and resources that help navigate the Bolivian legal system, particularly for vulnerable populations, including victims of human trafficking or undocumented migrants.

Lastly, several local law firms specialize in representing foreign visitors in Bolivia. These firms can provide comprehensive legal assistance tailored to the nuances of the local judicial system. Engaging a private attorney who speaks the visitor's language and understands their specific needs is crucial in overcoming the language barriers and legal complexities encountered in Bolivia. Foreign visitors should conduct thorough research to identify reputable legal firms during their stay. Online platforms, including legal directories (such as Legal 500 Latin America, Latin Lawyer 250, Lex Mundi, and PathLegal) often provide listings of qualified attorneys who specialize in various areas of law, including immigration, civil rights, and criminal defense. Referrals from the U.S. Embassy or other travelers can also serve as valuable recommendations.

Healthcare System and Medical Facilities

Foreign tourists in Bolivia can use both **public and private healthcare**. Public care is free but often has long waits and limited resources, especially in rural areas,[124] while private facilities offer higher quality and faster service at a greater cost. Travelers are advised to have **health insurance** and take preventive measures against risks like altitude sickness and mosquito-borne diseases.

Notable private facilities catering to foreigners include **Clinica Foianini** (Santa Cruz), **Centro Medico Especializado – CEMES** (La Paz), **Clinico Sirani** (Santa Cruz), and **Clinica Del Sur**, all offering modern services, emergency care, and English-speaking staff.

Access to Pre-Exposure Prophylaxis (PrEP) Treatment

In Bolivia, **PrEP is not officially available** and there is no national HIV prevention program for it. Access is limited to **private healthcare providers** in major cities like La Paz, Santa Cruz, and Cochabamba. Costs are relatively high, and eligibility is not formally defined, though private providers may prescribe it to HIV-negative individuals at high risk. Both residents and tourists can seek PrEP privately if a provider deems it appropriate.

---

124 https://wwwnc.cdc.gov/travel/destinations/traveler/none/bolivia

 ## Safety Precautions for LGBTQ+ Travelers

Bolivia is generally safe for LGBTQ+ travelers in major cities like La Paz and Santa Cruz de la Sierra, where there is a more progressive atmosphere and active LGBTQ+ communities. However, in rural areas and smaller towns, conservative attitudes may pose challenges, and public displays of affection could attract negative attention. While legal protections exist, discrimination and violence against LGBTQ+ individuals still occur, so travelers should exercise caution, especially in less urbanized regions.

Emergency Contact Numbers

- **Police:** 110
- **Ambulance:** 118
- **Fire Department:** 119
- **U.S. Embassy in La Paz:** +591-2-216-8000

Useful Emergency Phrases in Spanish

HELP! – ¡Ayuda! *(ah-YOO-dah)*

CALL AN AMBULANCE! – ¡Llame a una ambulancia! *(YAH-meh ah OO-nah am-boo-LAN-syah)*

I NEED A DOCTOR – Necesito un médico *(neh-seh-SEE-toh oon MEH-dee-koh)*

POLICE – Policía *(poh-lee-SEE-ah)*

I'M LOST – Estoy perdido/a *(ehs-TOY pehr-DEE-doh/dah)*

(Use "perdido" if you're male, "perdida" if you're female)

IT'S AN EMERGENCY – Es una emergencia *(ehs OO-nah eh-mehr-HEN-syah)*

173

INDIA

India is a diverse and vibrant democracy with a federal political system, where power is shared between the central government and individual states. The political landscape is characterized by a multi-party system, with major parties like the *Bharatiya Janata Party* (BJP) and the *Indian National Congress* shaping national politics. India is marked by deep cultural diversity, including various languages, ethnic groups, and regional identities. It also faces challenges related to poverty, inequality, and caste discrimination. The country has a rich history of arts, music, and literature, influenced by its ancient traditions and modern global interactions. Religiously, India is predominantly Hindu, but it is home to significant Muslim, Christian, Sikh, Buddhist, and Jain populations, with religion playing an important role in both personal and public life.

 ## Politics and LGBTQ+ Legislation

India is often considered a **conservative** country in many aspects, particularly when it comes to social issues such as gender roles, family structures, and religion. However, it also has liberal elements, especially in its democratic political system, economic policies, and urban areas where progressive views on issues like LGBTQ+ rights and women's empowerment are gaining ground.

India has made significant strides in LGBTQ+ rights, notably with the 2018 Supreme Court ruling that decriminalized homosexuality and affirmed privacy, autonomy, and identity for LGBTQ+ individuals. However, same-sex marriage remains unrecognized, and LGBTQ+ couples lack adoption rights. Transgender rights have also progressed, with legal recognition of a third gender and self-identification rights Despite these advances, discrimination continues in areas like employment and healthcare, due to the lack of comprehensive anti-discrimination laws.[125]

 **LGBTQ+ Scene**

Social acceptance of LGBTQ+ individuals in India varies widely. While rural areas often face intolerance and stigma, India's most LGBTQ+-friendly areas are primarily found in major urban centers like **Delhi, Mumbai, Bangalore**, and **Pune.** These cities host vibrant LGBTQ+ communities, with numerous support organizations, pride parades, and inclusive spaces such as bars, cafes, and clubs. Mumbai, particularly known for its inclusive culture, hosts one of the largest Pride parades in the country. Delhi and Bangalore also offer active LGBTQ+ scenes with advocacy groups, events, and safe spaces that foster visibility and acceptance. Since India's first Pride parade in 1999, over 21 cities now host Pride events. In 2023, festivals like the *KASHISH Mumbai Film Festival* and the *Chennai Pride Parade* highlighted progress, while some rural areas like Vasai-Virar and Dharmshala are beginning to host Pride marches as well, increasing LGBTQ+ visibility.

Beyond Pride Month, India's LGBTQ+ scene continues to thrive with year-round activities, support groups, and cultural events. LGBTQ+ community centers and organizations offer counseling, legal aid, and mental health support. In cities like Mumbai and Delhi, gay film festivals, art exhibitions, and theater productions provide platforms for LGBTQ+ voices, while social gatherings, workshops, and safe spaces for LGBTQ+ individuals foster ongoing solidarity.

---

125 https://fulbrightindiaguide.org.in/lgbtq-rights-in-india/

LGBTQ+-Related Crime

LGBTQ+-related crime in India includes violence, discrimination, and legal challenges. While the 2018 Supreme Court ruling decriminalized same-sex relationships, the lack of legal recognition for same-sex marriage leaves LGBTQ+ individuals vulnerable to violence, especially from family. Cases like Manoj's (see "True Story" below), who faced severe abuse after coming out as transgender, highlight the widespread issue. Many crimes go underreported due to fear of stigma and police discrimination. Hate crimes, particularly against transgender individuals, are common, with victims often facing police indifference. Social stigma also limits employment opportunities, pushing some into vulnerable situations like sex work.

True Story

The experience of 17-year-old Manoj sheds light on the severe violence and rejection faced by many transgender individuals in India. When Manoj, assigned female at birth, disclosed his identity as a man and expressed his love for a woman, the violent reaction from his family was heartbreaking. He described being physically assaulted, restrained, and threatened with death by his father, illustrating the extreme hostility that can accompany familial rejection in such contexts.[126]

LGBTQ+ and Prostitution

While prostitution itself is legal in India, activities such as brothel operation and solicitation are criminalized, creating a challenging environment for sex workers, including LGBTQ+ individuals. Economic vulnerability, particularly among transgender people, often forces many into sex work due to limited job opportunities and rejection from their

---

126 https://www.bbc.com/news/world-asia-india-66245194

families. Systemic discrimination and a lack of access to employment in traditional sectors contribute to this issue. Research suggests that around 62% of transgender individuals in India engage in some form of sex work.[127]

LGBTQ+ sex workers face significant health risks, including high rates of STIs and limited healthcare access due to stigma. They also endure violence from law enforcement, clients, and society, with many incidents going unreported, although activist organizations like the *National Network of Sex Workers* (NNSW) work to improve conditions through legal support, empowerment, and healthcare access.

LGBTQ+ and Jail System

The legal landscape for LGBTQ+ rights in India has progressed, notably with the decriminalization of consensual same-sex relations in 2018. However, data on LGBTQ+ representation in the prison system is limited, although studies suggest marginalized groups, including LGBTQ+ individuals, are overrepresented in prisons due to systemic discrimination. Between May 2018 and April 2019, around 214 transgender individuals were incarcerated in India, but comprehensive statistics are lacking.[128]

LGBTQ+ individuals, particularly transgender people, face severe discrimination and violence in Indian prisons. Transgender inmates are often housed in facilities that do not match their gender identity, increasing their risk of abuse and mistreatment. The lack of clear policies on housing LGBTQ+ prisoners often results in their treatment based on biological sex rather than gender identity and access to adequate medical care is another major issue.

---

127 https://pmc.ncbi.nlm.nih.gov/articles/PMC9879189/

128 https://www.washingtonblade.com/2024/07/31/
indian-home-ministry-directs-prisons-to-protect-transgender-inmates

 ## Arrested in India

When a foreigner is arrested in India, the police must notify the Ministry of External Affairs (MEA), especially for major crimes, so that the relevant consulate can offer legal representation. The arrest process follows the same procedures as for Indian citizens under the Code of Criminal Procedure, including informing the detainee of the charges, taking them to the police station, and presenting them before a magistrate within **24 hours**. Depending on the crime, the magistrate may grant bail or remand the individual to judicial custody until the trial.[129] If the foreigner is wanted in another country, an extradition process may be initiated through diplomatic channels, where the Indian government reviews the request and may issue an arrest warrant.

Bail

In India, bail is governed by the Criminal Procedure Code (CrPC) of 1973 and applies equally to citizens and foreign nationals. Offenses are classified as bailable (less severe) or non-bailable (serious crimes like murder, terrorism, or drug trafficking). Bail eligibility is assessed on a case-by-case basis, considering factors such as flight risk, crime severity, and public safety.

Foreign nationals often face additional challenges, including being perceived as flight risks, language barriers, unfamiliarity with the legal system, and difficulty accessing legal aid. Magistrates have broad discretion in granting bail, and bias against foreigners can occur.[130] Foreign detainees are advised to seek qualified lawyers, which can be found through online legal directories like LawRato, Justdial, and Vakilsearch, to improve their chances of a favorable outcome.

---

129 https://travel.gc.ca/travelling/advisories/
overview-of-the-criminal-law-system-in-india

130 https://travel.gc.ca/travelling/advisories/
overview-of-the-criminal-law-system-in-india

Legal Representation

In India, the right to legal representation is enshrined under Article 22 of the Constitution, which guarantees certain rights to individuals arrested or detained, including the right to consult and be defended by a legal practitioner of their choice. However, this right is not uniformly accessible to foreign detainees, who may face additional hurdles in navigating the legal landscape due to their status, language difficulties, and unfamiliarity with Indian laws.

When a foreign national is detained in India, they have the right to legal representation, which can be accessed through a local lawyer or by notifying their consulate for assistance in finding suitable counsel. The consulate must be informed of the arrest, as per the Vienna Convention on Consular Relations, allowing them to provide legal support and monitor the case. Detainees can hire a private lawyer or, if unable to afford one, request a court-appointed lawyer. However, the definition of "major crimes," which triggers automatic consular notification, is unclear in Indian law. Therefore, it is essential for the detainee to contact their embassy or consulate as soon as possible.

U.S. Embassy in New Delhi

Shantipath, Chanakyapuri
New Delhi - 110021
Phone: +91-11-2419-8000

One primary challenge faced by foreign detainees in accessing legal representation is the language barrier. Many detainees do not speak English or Hindi proficiently, making it difficult for them to effectively communicate with legal counsel and comprehend the legal proceedings (Migration and International Human Rights Law). Reports indicate that lack of translators and interpreters at detention facilities further exacerbates these difficulties, often leaving detainees without adequate support to understand their rights, the charges against them, or the implications of their legal situation.

Moreover, foreign detainees often report limited access to funds to secure legal representation. The inability to afford private legal counsel significantly hinders their ability to navigate intricacies of the legal system effectively. Although some non-profit organizations strive to provide legal aid, their resources are minimal compared to the growing number of detained foreign nationals. As a result, many detainees may find themselves relying on underfunded public defenders or non-governmental initiatives, which may not have the expertise or capacity to address their specific needs.

You home embassy is a good resource to help you retain qualified legal representation and most embassies provide a list of local attorneys that are capable to assist foreign detainees. Such a list by the U.S. state department can be found at **https://in.usembassy.gov/wp-content/uploads/sites/71/2017/05/2017-ATTORNEY-LIST.pdf.**

Healthcare System and Medical Facilities

Visitors to India can access both public and private healthcare, with major cities like Delhi, Mumbai, Chennai, and Bangalore hosting internationally accredited hospitals. While public services are available, they often require out-of-pocket payments, though costs are significantly lower than in Western countries, often between 60 and 90% cheaper.[131] India is a major destination for medical tourism, offering high-quality, affordable care with services in English and multilingual support. Notable hospitals include Apollo, Fortis, Max Healthcare, Medanta, and CMC Vellore, all providing advanced treatments, personalized international patient services, and streamlined processes. The government facilitates medical tourism through medical visa policies, allowing foreign patients to stay for the duration of their treatment.[132]

---

131 https://ghealth121.com/the-cost-advantage-of-medical-treatment-in-india

132 https://www.cgitoronto.gov.in/page/medical-visa

Access to Pre-Exposure Prophylaxis (PrEP) Treatment

PrEP in India is primarily oral, limited to high-risk populations, and mostly available through pilot programs, NGOs, and select government centers rather than as a standard public health service. Injectable PrEP is not approved. It is not covered by national health insurance, and costs (₹1,500–2,500 per month, ~$20–30 USD) can be high relative to local incomes. Availability is concentrated in urban areas, making access in rural regions difficult. Eligibility is based on HIV risk assessment, and non-residents or tourists must rely on private providers, paying out of pocket.

 ## Safety Precautions for LGBTQ+ Travelers

LGBTQ+ travelers to India should exercise caution, particularly in rural areas, due to conservative societal norms. While homosexuality is decriminalized, public displays of affection can still attract unwanted attention, so it's advisable to minimize such behaviors. Staying in LGBTQ+-friendly accommodations and traveling in groups can enhance safety, and solo travelers can reach out to local LGBTQ+ organizations for advice on safe spaces. It's also helpful to practice discretion in conversations and use gender-neutral language to navigate varying levels of acceptance. Utilizing resources like *Pink Vibgyor* or *IndjaPink* can provide tailored support for a smoother and more secure travel experience.

Emergency Contact Numbers

- **Police:** 110 or 112
- **Ambulance:** 102 or 112
- **Fire Department:** 101 or 112
- **U.S. Embassy in New Delhi:** +91-11-2419-8000

Useful Emergency Phrases in Hindi

The official language of India is Hindi, however English is also widely used for official and administrative purposes, and it serves as a subsidiary official language.

HELP! – मदद करो! *(ma-dad ka-ro!)*

CALL AN AMBULANCE! – एंब्युलेंस बुलाओ! *(em-bu-lens bu-lao!)*

I NEED A DOCTOR – मुझे डॉक्टर की जरूरत है *(mu-jhe dok-tar kee jar-oorat hai)*

POLICE – पुलिस *(po-lis)*

I'M LOST – मैं खो गया हूँ *(main kho gaya hoon)* [for males]

मैं खो गई हूँ *(main kho gayi hoon)* [for females]

IT'S AN EMERGENCY – यह आपातकाल है *(yah a-paat-kaal hai)*

 **ISRAEL**

Israel is a democratic state in the Middle East, with a parliamentary system of government. The political landscape is shaped by a multi-party system, with the Likud and Labor parties being prominent players, and issues like security, the Israeli-Palestinian conflict, and relations with neighboring countries dominating national discourse. Israel is socially diverse, with a mix of Jewish, Arab, Druze, and other minority populations, though tensions exist between these groups. Culturally, Israel blends Jewish heritage with influences from its diverse immigrant communities, particularly in music, art, and cuisine. Religion is integral to both national identity and daily life in Israel, where Judaism is the dominant faith, alongside significant populations of Muslims, Christians, and other religious groups.

 ## Politics and LGBTQ+ Legislation

Israel is generally considered a **liberal** country in terms of its democratic values, civil society, and economic policies. However, it also has **conservative** elements, especially due to the influence of Orthodox Judaism on issues like marriage and education. The country features a mix of liberal and conservative factions, with urban areas typically more progressive and rural or religious communities tending to hold more conservative views.

Nevertheless, LGBTQ+ rights and legislation in Israel are considered among the most progressive in the Middle East. Same-sex sexual activity has been legal since 1988, and same-sex marriages performed abroad are recognized, though domestic civil marriages are not allowed due to religious laws. Same-sex couples have the right to adopt children and access IVF, though societal discrimination persists. Anti-discrimination laws protect LGBTQ+ individuals in employment, education, and public services, but enforcement can be inconsistent. Transgender individuals can change their legal gender, though it requires medical approval. LGBTQ+ people can serve openly in the Israeli military, which has policies to support them.[133]

 ## LGBTQ+ Scene

The LGBTQ+ scene in Israel has gained significant visibility and prominence, particularly in urban areas like **Tel Aviv**. Labeled as the "gay capital" of the Middle East and reputed for its open-minded and accepting atmosphere, Tel Aviv is recognized as the vibrant epicenter of LGBTQ+ culture in the country. Approximately 25% of the city's population identifies as LGBTQ+, contributing to a thriving night scene and

---

133 https://en.wikipedia.org/wiki/LGBTQ+_rights_in_Israel

annual events that attract both local and international visitors.[134] The city boasts an array of gay bars and clubs and hosts one of the largest Pride parades in the world, attracting over 250,000 participants each year.[135] The sense of safety and acceptance here has made it a popular destination for LGBTQ+ tourism.

While Tel Aviv is renowned for its vibrant night LGBTQ+ scene and openness. **Jerusalem** is more conservative due to its religious demographics, and its LGBTQ+ community faces challenges. The city's Pride event is more of a protest, reflecting local tensions. **Haifa**, known as the "City of Coexistenceis more inclusive and hosts events for a diverse audience, while **Eilat**, a southern resort town, offers a laid-back, welcoming atmosphere for LGBTQ+ visitors with local gay clubs and a pride event. Beyond Pride Month, LGBTQ+ advocacy in Israel extends through initiatives, support groups, social events, and ongoing legal and societal challenges.

 **LGBTQ+-Related Crime**

LGBTQ+ hate crimes in Israel have seen a troubling rise, with violent incidents increasing by 28% in the first ten months of 2023 compared to the same period in 2022.[136] Many of these attacks occur in public spaces, highlighting the vulnerability of the LGBTQ+ community. The surge in violence is partly attributed to political tensions, with homophobic statements from public figures and political leaders fueling hostility toward the community. LGBTQ+ involvement in protests government policies has also led to backlash from extremist groups. Compounding the issue, the Israeli Education Ministry's decision to cut funding for LGBTQ+ tolerance programs by 85% has resulted in the cancellation

134 https://www.touristisrael.com/gay-tel-aviv-for-beginners/5686/

135 https://www.masaisrael.org/pride-2024-israel

136 https://www.haaretz.com/israel-news/2024-05-30/ty-article/.premium/anti-lgbtq-violence-spiked-in-israel-during-judicial-overhaul-protests-report-finds/0000018f-c87e-da41-a9cf-d97ef2c50000

of thousands of educational workshops, reducing efforts to combat homophobia and foster understanding among younger generations.[137]

True Story

Sephardic Chief Rabbi Shlomo Amar recently claimed that the recent earthquakes in Israel were divine punishment for the rise in LGBTQ+ rights, particularly gay marriage, citing a Talmudic passage. His remarks, which echoed previous homophobic statements, sparked controversy, including criticism from openly gay Channel 13 News anchor Ori Qual, who condemned Amar for blaming the LGBTQ+ community for societal issues and called for his accountability.[138]

LGBTQ+ and Prostitution

Prostitution in Israel has undergone significant legal changes, particularly with the introduction of the "Nordic Model" in 2018, **which criminalizes the purchase of sex but decriminalizes the sale**. This legislation aims to reduce prostitution by targeting clients rather than sex workers themselves. However, LGBTQ+ individuals, particularly transgender women, often find themselves disproportionately affected by these laws, as they may lack alternative means of financial support, leading some to enter sex work.

Studies indicate that a notable percentage of transgender individuals in Israel engage in sex work, often as a means of survival rather than choice. Societal discrimination and limited employment opportunities contribute significantly to these circumstances, exacerbating vulnerability among LGBTQ+ youth, especially trans women. While there is growing public support for LGBTQ+ rights in Israel, there remains a

---

137 https://www.jpost.com/israel-news/article-794666

138 https://www.jpost.com/israel-news/article-732914

significant gap in societal acceptance of sex work, often viewed through a lens of morality rather than as a nuanced social issue.[139]

LGBTQ+ and Jail System

Statistics regarding the exact representation of LGBTQ+ individuals in Israeli prisons are not widely available. The available information primarily focuses on broader correctional system statistics rather than on LGBTQ+ specific data. For instance, the total prison population in Israel was reported to be approximately 19,756 individuals as of December 2023. Among these, the specific representation of LGBTQ+ individuals, particularly transgender prisoners, is often overlooked or not explicitly documented in official statistics.[140]

However, it is understood that LGBTQ+ inmates, particularly transgender individuals, experience higher rates of incarceration due to systemic issues such as social marginalization and lack of economic opportunities. LGBTQ+ inmates, especially those who are transgender, often encounter significant vulnerabilities, including increased risk of violence and sexual harassment both from other inmates and prison staff. Studies indicate that lesbian, gay, bisexual, transgender, and queer individuals in prison face a range of difficulties such as sexual assault and inadequate medical care.

 **Arrested in Israel**

When a foreign visitor is arrested in Israel, the initial process involves law enforcement officers executing an arrest based on suspicion of a crime. This can range from minor offenses, such as violations of local laws or regulations, to more severe allegations. Upon arrest, authorities are required to inform the detainee of the specific charges being laid

---

139 https://www.jpost.com/israel-news/article-809634

140 https://www.prisonstudies.org/country/israel

against them without unnecessary delay. This aspect is crucial for foreign visitors, as understanding the nature of the charges is vital for their defense.

A significant point to remember is that the arrest process might involve police questioning, where individuals have the right to remain silent. It is advisable for detainees not to engage in discussions without legal representation present, as anything stated during questioning can be used against them in court. The lack of awareness about this right can lead to inadvertent admissions that may complicate their legal standing.

Much like in other countries, foreign visitors in Israel enjoy several rights once arrested: the right to consult with a lawyer of their choice immediately upon arrest; the right to consular assistance; the right to be informed of charges; and the right to a prompt hearing. The legal framework in Israel mandates a prompt appearance of detainees before a judge, typically within **48 hours** of arrest.

Despite these rights, foreign visitors may encounter systemic challenges. One prevalent issue is the language barrier. Many detainees may not speak Hebrew or Arabic fluently, which can hinder their ability to understand the proceedings and communicate effectively with legal representatives. This barrier emphasizes the importance of requesting access to interpreters during critical moments of the arrest and interrogation process. Most foreign embassies and consulates in Israel can provide a list of English-speaking attorneys in the area. If the list is not readily available through online search, contact the embassy or consulate directly.

U.S. Embassy in Jerusalem
14 David Flusser
Jerusalem 9378322, Israel
Phone: +972-02-630-4000

There can sometimes be delays in accessing legal representation due to the complexities of the legal system, necessitating that detainees are proactive in requesting their rights through their representation or consular officials. Additionally, some reports have emerged indicating that foreigners might be treated differently than Israeli citizens, which raises concerns about fairness and equality under the law.

Bail

In Israel, there is **no traditional bail system** like in many Western countries. Instead, detainees' release is determined by a Detention Review Tribunal, which assesses the legality of detention rather than setting financial bail. Decisions are made by judges based on the nature of the offense and other case factors, with reviews typically occurring within 96 hours. The judicial system is adversarial, without juries, and includes both secular and religious courts. Legal information can be difficult to access in English, but resources include the Israeli Ministry of Justice, the Israel Bar Association, and local police departments for guidance on legal procedures and rights.

You can learn more about Israel's bail system by contacting the Judicial Authority at **https:// www.gov.il/en/departments/ the_judicial_authority.**

Legal Representation

Having competent legal representation can significantly influence the outcome of a case. Foreign visitors should seek attorneys who specialize in criminal law and are familiar with the nuances of representing international clients in Israel. Many embassies maintain lists of local legal aid services that can assist travelers facing legal challenges. Engaging a lawyer can help ensure that rights are upheld and that individuals receive a fair trial.

In Israel, the right to legal representation is fundamental; however, foreign visitors often encounter unique challenges in accessing qualified legal counsel. While they are entitled to engage a lawyer of their choice, the availability of such assistance can be limited, especially for those not fluent in Hebrew or Arabic. This language barrier can severely hinder effective communication with legal representatives, leading to misunderstandings and misinterpretations of legal advice.

Legal aid services in Israel are typically organized for residents, with fewer provisions explicitly tailored for foreign detainees. Organizations such as the Public Defender's Office provide representation for those in need, but this service can be overwhelmed by demand, risking delays in securing adequate legal representation. Moreover, many foreign visitors may not be fully aware of the legal aid services available to them, further complicating their situations.

Thus, home embassies and consulates play a crucial role in providing support to foreign detainees. Under international law, consular officials are mandated to assist their nationals in distress, which includes providing legal referrals and ensuring that detainees are treated humanely while in custody. The U.S. Embassy, for example, is required to be notified promptly if an American citizen is arrested, allowing it to offer necessary assistance, including legal referrals and contact with family members. Keep in mind that the effectiveness of consular assistance can vary widely depending on the political context and the nature of the allegations against the detainee. Challenges arise when detainees face politically charged circumstances, such as protests or involvement with controversial organizations; in these cases, consular representatives may have limited influence on legal proceedings or outcomes.

Healthcare System and Medical Facilities

Foreign visitors in Israel cannot access the universal healthcare system and must use private medical facilities, which provide high-quality care but require direct payment. Tourists are strongly advised to obtain travel health insurance to cover potential emergency or unexpected medical costs. Notable private and international-friendly hospitals include Terem and Bikur Rofeh for emergency services, as well as Hadassah Medical Center in Jerusalem and Sheba Medical Center in Ramat Gan, which offer specialized treatments, international patient support, and language assistance. Travelers should be prepared for upfront payments and may need guidance navigating the healthcare system.[141]

---

141 https://www.commonwealthfund.org/international-health-policy-center/
countries/israel

Access to Pre-Exposure Prophylaxis (PrEP) Treatment

PrEP in Israel is legally available only in oral form; injectable PrEP is not approved. Since 2020, oral PrEP is included in the national health basket and covered under Israel's universal healthcare system (Kupot Holim), though users pay a monthly co-payment of about $84–$103 USD. Access through public HMOs requires a referral from a primary care doctor or infectious disease specialist. Private clinics, mainly in cities like Tel Aviv, also provide PrEP, with one-month supplies costing up to 2,400 ILS (~$700 USD), though generics and online options can reduce this to ~$30 USD. Eligibility is based on HIV-negative individuals at high risk, but public subsidies are limited to Israeli residents. Non-residents and tourists must access PrEP privately, paying out-of-pocket, though personal import with a prescription is permitted.

 ## Safety Precautions for LGBTQ+ Travelers

While urban areas are welcoming, visitors should exercise caution in more conservative regions. Areas such as Jerusalem, particularly certain neighborhoods with strong religious communities, may exhibit less acceptance of LGBTQ+ identities and LGBTQ+ travelers are encouraged to use discretion regarding public displays of affection.

It's always a good idea to research local dynamics, stay informed of events and connect with local LGBTQ+ organizations that can help travelers navigate their experiences more safely.

Emergency Contact Numbers

- **Police:**
- **Ambulance:**
- **Fire Department:**
- **U.S. Embassy in Jerusalem:** +972-02-630-4000

Useful Emergency Phrases in Hebrew and Arabic

The official languages of Israel are **Hebrew** and **Arabic**. Hebrew is the primary language spoken by the majority of the population and is used in government, education, and daily life. Arabic is also an official language, particularly spoken by the Arab population of Israel.

Hebrew:

HELP! – הרזע! (*ez-RAH!*)

CALL AN AMBULANCE! – סנלובמא ארקת! (*tik-RAH am-boo-LAHNS!*)

I NEED A DOCTOR – אפור ךירצ ינא (*a-NEE tsa-REEKH ro-FEH*) [for males]

אפור הכירצ ינא (*a-NEE tsree-KHAH ro-FEH*) [for females]

POLICE – הרטשמ (*meesh-TAH-rah*)

I'M LOST – דובא ינא (*a-NEE a-VOOD*) [for males]

הדובא ינא (*a-NEE a-VOO-dah*) [for females]

IT'S AN EMERGENCY – םוריח הז (*zo chee-ROOM*)

Arabic:

HELP! – ةدعاسم! (*mu-sa-AH-dah!*)

CALL AN AMBULANCE! – فاعسإلاب لصتا! (*it-tasl bil is-'aaf!*)

I NEED A DOCTOR – بيبط ىلإ جاتحأ (*ah-TAJ ila TAH-beeb*)

POLICE – ةطرش (*SHOR-tah*)

I'M LOST – عئاض انأ (*ana DAA-ih*) [for males]

ةعئاض انأ (*ana DAA-i-ah*) [for females]

IT'S AN EMERGENCY – ئراوط ةلاح هنإ (*in-nahu HA-lah-tah TAW-ah-ree*)

LGBTQ+ HOSTILE COUNTRIES
(Low Safety)

PART 3

LGBTQ+ HOSTILE COUNTRIES

In these countries, LGBTQ+ individuals face significant legal, social, and cultural challenges. Same-sex relationships may be criminalized or heavily stigmatized, and LGBTQ+ people may experience legal discrimination, violence, or harassment. In some cases, LGBTQ+ people face the threat of imprisonment, physical harm or even death. Public expressions of LGBTQ+ identity are dangerous. Social acceptance is low, and advocacy for LGBTQ+ rights may be met with hostility. PrEP is generally unavailable or unsafe to access in LGBTQ+ hostile countries due to legal restrictions and stigma. In some of these countries, seeking or using PrEP may expose individuals to legal or social risks, and public access is extremely limited or non-existent.

Countries in this group include UAE, Saudi Arabia, Yemen, Qatar (in the Middle East); Malaysia and Afghanistan (in Southeast Asia); Egypt, Uganda, and Nigeria (in Africa); and Russia (in Europe/Asia).

 ## UNITED ARAB EMIRATES

The United Arab Emirates (UAE) is a federation of seven emirates located on the southeastern corner of the Arabian Peninsula, known for its modern architecture, luxury lifestyle, and rapid economic development. Home to iconic landmarks like the Burj Khalifa and the Sheikh Zayed Grand Mosque, the UAE offers a blend of rich cultural heritage and cutting-edge innovation, attracting millions of tourists and expatriates from around the world.

Politics and LGBTQ+ Legislation

The United Arab Emirates (UAE) is a federal presidential elective constitutional monarchy made up of seven emirates, each governed by hereditary rulers, with real power concentrated in the ruling families and no political parties allowed. UAE is considered **conservative** when it comes to social issues, reflecting its Islamic traditions and cultural values. The country maintains strict laws regarding freedom of expression, sexual orientation, and personal behavior.

The legal system in the UAE, grounded in conservative Sharia law, is strict, particularly in comparison to many Western legal frameworks, and includes stringent penalties for a wide range of offenses, particularly those linked to morality and public order. **LGBTQ+ rights in the UAE are severely limited, as homosexuality is illegal** and subject to imprisonment, typically initiated only by complaints from male guardians or spouses. Public displays of affection, cross-dressing, and expressions of LGBTQ+ identities can result in harassment and legal penalties, reflecting a conservative societal attitude that suppresses open discussion of sexual orientation and gender identity. For example, engaging in consensual same-sex sexual acts can lead to a minimum prison sentence of six months. While specific laws have relaxed somewhat, men who dress as women in public or enter spaces designated for women may be imprisoned for up to one year and fined up to AED 100,000 (approximately $27,200). Consequently, many LGBTQ+ individuals face significant challenges and live in fear of expressing their identities in a cultural context that strongly adheres to traditional values.[142]

---

142 https://en.wikipedia.org/wiki/
   LGBTQ+_rights_in_the_United_Arab_Emirates

 ## LGBTQ+ Scene

There are no official LGBTQ+ events in the United Arab Emirates (UAE) due to strict anti-homosexuality laws and cultural stigma. This repressive environment makes public displays of LGBTQ+ identities impossible. While some informal underground gatherings may occur among expatriates, they are secretive and carry significant legal risks. The absence of formal organizations and community support further hinders the visibility and rights of LGBTQ+ individuals in the UAE.

 ## LGBTQ+-Related Crime

Hate crimes against LGBTQ+ individuals in UAE manifest in various forms, reflecting a combination of legal enforcement, societal attitudes, and cultural stigmas. Instances of physical violence, harassment, and psychological intimidation are common. Victims may face violence not only law enforcement but also from private individuals who feel empowered by a legal system that does not protect marginalized groups. There have been accounts of individuals being beaten or otherwise harmed as a result of their sexual orientation or gender expression, contributing to a pervasive culture of fear.

Authorities often utilize entrapment to target LGBTQ+ individuals, especially through dating apps and social media. Reports suggest that individuals are lured into situations where they can be arrested and face prosecution based on their sexual orientation. During arrests, many have experienced police brutality, including physical abuse and the coercion to provide confessions.

 ## Discrimination and Violence

Beyond legal and physical violence, discrimination permeates everyday life for LGBTQ+ individuals in the UAE. Instances of job loss, eviction, and rejection by family members due solely to an individual's sexual orientation or gender identity are often reported, compounding the trauma experienced by those targeted. Additionally, there are accounts of forced conversion therapy and coercive rehabilitation practices aimed at changing an individual's sexual orientation, which are inherently abusive and violate human rights.[143]

True Story

Two Singaporean nationals, Nur Qistina Fitriah Ibrahim and Muhammad Fadli Bin Abdul Rahman, were arrested at Yas Mall in Abu Dhabi in August 2017 for allegedly dressing in a manner deemed feminine. Following their arrest, they were sentenced to one year in prison for "attempting to resemble women" and later deported back to Singapore after spending time in custody.[144]

LGBTQ+ and Prostitution

Saudi Arabia strictly prohibits prostitution under Sharia law, with violations resulting in imprisonment, fines, and deportation for foreign nationals. While flogging was abolished in April 2020, the legal framework remains severe in addressing sexual conduct outside marriage.

The kingdom's broad legal definition encompasses any sexual activity outside lawful marriage, including consensual same-sex relations,

---

143 https://www.humandignitytrust.org/country-profile/united-arab-emirates

144 https://www.ksl.com/article/45533541/
    uae-imprisons-transgender-singaporean-friend-for-their-look

creating particularly dangerous circumstances for LGBTQ+ individuals who face prosecution for adultery, fornication, or sodomy.

The intersection of anti-prostitution and anti-homosexuality laws compounds marginalization for LGBTQ+ citizens. Limited employment opportunities and societal discrimination often force vulnerable individuals into high-risk situations, potentially including sex work as survival. Combined with documented harassment, torture, and severe punishment of LGBTQ+ individuals, this creates an atmosphere of fear preventing victims from seeking help or reporting abuse.

This legal landscape traps marginalized populations in vulnerability cycles, where laws intended to regulate moral conduct push at-risk individuals into dangerous circumstances while simultaneously criminalizing their existence and survival strategies.

LGBTQ+ and Jail System

UAE prisons are generally well-equipped with the necessary infrastructure to accommodate inmates, including facilities for physical activity and mental health support. Inmates have access to medical services, though the quality and timeliness of healthcare can vary depending on resources. The UAE has legal frameworks in place to protect prisoners' rights, including protections against torture and mistreatment, but some instances of mistreatment and poor conditions have been reported.

LGBTQ+ individuals, particularly those who identify as transgender or non-binary, are incarcerated at markedly higher rates than the general population. Data indicate that LGBTQ+ adults are three times more likely to be incarcerated than their heterosexual counterparts. Moreover, one in six transgender individuals reports being incarcerated at some point in their lives.[145] LGBTQ+ inmates are more likely to face violence from staff and fellow inmates, often being targeted due to their sexual orientation or gender identity and many LGBTQ+ inmates are denied gender-affirming treatments, which contributes to mental health crises among this population.

---

145 https://www.aclu.org/news/lgbtq-rights/
    pride-has-always-been-about-ending-mass-incarceration

 ## Arrested in UAE

The arrest process in the United Arab Emirates (UAE) involves several structured steps to ensure adherence to local laws while protecting individual rights. An arrest can occur if a law enforcement officer witnesses a crime, receives a complaint, or has reasonable suspicion of involvement in criminal activity. Upon arrest, individuals are taken to a police station where they are informed of the charges against them and their rights, including the right to legal representation and consular access if they are foreign nationals. Typically, a suspect can be detained for up to **48 hours** without formal charges, during which time they may be interrogated. After this initial period, the case is referred to the public prosecutor, who determines whether to file formal charges, grant bail, or extend the detention for further investigation. If charged, the individual will face trial in a court where proceedings occur without a jury, guided solely by the evidence presented.[146]

Bail

The United Arab Emirates (UAE) has a structured bail system that allows individuals to secure temporary release while awaiting trial, primarily through personal and financial guarantees. After an arrest, detainees can apply for bail during initial hearings, where the public prosecutor assesses factors such as the nature of the charges and flight risk before granting or denying the request. Personal guarantees typically involve surrendering documents like a passport, while financial guarantees require a monetary bond determined by the court. Bail can be revoked if the accused fails to comply with conditions imposed by the court or if new evidence emerges against them, reflecting the UAE's approach to balancing individual rights with public safety.[147]

146 https://paoli.legal/arrested-in-the-uae/

147 https://kslegal.law/bail-in-the-uae/

Legal Representation

In the United Arab Emirates (UAE), foreign nationals have the right to appoint a licensed lawyer to represent them during legal proceedings, and if they lack the financial means for legal counsel, the court may appoint a public defender, especially in serious cases. The appointment of legal representatives must follow regulatory requirements, as lawyers must be registered to practice within the UAE. Additionally, legal aid services are available to assist low-income individuals, providing free consultations and support for eligible expatriates. However, challenges such as language barriers and cultural differences can complicate the legal landscape for foreigners, necessitating expertise in relevant laws and practices to ensure effective representation.

Finding an English-speaking attorney in the United Arab Emirates is generally considered to be relatively easy, especially in major urban centers like Dubai and Abu Dhabi. The country has a diverse expatriate population, and as such, the demand for legal services in English is significant. To obtain the list of English-speaking attorneys, individuals can visit the U.S. Embassy's official website or direct inquiries to the embassy's consular section. The embassy's resources provide guidance on selecting a legal representative, as well as important considerations regarding the legal process in the UAE. It is always a good idea to contact your home embassy if in need of legal assistance as they can provide you with a list of local English-speaking attorneys and guide you through the legal system.

U.S. Embassy in Abu Dhabi
Phone: +971-2-414-2200
Emergency After-Hours Phone:
+971-0-2-414-2200
Fax: +971-2-414-2241
Email: abudhabiacs@state.gov
Address: Embassies District, Plot 38, Sector
W59-02, Street No. 4, Abu Dhabi, U.A.E.

Additionally, various online legal directories and platforms offer comprehensive listings of attorneys, allowing individuals to filter by language and expertise. Likewise, law firm websites provide valuable information about services and legal specialties.

Healthcare System and Medical Facilities[148]

The United Arab Emirates has established itself as a premier healthcare destination, offering world-class medical services through a network of modern facilities staffed by internationally trained professionals. The system's accessibility to foreign patients is enhanced by widespread English fluency among medical staff and numerous hospitals holding Joint Commission International accreditation, ensuring adherence to global healthcare standards.

Among the standout medical institutions are Rashid Hospital, recognized as Dubai's highest-rated facility with exceptional emergency and trauma services, and the American Hospital Dubai, which operates as part of the Mayo Clinic Care Network to provide access to cutting-edge medical protocols. Dubai Healthcare City houses Mediclinic City Hospital, offering comprehensive inpatient and outpatient services, while Cleveland Clinic Abu Dhabi serves as a specialized center for cardiac and digestive disease treatments.

The healthcare landscape operates primarily through private facilities, creating a two-tiered system where UAE nationals enjoy free public healthcare while expatriates typically require health insurance coverage and face fees for services. Foreign patients can choose between public hospitals, which offer more affordable care but with longer waiting periods, and private institutions that provide expedited service with broader specialist availability. The system accommodates international patients through multilingual staff and flexible payment arrangements, including cash, credit cards, insurance plans, and installment options for major medical expenses.

---

148 https://www.flyreva.com/blog/best-international-hospitals-in-the-world/
international-hospitals-in-the-uae

 # Safety Precautions for LGBTQ+ Travelers

Traveling to the United Arab Emirates (UAE) as an LGBTQ+ individual requires careful consideration of local laws and cultural attitudes. While the UAE is known for its modernity and vibrant cities, it maintains strict laws against same-sex relationships and gender non-conformity, making it essential for visitors to prioritize their safety. LGBTQ+ individuals traveling to the UAE should prioritize their safety by understanding local laws, avoiding public displays of affection, engaging in discreet online behavior, and utilizing known LGBTQ+-friendly venues.

Emergency Contact Numbers

- **Police:** 999
- **Ambulance:** 998
- **Fire Department:** 997
- **U.S. Embassy in Abu Dhabi:** +971-2-414-2200

Useful Emergency Phrases in Arabic

HELP! – مساعدة! *(mu-sa-AH-dah!)*

CALL AN AMBULANCE! – اتصل بالإسعاف! *(it-tasl bil is-'aaf!)*

I NEED A DOCTOR – أحتاج إلى طبيب *(ah-TAJ ila TAH-beeb)*

POLICE – شرطة *(SHOR-tah)*

I'M LOST – أنا ضائع *(ana DAA-ih)* [for males]

أنا ضائعة *(ana DAA-i-ah)* [for females]

IT'S AN EMERGENCY – إنه حالة طوارئ *(in-nahu HA-lah-tah TAW-ah-ree)*

SAUDI ARABIA

Saudi Arabia is considered a very conservative country, particularly in terms of social norms and practices. The societal structure is heavily influenced by Wahhabi Islam, which promotes strict interpretations of Islamic law. Saudi Arabia, officially known as the Kingdom of Saudi Arabia, is a vast country located on the Arabian Peninsula, renowned for being the birthplace of Islam and home to its two holiest cities, Mecca and Medina. The nation has a significant economy primarily driven by oil production, and it features a rich cultural heritage shaped by Islamic traditions and tribal customs.

Politics and LGBTQ+ Legislation

Saudi Arabia is considered **highly conservative**, with strict interpretations of Wahhabi Islam shaping its social policies, including limitations on women's rights, severe restrictions on LGBTQ+ individuals, and tight controls on freedom of expression and religious practice. Public life is heavily regulated, and personal freedoms are more restricted compared to many other countries.

Saudi Arabia is an absolute monarchy, with the King serving as both head of state and government. King Salman has ruled since 2015, with his son, Crown Prince Mohammed bin Salman (MBS), regarded as the de facto ruler. The country's political system blends traditional tribal customs with Islamic law (Sharia), based on the Quran and Sunnah. Saudi Arabia lacks a formal constitution, and its laws are primarily shaped by religious scholars. There are no political parties or elections, limiting political participation to the royal family and advisory councils. The government operates under authoritarian rule, with significant influence from the royal family and religious authorities.

This framework significantly impacts the treatment of LGBTQ+ individuals, who live under the constant threat of severe legal penalties and societal discrimination. LGBTQ+ individuals face severe legal consequences due to the country's strict adherence to Sharia law. **Same-sex activity and gender non-conformity are criminalized, with penalties including imprisonment, flogging, or even the death penalty in some cases.**[149] LGBTQ+ individuals have been subjected to arrests, torture, and human rights violations without legal protection. Transgender people face discrimination, with laws criminalizing gender expression, leading to arrests based on appearance and dress codes. Despite some attempts by the Saudi Tourism Authority to project a more inclusive image, strict enforcement of these laws persists, and societal attitudes remain hostile due to conservative Islamic values. As a result, LGBTQ+ individuals live in fear, and public support for LGBTQ+ rights is suppressed.[150]

 ## LGBTQ+ Scene

There are no official LGBTQ+ events in Saudi Arabia due to the country's stringent anti-homosexuality laws and cultural stigma surrounding LGBTQ+ identities. While some informal and underground gatherings may occur, they operate in secrecy and with great caution, as any public acknowledgment of LGBTQ+ identities could lead to serious legal repercussions.

 ## LGBTQ+-Related Crime

Under Saudi law, **same-sex sexual activity is illegal** and can result in severe punishments. This includes the potential for the **death penalty and lengthy prison sentences**, often handed down arbitrarily by judges who interpret Islamic law. Reports indicate that enforcement of

---

149 https://www.humandignitytrust.org/country-profile/saudi-arabia

150 https://en.wikipedia.org/wiki/LGBTQ+_rights_in_Saudi_Arabia

anti-LGBTQ+ laws is frequent, and those suspected of homosexuality or gender non-conformity face significant harassment, including arrest and torture by law enforcement.

There have been several high-profile cases of violence and discrimination against LGBTQ+ individuals in Saudi Arabia. For instance, in 2017, a raid led to the arrest of 35 transgender individuals at a party, where two women were reportedly beaten to death by police. This incident exemplifies the level of violence sanctioned by authorities against LGBTQ+ individuals.[151]

Additionally, hate crimes perpetrated by society reflect deep-seated homophobia. Reports show consistent incidents of assault, harassment, and discrimination against LGBTQ+ persons in various aspects of life, including employment and healthcare. However, precise statistics regarding arrests or hate crimes are difficult to obtain due to the underground nature of LGBTQ+ communities and societal stigma that discourages reporting such incidents.[152]

LGBTQ+ and Prostitution

Prostitution is illegal in Saudi Arabia and is strictly punishable under Sharia law. Those found guilty of engaging in prostitution can face severe penalties, including imprisonment, fines, and deportation for foreign nationals. Historically, floggings were also a common punishment, but this practice was officially abolished in April 2020.[153]

The legal definition of prostitution in Saudi Arabia is broadly tied to any sexual activity outside of lawful marriage, encompassing both voluntary sex work and consensual same-sex relations, which further complicates the situation for LGBTQ+ individuals.

---

151 https://www.newsweek.com/saudi-arabia-pakistan-transgender-lgbt-transgender-rights-hate-crimes-564544

152 https://www.humandignitytrust.org/country-profile/saudi-arabia

153 https://en.wikipedia.org/wiki/Prostitution_in_Saudi_Arabia

In Saudi Arabia, individuals involved in prostitution can be prosecuted for adultery, fornication, or sodomy, all of which carry severe penalties. LGBTQ+ individuals, who already face criminalization of same-sex activity, are particularly vulnerable in this context. The intersection of laws against homosexuality and prostitution exacerbates their marginalization, pushing many into risky situations where they may turn to sex work due to limited employment options and societal discrimination. Reports of harassment, torture, and even execution of LGBTQ+ individuals further increase their risks. The stigma surrounding both prostitution and homosexuality prevents many from seeking help or reporting abuse, perpetuating a culture of fear and silence.

LGBTQ+ and Jail System

Living conditions in Saudi prisons are frequently described as harsh. Reports indicate chronic overcrowding, with detainees often forced to share limited space in unhygienic facilities. Poor sanitation is a common issue, leading to the spread of infectious diseases among inmates. Many prisons lack basic necessities such as adequate food, water, and access to healthcare, resulting in severe health issues for the inmates.[154]

Human rights organizations report widespread torture and mistreatment of prisoners in Saudi Arabia, particularly during interrogations. Many inmates, including political activists and opponents, face psychological and physical abuse, long periods of solitary confinement, and forced labor. While the authorities claim to provide medical care, reports highlight systemic neglect, with inadequate healthcare and critical conditions often going untreated, leading to deaths in custody. Rehabilitation programs exist but are poorly implemented, focusing more on punishment than on genuine reform.

The information regarding the LGBTQ+ population in Saudi prisons is limited and often difficult to obtain due to the secretive nature of law enforcement and the stigma associated with homosexuality in the country. According to various sources, significant numbers of LGBTQ+

154 https://www.alqst.org/uploads/Shrouded-in-Secrecy-En.pdf

individuals have been arrested in recent years. For example, reports from human rights organizations indicate that around 260 arrests related to same-sex sexual activity occurred within a single year. In addition, there have been consistent accounts of targeted crackdowns against LGBTQ+ gatherings, leading to mass arrests. As expected under circumstances, LGBTQ+ individuals in Saudi Arabian prisons endure severe human rights abuses, including arbitrary arrests and harsh penalties under strict anti-homosexuality laws, fueled by pervasive societal stigma.

 ## Arrested in Saudi Arabia

In Saudi Arabia, arrests can be made for a wide range of offenses under strict Sharia law, including social behavior deemed inappropriate, drug offenses, and violations of moral conduct. Arrests may result from tip-offs, surveillance, or raids by law enforcement agencies like the police or the *Committee for the Promotion of Virtue and the Prevention of Vice*. Officers can detain individuals without a warrant, especially for offenses related to public morality or safety.

Once detained, individuals can be held for up to **24 hours** without formal charges, and the detention may be extended for up to six months for serious crimes, particularly those related to security. Access to legal representation and consular services is often delayed, and statements made during detention may be used against detainees in court. Trials in Saudi Arabia are held without juries, with a judge having ultimate discretion. The accused has the right to legal representation, but cross-examination and some defenses may not be allowed. Verdicts are based on evidence, including testimony from law enforcement and the accused's statements, but the judicial process often lacks stringent evidentiary standards, raising concerns about fairness.

If convicted, penalties range from fines and deportation for foreign nationals to imprisonment, corporal punishment, or even the death penalty, depending on the offense's severity.[155]

---

155 https://mytfc.com/Police-Arrests-Saudi-Arabia

One of the first steps you should take is to contact your home country's embassy or consulate in Saudi Arabia. They can provide guidance, support, and resources to assist you in navigating the local legal system.

U.S. Embassy Riyadh
Abdullah Ibn Hudhafah As Sahmi Street
Rondabout no. 9, Diplomatic Quarter
Riyadh, Saudi Arabia
Telephone: +966-11-488-3800

In addition, you should reach out to the nearest consulate if you are in Jeddah or Dhahran.

Bail

Saudi Arabia has a bail system, but it functions under Sharia law and relies heavily on judicial discretion, making it less standardized and transparent than in Western systems. Judges decide bail based on factors like the offense, flight risk, and community ties. When granted, bail usually involves a financial guarantee (cash or property) and may include restrictions such as passport surrender or movement limits. The lack of standardized procedures leads to inconsistent outcomes, and bail is often denied for serious offenses, particularly drug-related or moral crimes.

Legal Representation

Foreigners arrested in Saudi Arabia have the right to legal representation, but this right is limited compared to Western systems. They can request a lawyer during investigations and trials, though access may be hindered by judicial discretion, language barriers, and difficulties finding qualified attorneys for non-Arabic speakers. Detainees may also face **incommunicado detention**, preventing contact with family or legal counsel during early investigations. Foreign embassies often assist by providing lists of local English-speaking lawyers, making early embassy contact crucial for securing proper representation.

Healthcare System and Medical Facilities

Saudi Arabia's healthcare system, overseen by the Ministry of Health, combines public and private sectors. Citizens and some expatriates receive free care, but foreign visitors must rely on private hospitals and valid health insurance, as public facilities do not offer free services to them. The government invests heavily in healthcare (about 14.4% of its budget) and is modernizing infrastructure under Vision 2030 to boost quality and medical tourism. Private hospitals like King Faisal Specialist Hospital, Saudi German Hospital, and the International Medical Center in Jeddah are popular with foreigners for their advanced care and shorter wait times. Emergency services are accessible by dialing 997.

 ## Safety Precautions for LGBTQ+ Travelers

Traveling to Saudi Arabia as an LGBTQ+ individual requires a cautious approach due to the country's strict laws and cultural attitudes towards sexual orientation and gender identity. Although recent shifts in tourism policies suggest a more welcoming stance, the legal framework remains deeply rooted in conservative interpretations of Sharia law that criminalize same-sex relationships and non-conforming gender identities.

LGBTQ+ travelers should exercise caution, maintaining discretion in public by avoiding displays of affection or discussions about sexual orientation, and dressing according to local customs. When booking accommodation, it is important to choose reputable hotels that cater to international tourists and avoid places where privacy may be at risk.

Emergency Contact Numbers

- **General Emergency:** 112
- **Police:** 999
- **Ambulance:** 997

- **Fire Department:** 998
- **U.S. Embassy in Riyadh:** +966-11-488-3800

Useful Emergency Phrases in Arabic

HELP! – مساعدة! *(mu-sa-AH-dah!)*

CALL AN AMBULANCE! – اتصل بالإسعاف! *(it-tasl bil is-'aaf!)*

I NEED A DOCTOR – أحتاج إلى طبيب *(ah-TAJ ila TAH-beeb)*

POLICE – شرطة *(SHOR-tah)*

I'M LOST – أنا ضائع *(ana DAA-ih)* [for males]

أنا ضائعة *(ana DAA-i-ah)* [for females]

IT'S AN EMERGENCY – إنه حالة طوارئ *(in-nahu HA-lah-tah TAW-ah-ree)*

YEMEN

Yemen, located on the southern tip of the Arabian Peninsula, is a country with a complex geopolitical landscape, marked by ongoing conflict and instability, particularly since the 2014 Houthi insurgency. Known for its rich history, ancient architecture, and cultural heritage, it is home to diverse ethnic groups and traditions. The majority of Yemenis follow Islam, predominantly Sunni in the south and Zaydi Shia in the north, contributing to the country's religious and political divisions.

 ## Politics and LGBTQ+ Legislation

Yemen is a deeply conservative society shaped by Islamic law and tribal traditions, with strict limits on women's rights, expression, and especially LGBTQ+ rights. Same-sex activity is criminalized with punishments ranging from lashes to imprisonment, and even the death penalty for married individuals. Since the civil war began in 2015, state functions have collapsed, armed groups hold power, and human rights abuses have worsened. LGBTQ+ people face extreme stigma, arbitrary arrests, torture, and violence from both Houthi and anti-Houthi forces, often with impunity.

 ## LGBTQ+ Scene

There are no LGBTQ+ events in Yemen due to the harsh legal and social environment that criminalizes homosexuality, leading to severe penalties, including the death penalty. The negative societal attitudes create an atmosphere of fear and isolation, making any public expression or organization of events impossible. Consequently, LGBTQ+ individuals in Yemen face significant risks and hardships, with no visible community or support network.

 ## LGBTQ+-Related Crime

The situation for LGBTQ+ individuals in Yemen is dire, characterized by systemic discrimination and violence. The landscape of hate crimes against the LGBTQ+ community is exacerbated by the ongoing civil conflict, which has created a vacuum of legal protections and heightened societal hostility.

Recent instances highlight the brutality of the situation. In early 2024, a Houthi court sentenced 32 men, with nine facing the death penalty for charges including sodomy, in what was described as a mass trial lacking due process. In another case, 13 students were sentenced to death for allegedly "spreading homosexuality". There are also reports of vigilante killings, with at least eight individuals reportedly murdered on the streets under accusations of being homosexual, attributed to gangs like Al-Qaeda exploiting the chaos for acts of violence.[156]

True Story

In January and February 2024, Huthi-run courts in Yemen sentenced over 40 individuals, including 13 students, to death, flogging, or imprisonment on charges related to homosexuality. Nine people were sentenced to death by stoning or crucifixion, while others received prison terms or flogging for "spreading immorality" or engaging in same-sex conduct. Amnesty International condemned these actions as cruel, inhumane, and aimed at instilling fear, calling for the immediate release of those imprisoned and the repeal of laws criminalizing LGBTQ+ behavior. The organization emphasized that public flogging and execution violate international human rights standards and must be stopped.[157]

LGBTQ+ and Prostitution

Prostitution is criminalized under Islamic law, and those caught engaging in sex work may face harsh penalties enforced by the judiciary. The legal consequences can range from long prison sentences to corporal punishment. The ongoing conflict in Yemen has fueled a severe humanitarian crisis, leading to widespread displacement and economic hardship, with many women and children, especially refugees from

---

156 https://www.humandignitytrust.org/country-profile/yemen

157 https://www.amnesty.org.uk/press-releases/yemen-huthi-authorities-sentence-seven-stoning-and-two-crucifixion-homosexual-crimes

Somalia and Ethiopia, turning to sex work as a means of survival. Vulnerable individuals are often coerced into prostitution, facing violence and exploitation, while sex trafficking has become a significant issue.[158] Women and children are trafficked under false pretenses of employment, and children are particularly at risk, facing sexual exploitation both within Yemen and while being trafficked to other countries, such as Saudi Arabia.

Another vulnerable group are LGBTQ+ individuals who engage in prostitution and who face significant violence and discrimination, both from clients and from law enforcement. Activists and human rights organizations have documented instances of arbitrary arrests, torture, and extrajudicial killings of LGBTQ+ individuals in Yemen, particularly in Houthi-controlled areas.[159]

LGBTQ+ and Jail System

The jail system in Yemen is severely compromised due to the ongoing civil war, which has led to overcrowding, inadequate facilities, and widespread human rights violations. Many prisons are controlled by various armed groups, including the Houthis, leading to dire conditions where inmates face torture, ill-treatment, and inadequate medical care, often without proper legal representation. The lack of classification within facilities exacerbates safety risks, housing dangerous offenders alongside lesser criminals and pre-trial detainees.[160]

Prisons in Yemen, particularly those under Houthi control, are notorious for their inhumane conditions. Reports indicate that LGBTQ+ detainees face extreme violence and discrimination, including torture and sexual violence. Human rights organizations have documented instances

---

158 https://www.reuters.com/article/world/
    desperate-somalis-turn-to-prostitution-in-yemen

159 https://lawsandpolicies.unaids.org/jointanalysis

160 https://www.usip.org/publications/2015/03/prisons-yemen

of prisoners being subjected to public flogging in front of crowds, often used as a method of state-sanctioned humiliation and control.[161]

 ## Arrested in Yemen

Foreigners in Yemen face arbitrary arrests, often without clear charges or warrants, and limited access to legal or consular support. Detainees can be held up to 30 days without charge, but extensions are common—especially in political or security cases—resulting in prolonged detention without trial. Incommunicado detention, informal prisons, torture, and human rights abuses are widespread, making the arrest process highly dangerous for foreign nationals.

Bail

Yemen has a bail system established under its legal framework, allowing the possibility of release for individuals charged with non-serious offenses. However, its implementation is inconsistent due to the ongoing civil conflict, which has weakened the judicial system and complicated legal proceedings. The discretionary nature of bail decisions, influenced by factors such as the type of offense and political considerations, often leads to challenges in accessing bail. Corruption within the legal system further exacerbates these issues, resulting in many detainees remaining in prolonged pretrial detention without effective recourse to bail options.

Legal Representation

Yemen legally recognizes the right to legal representation; however, its effective implementation is severely hindered by ongoing conflict. Foreigners are theoretically entitled to legal representation, as stipulated in the country's judicial framework, which aims to provide legal

---

161 https://www.amnesty.org/en/latest/news/2024/02/yemen-huthis-must-stop-executions-and-release-dozens-facing-lgbti-charges

assistance regardless of nationality. However, the actual realization of this right is hindered by various challenges, including a limited number of available attorneys, particularly in conflict-affected regions, and financial barriers due to varying legal fees. The process of securing legal counsel often requires foreign nationals to rely on referrals or legal aid organizations, while language barriers further complicate communication, as proceedings are conducted in Arabic. Additionally, foreigners face inconsistent legal practices, corruption within the judicial system, and the risk of arbitrary detention without due process, all of which significantly impede their access to effective legal representation.

If you are arrested in Yemen, you should immediately request that local authorities notify your embassy or consulate to secure diplomatic support. Since the U.S. Embassy in Sana'a is closed, U.S. citizens should contact the nearest embassies in Saudi Arabia, Djibouti, or Egypt for assistance.

U.S. Embassy in Saudi Arabia

Abdullah Ibn Hudhafah As Sahmi
Street Roundabout no. 9, Diplomatic
Quarter, Riyadh, Saudi Arabia
Phone: +966-11-488-3800
Emergency After-Hours Phone: +966-11-488-3800

U.S. Embassy in Djibouti

Lot 350-B Haramouss B.P. 185, Djibouti
Phone: +253-21-49-5300.
Email: ConsularDjibouti@state.gov

U.S. Embassy in Egypt

5 Tawfik Diab Street, Garden City, Cairo, Egypt
Phone: +20-2-2797-3300
Email: consularcairoacs@state.gov

Additionally, individuals should seek information about the reason for their arrest and obtain legal representation as soon as possible by requesting a list of local attorneys from your consulate. You can also find this information at **www.thelawyersglobal.org/law-firms/country/ yemen.**

Engaging with local non-governmental organizations may also provide further legal assistance.

Yemen Accountability Project

10900 Euclid Ave., Cleveland,
OH 44106, United States
Email: Contact via their website
Phone: +216-368-8700

UNHCR Office in Yemen

Street No. 38, Off Algerian Street,
Building No. 2, Sana'a, Yemen
P.O. Box 12093, Sana'a, Yemen
Email: sanaacom@unhcr.org
Phone: +967-1-205-300

Healthcare System and Medical Facilities

Yemen's healthcare system is severely compromised by ongoing conflict, economic collapse, and humanitarian crises, with only about half of health facilities fully operational. Over 19 million residents lack access to essential care, and preventable diseases are rising due to poor vaccination coverage and malnutrition. International organizations and NGOs provide some emergency services, but resources are insufficient. Despite these challenges, a few hospitals and clinics in Sana'a—including Saudi German Hospital, Modern European Hospital, University of Science and Technology Hospital, and Yemen International Hospital—offer services in English and aim to meet international standards. NGO-run health centers also provide basic and emergency care, particularly for displaced populations. Travelers are advised to confirm whether the facility can treat them before seeking care.

 ## Safety Precautions for LGBTQ+ Travelers

LGBTQ+ travelers considering a visit to Yemen must exercise extreme caution due to stringent laws and societal attitudes against homosexuality. It is crucial to avoid public disclosures of sexual orientation, refrain from public displays of affection, and remain discreet in all interactions. Understanding local laws is essential, given the severe penalties for same-sex activity, and travelers should stay alert to their surroundings. Having an exit plan, staying updated on government travel advisories, and considering group travel for added safety are recommended.

Emergency Contact Numbers

- **Police:** 199
- **Ambulance:** 194
- **Fire Department:** 191
- **U.S. Embassy in Egypt:** +20-2-2797-3300

Useful Emergency Phrases in Arabic

HELP! – مساعدة! *(mu-sa-AH-dah!)*

CALL AN AMBULANCE! – اتصل بالإسعاف! *(it-tasl bil is-'aaf!)*

I NEED A DOCTOR – أحتاج إلى طبيب *(ah-TAJ ila TAH-beeb)*

POLICE – شرطة *(SHOR-tah)*

I'M LOST – انا ضائع *(ana DAA-ih)* [for males]

انا ضائعة *(ana DAA-i-ah)* [for females]

IT'S AN EMERGENCY – إنها حالة طوارئ *(in-nahu HA-lah tah TAW-ah-ree)*

218

QATAR

Qatar is an influential monarchy in the Gulf, where cultural heritage and modern development are shaped by Islamic traditions, with its strategic location and natural gas resources enhancing its geopolitical significance. The country is characterized by conservative social norms, with strict regulations influenced by Islamic law governing public behavior, dress codes, and alcohol consumption. Despite some progress in political participation and women's rights, Qatar maintains a steadfast adherence to traditional values, significantly impacting the lives of its citizens and residents.

 ## Politics and LGBTQ+ Legislation

Qatar is a conservative, Islamic-ruled country with strict social norms and limited civil liberties. Governed by an authoritarian monarchy under Emir Sheikh Tamim bin Hamad Al Thani, political rights are restricted, and political parties are banned. LGBTQ+ individuals face severe legal risks: same-sex sexual activity is criminalized, punishable by imprisonment, with the death penalty theoretically possible for Muslims, and no legal protections or recognition exist for LGBTQ+ relationships.

True Story

Human Rights Watch has reported on the systematic abuse of LGBT people by Qatar's Preventive Security Department, including arbitrary arrests, beatings, sexual harassment, and forced participation in conversion therapy. Between 2019 and 2022, LGBT detainees were subjected to cruel treatment, including physical violence, verbal abuse, and privacy violations such as unlawful phone searches. As Human

Rights Watch's Rasha Younes stated, "While Qatar prepares to host the World Cup, security forces are detaining and abusing LGBT people simply for who they are, apparently confident that the security force abuses will go unreported and unchecked." The organization has called for an end to impunity for these abuses, the repeal of discriminatory laws, and the release of all LGBT individuals detained solely for their sexual orientation or gender identity.[162]

 ## LGBTQ+ Scene

There are no LGBTQ+ events in Qatar due to the country's severe legal restrictions and cultural stigma surrounding homosexuality. Homosexuality is criminalized, with penalties including imprisonment, which creates a hostile environment for any form of public LGBTQ+ expression. The prevailing negative societal attitudes further inhibit organized activities, making it impossible for LGBTQ+ individuals to openly gather or celebrate their identities. Any interactions within the LGBTQ+ community tend to be underground and highly secretive.

 ## LGBTQ+-Related Crime

In Qatar, LGBTQ+ individuals face a hostile environment marked by legal discrimination and societal stigma, which contributes to an increase in hate crimes. Reports indicate that hate crimes against LGBTQ+ individuals can take various forms, including verbal abuse, physical violence, and arbitrary arrests based solely on one's sexual orientation or gender identity. Human Rights Watch has documented instances of law enforcement detaining LGBTQ+ individuals, subjecting them to mistreatment, and even forcing them into conversion therapy as part of

---

162 https://www.hrw.org/news/2022/10/24/
qatar-security-forces-arrest-abuse-lgbt-people

detention conditions. However, accurate statistics on hate crimes are difficult to compile due to underreporting, fear of retaliation, and a lack of legal protection for victims.

LGBTQ+ and Prostitution

Prostitution is illegal in Qatar, with penalties that can include imprisonment, yet it still occurs discreetly in venues like bars and hotels despite crackdowns on the practice. LGBTQ+ individuals face additional challenges in this context, as homosexuality is also criminalized, leading to severe legal consequences, including possible death penalties for Muslim individuals. Many LGBTQ+ individuals, often marginalized and economically vulnerable, may be coerced into sex work, exposing them to heightened risks of exploitation and violence while lacking legal protections. The intersection of these factors creates a precarious environment for LGBTQ+ sex workers, who may be reluctant to seek help due to fear of arrest and discrimination, highlighting the urgent need for reform and greater advocacy for their rights.[163]

LGBTQ+ and Jail System

Qatar's prison system, primarily managed by the Ministry of Interior, includes facilities like the Central Prison, which has seen modernization efforts yet faces significant challenges, including overcrowding and allegations of mistreatment. Inmates generally have access to basic necessities such as food, water, and medical care. The prison provides three meals a day, typically consisting of rice and meat, and special dietary requirements can be accommodated. Inmates also have some legal rights, such as access to legal counsel and visitors; however, these rights are often limited in practice.

Reports indicate that conditions vary widely and that LGBTQ+ prisoners often experience a range of abuses, including physical violence,

163 https://www.hrw.org/news/2022/10/24/
    qatar-security-forces-arrest-abuse-lgbt-people

sexual harassment, and psychological torture. *Human Rights Watch* documented six cases of severe beatings and five instances of sexual harassment in police custody from 2019 to 2022, highlighting the harsh realities faced by those detained solely for their sexual orientation or gender expression. Detainees have reported being subjected to physical abuse, including slapping, kicking, and other forms of violence that frequently result in injuries.[164]

 ## Arrested in Qatar

In Qatar, arrests and detention are governed by Sharia-based laws, which allow authorities to detain individuals—including visitors—for offenses that may be legal elsewhere, such as violations of local customs or morality codes. Under the Protection of Society Law, detainees can be held without charges for up to six months, though they are generally supposed to appear before a judge within 24 hours. LGBTQ+ individuals and those violating cultural norms (e.g., public affection, dress codes, or intoxication) face heightened risk of arrest and mistreatment. Legal representation can be limited, making embassy assistance critical. Embassies can provide guidance, access to local attorneys, and family notification. Human rights organizations note that the legal process is not flexible and enforcement is strict, so visitors must exercise caution to avoid inadvertent violations.

U.S. Embassy Doha

Building 1, Diplomatic Area
Doha, Qatar
Main Phone Number: +974-4496-6000

After-Hours Emergency Phone Number: +974-4496-6000 (

Email: ACSDoha@state.gov (for General Inquiries), or ConsularDoha@ state.gov (for Consular Issues)

---

164 https://www.hrw.org/news/2022/10/24/
qatar-security-forces-arrest-abuse-lgbt-people

Bail

Qatar's bail system allows individuals facing criminal charges, including both Qatari citizens and foreign nationals, the opportunity for temporary release while awaiting trial. Governed by the Qatari Penal Code, the bail process requires that defendants demonstrate they do not pose a flight risk, with evaluations based on the nature of the offense and their community ties. The Public Prosecution plays a crucial role by facilitating bail applications and collecting bail amounts, which can be paid through various channels. However, foreign nationals may face additional challenges, such as language barriers and unfamiliarity with local laws, complicating their ability to navigate the bail process effectively.[165]

Legal Representation

Visitors to Qatar who encounter legal issues have access to various legal representation options to help navigate the local legal system. It is crucial for individuals in this situation to understand their rights and the different types of legal representatives available, which can make a significant difference in resolving legal matters effectively

In Qatar, the legal representation can come from several sources, including:[166]

- **Lawyers:** These are the most common legal representatives who can provide comprehensive legal services, including advising on rights, representing clients in court, and negotiating settlements. Lawyers in Qatar often specialize in various areas such as criminal law, commercial law, and family law.

- **Legal Consultants:** While they are not licensed to represent clients in court, legal consultants offer valuable advice on non-litigious matters like contract drafting and dispute resolution.

- **Notaries Public:** These professionals can certify and authenticate documents, providing legal advice on non-contentious matters, which can be beneficial for visitors needing document verification.

---

165 https://lawyers974.com/blog/criminal-lawyer-in-qatar

166 https://lawyers974.com/blog/legal-representation-in-qatar

Visitors in Qatar have the right to legal counsel, which includes the ability to contact a lawyer if arrested or detained. This right is protected under Qatari law, and proper legal representation can help ensure that visitors' rights are upheld throughout legal proceedings. Legal aid services are also available for those who cannot afford private legal representation. The Qatar International Court and Dispute Resolution Centre offers a pro bono service to individuals needing legal assistance related to civil and commercial disputes.[167]

Qatar has a variety of English-speaking attorneys available specializing in different areas of law. Some notable law firms in Qatar known for their English-speaking legal services include:

- **Al Tamimi & Company:** One of the largest law firms in the Middle East, offering a wide range of legal services with expertise in various fields.

- **Clyde & Co:** A prominent international law firm specializing in sectors such as construction, insurance, and commercial law.

- **Quinn Emanuel Urquhart & Sullivan, LLP:** This firm is recognized for its litigation and arbitration practices and has a team experienced in handling complex legal issues.

Healthcare System and Medical Facilities

Qatar's healthcare system combines public and private sectors under the Ministry of Public Health. The public sector, led by Hamad Medical Corporation (HMC), provides free or low-cost care for citizens and nominal fees for expatriates, while the private sector offers faster access and specialized services, mainly for expatriates and visitors. The system is highly rated in the Middle East, with significant investments in modern facilities, technology, and patient safety. Health insurance is mandatory for expatriates, and many facilities have English-speaking staff. Key hospitals include Hamad General Hospital (comprehensive care), Al Ahli Hospital (private, multilingual services), the American Hospital in Doha (American standards, preventive and urgent care), and The View Hospital (modern facilities and international patient focus).

---

167 https://www.qicdrc.gov.qa/services/pro-bono

 # Safety Precautions for LGBTQ+ Travelers

LGBTQ+ travelers visiting Qatar should exercise caution due to the country's strict laws against homosexuality and conservative cultural norms. It is essential to refrain from public displays of affection and to familiarize oneself with local customs to avoid attracting unwanted attention or legal repercussions. Utilizing discreet communication methods and considering hotel policies regarding same-sex couples can enhance safety. Additionally, travelers should know local emergency numbers and the locations of their embassies for support in case of any issues. By remaining respectful and aware of their surroundings, LGBTQ+ individuals can navigate their visit to Qatar more safely and enjoyably.

Emergency Contact Numbers

- **Police/Ambulance/Fire Department:** 999
- **U.S. Embassy in Doha:** +974-4496-6000

Useful Emergency Phrases in Arabic

HELP! – مساعدة! *(mu-sa-AH-dah!)*

CALL AN AMBULANCE! – اتصل بالإسعاف! *(it-tasl bil is-'aaf!)*

I NEED A DOCTOR – أحتاج إلى طبيب *(ah-TAJ ila TAH-beeb)*

POLICE – شرطة *(SHOR-tah)*

I'M LOST – أنا ضائع *(ana DAA-ih)* [for males]

أنا ضائعة *(ana DAA-i-ah)* [for females]

IT'S AN EMERGENCY – إنه حالة طوارئ *(in-nahu HA-lah-tah TAW-ah-ree)*

MALAYSIA

Malaysia is a Southeast Asian country known for its cultural diversity, combining Malay, Chinese, Indian, and indigenous influences. It has a constitutional monarchy with a unique system of rotating rulers from its 13 states and a rapidly developing economy, particularly in technology, manufacturing, and tourism. While it boasts a rich natural landscape, from rainforests to tropical islands, Malaysia also faces challenges with political stability, human rights issues, and its legal stance on LGBTQ+ rights.

 ## Politics and LGBTQ+ Legislation

Malaysia is generally considered a **conservative** country, especially with regards to social issues. The country's political landscape poses significant challenges for LGBTQ+ rights due to a dual legal system that enforces both secular and Islamic laws, which criminalize same-sex relationships and impose severe penalties, particularly under Sharia law for Muslims. Major political coalitions, such as *Barisan Nasional* and *Pakatan Harapan*, maintain conservative positions influenced by Islamic teachings, leading to a lack of legal protections for LGBTQ+ individuals. The rigid legal framework includes severe punishments like imprisonment for up to 20 years under the Penal Code and additional penalties under Sharia law, creating an environment rife with discrimination, harassment, and fear that severely restricts the rights and safety of the LGBTQ+ community in Malaysia.

 ## LGBTQ+ Scene

The annual *Seksualiti Merdeka* (Independent Sexuality) festival has been a key platform for LGBTQ+ activism in Malaysia since its inception in 2008. However, it faced a ban from the authorities in 2011 and has been consistently targeted by police raids in subsequent years. In 2017, a pride march organized by Taylor's University was cancelled due to Islamist pressure, reflecting the increasing challenges faced by LGBTQ+ activists trying to express their identities publicly.

In recent years, LGBTQ+ events have faced imposed censorship and crackdowns. For instance, in 2022, a Halloween-themed drag event was raided by authorities, resulting in arrests and highlighting the volatile nature of LGBTQ+ expression in Malaysia. Similarly, international incidents where foreign artists have expressed support for LGBTQ+ rights, like the incident involving the band The 1975 during a performance, have caused government backlash, further isolating the local community.[168]

 ## LGBTQ+-Related Crime

Reports indicate a rising trend in violence against LGBTQ+ individuals, particularly targeting transgender women. For instance, a troubling number of murder cases involving transgender women have come to light, with at least 11 reported murders from 2007 to 2016, highlighting the severe risks this community faces. Tragically, attacks are often brutal; in 2018, the murder of a transgender woman in Klang raised alarm about escalating violence, and authorities have frequently been criticized for prematurely classifying such homicides as non-hate crimes.[169]

---

168 https://www.reuters.com/world/asia-pacific/
lgbtq-fears-grow-malaysia-islamists-shatter-reform-hopes-2023-08-21

169 https://www.hrw.org/news/2019/06/25/
deceased-cant-speak-herself-violence-against-lgbt-people-malaysia

A prominent case involved another trans woman who was beaten to death, further fueling concerns about the safety of transgender individuals in Malaysia, particularly those engaged in sex work who are often seen as more vulnerable.

Hostility towards LGBTQ+ individuals is widespread, driven by cultural and religious attitudes, resulting in harassment, discrimination, and violence from both civilians and law enforcement. Many incidents of violence, such as a widely publicized case of a group assaulting someone over perceived same-sex behavior, often go unreported due to fear of further discrimination, a lack of legal protections, and societal stigma. This leaves many LGBTQ+ individuals without the support or recourse to address their experiences of abuse.[170]

LGBTQ+ and Prostitution

Prostitution in Malaysia is officially prohibited, yet it remains widespread and operates largely underground, with a notable population of sex workers estimated at around 150,000 in 2014. While engaging in prostitution itself is not explicitly illegal, various related activities, such as soliciting and operating brothels, are criminalized under the Penal Code and Sharia law, leading to significant enforcement challenges and legal ambiguities. The Malaysian sex industry includes both local and foreign workers, many of whom are vulnerable due to economic hardship and trafficking.

Societal attitudes toward sex work are predominantly negative, resulting in discrimination and violence against sex workers, who often lack legal protections and adequate healthcare. Health risks, particularly in relation to sexually transmitted infections, are prevalent among sex workers, with around 7,500 estimated to be living with HIV.[171] Despite some efforts by NGOs to provide support, the overall response to the challenges faced by sex workers remains limited, highlighting the urgent need for legal reform and public health initiatives to protect their rights and well-being.

---

170 https://tinyurl.com/24dzbtnw

171 https://legaladvice.com.my/prostitution-malaysia

True Story

Ahnbhalagan Muthu's death in Penang Prison highlights critical issues within Malaysia's prison system. Serving a three-year sentence for burglary, he died just months into his incarceration, with officials attributing his death to suicide. However, his wife, Deviga, claimed that "his body showed signs he had been beaten," raising serious concerns about inmate treatment. Muthu's case is not isolated; official reports indicate 257 deaths in custody between 2002 and 2016. As politician P Ramasamy noted, "There have been too many deaths in custody," emphasizing the urgent need for reform and accountability in Malaysia's correctional facilities. His death reflects the systemic neglect that demands immediate action.[172]

LGBTQ+ and Jail System

Malaysia's prison system comprises about 30 facilities, housing around 87,000 inmates as of November 2024, far exceeding the official capacity of 74,000, resulting in significant overcrowding (17.6%).

This overpopulation leads to inadequate living conditions, limited resources, and difficulties in delivering effective rehabilitation programs. LGBTQ+ individuals, particularly vulnerable within this system, face severe mistreatment, including physical and psychological abuse, harassment, and forced "conversion therapy." This mistreatment is fueled by both the criminalization of homosexuality under Section 377A of the Penal Code and broader societal stigma, which creates a hostile environment for LGBTQ+ prisoners and leaves them without adequate legal protections or support.[173]

---

172 https://www.prison-insider.com/en/articles/
    malaisie-abuse-collusion-and-obstruction-malaysia-s-prison-problems

173 https://www.prisonstudies.org/country/malaysia

 **Arrested in Malaysia**

The arrest process for foreigners in Malaysia is governed by the Immigration Act and the Criminal Procedure Code, which grant immigration officers and police the authority to conduct arrests for law violations. Upon arrest, individuals must be notified of the reasons for their detention and have the right to contact their embassy. They must be presented before a magistrate within 24 hours, although extensions can occur under certain conditions. Foreign detainees are entitled to legal representation, but access to counsel may be delayed for up to **48 hours** if deemed necessary by police. While the legal framework aims to protect the rights of foreigners during detention, reports indicate inconsistencies in the implementation of these rights, including issues related to transparency, access to family and legal aid, and healthcare. Ultimately, there is a need for systemic reforms to ensure fair treatment of all detainees within Malaysia's legal system.[174]

Bail

The bail system in Malaysia is governed by the Criminal Procedure Code and classifies offences into bailable, non-bailable, and unbailable categories, determining the eligibility for bail and the discretion of the court. Bailable offences guarantee the right to bail, while non-bailable offences are at the court's discretion, and unbailable offences, typically severe crimes, preclude bail entirely. The application process involves filing a request in court, followed by a hearing where factors like the severity of the crime and flight risk are assessed. If granted, bail may come with conditions such as regular reporting to authorities or surrendering travel documents. One significant requirement is that the bailor must be a Malaysian citizen.[175] However, challenges persist, including inconsistencies in bail decisions and accessibility issues for those from lower socio-economic backgrounds.

---

174 https://icms.edu.my/the-general-overview-of-the-arrest-procedure/

175 https://www.kehakiman.gov.my/en/procedures-criminal-cases

Legal Representation

Access to legal representation for foreigners in Malaysia is governed by constitutional and legal provisions that affirm their rights, as outlined in Article 5(3) of the Federal Constitution. However, foreigners face several challenges, including language barriers that hinder effective communication, a limited understanding of their legal rights, and difficulties in obtaining legal aid due to their immigration status. While local legal aid organizations and consular services can provide support, the complexity of navigating the Malaysian legal system often poses significant obstacles. To enhance access to justice, it is crucial to improve awareness of legal rights, provide better resources, and facilitate communication for foreign nationals.[176]

If you are arrested as a foreigner in Malaysia, the first step is to contact your home country's embassy or consulate, as they can provide vital assistance, including legal representation and guidance on local laws. Inform the arresting officers of your intent to reach your embassy immediately after detention.

U.S. Embassy Kuala Lumpur

376, Jalan Tun Razak, 50400
Kuala Lumpur, Malaysia
Phone Number: +60-3-2168-5000
Website: my.usembassy.gov.

Additionally, you can reach out to the *Ministry of Foreign Affairs Malaysia* at +603-8887-4000 for further assistance. Be prepared to provide identification and details about your arrest, including the time and location. It's essential to understand your rights, such as the right to remain silent and the right to legal counsel, and to document any relevant incidents during your arrest. Taking these steps will help ensure that your legal rights are protected throughout the process.

---

176 https://jpp.org.pk/report/
primer-for-lawyers-representing-foreign-prisoners-in-malaysia/

Healthcare System and Medical Facilities

Malaysia has a dual healthcare system with public and private sectors. Public healthcare is tax-funded, providing low-cost access to essential services through roughly 148 government hospitals, though rural areas face accessibility challenges and longer waits. Private hospitals, numbering around 207, offer faster, higher-quality care at competitive costs and cater extensively to medical tourists. Foreign visitors must pay for public services and are encouraged to have travel insurance; private hospitals provide internationally accredited care with English-speaking staff. Key facilities serving foreign patients include Prince Court Medical Centre, Gleneagles Kuala Lumpur, and Sunway Medical Centre, all offering advanced treatments and dedicated support for international patients.

 ## Safety Precautions for LGBTQ+ Travelers

LGBTQ+ travelers to Malaysia should prioritize safety by adhering to local laws and cultural norms, as the country has strict regulations against same-sex relations and lacks legal protections for LGBTQ+ individuals. It is advisable to avoid public displays of affection and to be discreet about one's sexual orientation to minimize the risk of harassment or legal repercussions. Forming social connections with locals should be approached cautiously, particularly outside LGBTQ+-friendly spaces, and travelers should research accommodations that welcome LGBTQ+ guests. Additionally, knowing emergency contacts, including local embassy numbers, and exercising respect for local customs can enhance safety and ensure a more enjoyable experience while navigating Malaysia's complex social landscape.

Emergency Contact Numbers

- **Police:** 999
- **Ambulance:** 999 or 991
- **Fire Department:** 999 or 994
- **U.S. Embassy in Kuala Lumpur:** +60-3-2168-5000

Useful Emergency Phrases in Malay

HELP! – Tolong! *(toh-LOHNG!)*

CALL AN AMBULANCE! – Panggil ambulans! *(pang-GIL am-boo-LAHNS!)*

I NEED A DOCTOR – Saya perlu doktor *(SAH-yah per-LOO dok-TOR)*

POLICE – Polis *(POH-lees)*

I'M LOST – Saya sesat *(SAH-yah seh-SAHT)*

IT'S AN EMERGENCY – Ini kecemasan *(EE-nee keh-chem-AH-sahn)*

 # AFGHANISTAN

Afghanistan is a landlocked country in South Asia, characterized by its rugged mountainous terrain and a diverse mix of ethnicities and cultures. With a rich history that includes influences from Persian, Greek, and Islamic civilizations, Afghanistan has long been a center of trade and cultural exchange, despite facing significant challenges due to political instability and conflict.

 ## Politics and LGBTQ+ Legislation

Afghanistan is predominantly **conservative**, with over 99% of the population identifying as Muslim. Homosexuality is viewed as taboo and often associated with criminality and moral corruption. The political and legal status of LGBTQ+ individuals in Afghanistan has undergone drastic changes in recent years, particularly after the Taliban regained power in August 2021. Afghanistan's legal framework regarding LGBTQ+

individuals is predominantly shaped by Sharia law, which governs the legal system under Taliban rule. Same-sex sexual activity is criminalized, with the maximum penalty being death.[177] The 2018 Penal Code explicitly criminalizes same-sex relations and outlines severe punishments, including stoning or death by "wall-toppling," reflecting a harsh interpretation of Islamic law.

 ## LGBTQ+ Scene

There are no LGBTQ+ events in Afghanistan due to the severe repression faced by LGBTQ+ individuals, particularly following the Taliban's takeover in 2021.The Taliban criminalize same-sex relations under Sharia law, imposing harsh penalties, including execution, which creates an atmosphere of fear and prohibits any public gatherings or activism. Individuals within the LGBTQ+ community often lead clandestine lives to ensure their safety, and informal support networks have largely collapsed. International organizations continue to advocate for LGBTQ+ rights and provide assistance to those seeking asylum, but the current environment makes organizing events impractical and extremely dangerous.

 ## LGBTQ+-Related Crime

Reports indicate a significant rise in violence against the LGBTQ+ community, particularly targeting individuals based on their sexual orientation or gender identity. Many LGBTQ+ Afghans have reported experiences of extreme violence, including mob attacks, sexual assaults, and extrajudicial killings.[178] For example, a recent report noted cases of gang rapes and brutal physical assaults perpetrated by Taliban members and

---

177 https://www.humandignitytrust.org/country-profile/afghanistan

178 https://www.hrw.org/news/2022/01/26/
   afghanistan-taliban-target-lgbt-afghan

others supported by the regime.[179] Other accounts document cases of neighbors and family members hunting down and even killing suspected LGBTQ+ individuals in order to "restore family honor", driven by fear of Taliban reprisals.

LGBTQ+ and Prostitution

Under Taliban rule, same-sex sexual activity is criminalized, with penalties that can include death under a strict interpretation of Sharia law. Prostitution is also illegal in Afghanistan, and those caught can face significant prison sentences ranging from five to fifteen years.[180]

LGBTQ+ persons are uniquely vulnerable in the context of prostitution. Reports indicate that in the absence of societal acceptance, individuals may turn to sex work as a last resort to escape poverty and homelessness—especially given the lack of protection under the law and the absence of support networks. Many LGBTQ+ individuals, particularly young gay men, may be coerced into prostitution as a means of survival due to socio-economic pressures and the threat of violence if they do not conform to heterosexual norms.

A particularly troubling practice in Afghanistan is known as "bacha bazi," wherein young boys are often exploited sexually by older men, sometimes under the guise of male dance competitions.[181] Despite being illegal, bacha bazi is culturally entrenched and remains a practice that sees little justice or accountability for the perpetrators.

---

179 https://www.jurist.org/features/2024/11/08/hidden-atrocities-the-unseen-struggle-of-afghanistans-lgbtq-community-under-taliban-rule-report-and-interview

180 https://en.wikipedia.org/wiki/Prostitution_in_Afghanistan

181 https://www.humanium.org/en/bacha-bazi-severe-child-abuse-disguised-as-an-afghani-custom/

LGBTQ+ and Jail System

Afghan prisons are extremely overcrowded and under-resourced, with inhumane conditions, poor sanitation, insufficient food, and limited medical care. Arbitrary detention is common, with many held without trial, and legal protections are largely ignored—especially under Taliban rule. Vulnerable groups, including women, juveniles, and LGBTQ+ individuals, face severe mistreatment. LGBTQ+ detainees are particularly at risk of violence, sexual assault, and discrimination from both guards and fellow inmates.

 ## Arrested in Afghanistan

When a person is arrested in Afghanistan, the process typically begins with law enforcement officials, such as the police or the Taliban security forces, detaining an individual. Arrests can occur with or without a warrant; however, warrants are rarely upheld under the current regime. Individuals are generally taken into custody at the location of the alleged offense, often without formal notification of their rights or the reasons for their arrest, leading to a significant lack of due process.

Upon arrest, detainees may experience immediate mistreatment. Many are not taken directly to official law enforcement facilities but instead are held in unofficial locations, where various forms of abuse and coercion can occur, including torture. The Taliban has been reported to allow for prolonged detention that exceeds lawful limits without judicial oversight, resulting in individuals being held for extended periods without charges being filed.

After the initial detention, the arrested individual is supposed to be presented before a court within legal timeframes; however, this rarely happens in practice. When detainees finally appear in front of a judicial authority, the process often lacks transparency and fairness. Legal representation can be minimal, with many defendants encountering defense attorneys only at the start of trial proceedings, further complicating their ability to mount an effective defense.

Bail

In Afghanistan, the bail system is limited and often does not function effectively, particularly under the Taliban regime, which has prioritized punitive measures over judicial reforms. Historically, bail as a judicial option existed, but the political instability and ongoing conflicts have disrupted its application. Currently, individuals facing arrest may have little hope for bail, as many are held without charges or are denied pre-trial release under current Taliban practices.[182]

Legal Representation

In Afghanistan, individuals have the right to hire lawyers, but access to competent legal representation is limited due to resource constraints, intimidation, and the Taliban's restrictive environment. Many previously active lawyers, especially in criminal or human rights cases, have left or have gone into hiding.

English-speaking attorneys are scarce, but some firms, such as Afghanistan Lawyers International, Divan Law Firm, and Kabul Legal Group, provide services for both locals and international clients. Arrested individuals should contact their embassy (often outside Afghanistan) and local or international legal aid organizations, like the Afghan Legal Aid and Pathways Project, Amnesty International, or the Red Cross, to obtain guidance and support. Prompt action is crucial for navigating legal challenges effectively.

Healthcare System and Medical Facilities

Access to medical care for foreigners in Afghanistan is complex due to the political situation and varying quality of healthcare facilities. However, several key hospitals and medical facilities cater specifically to expatriates and have English-speaking staff.

---

182 https://www.amnesty.org/en/wp-content/uploads/2021/06/
asa110172003en.pdf

Afghanistan has over 100 hospitals, both government and private, particularly in urban centers like Kabul. Despite improvements, the quality and availability of care can differ significantly. Major hospitals include:

- **French Medical Institute for Children (FMIC):** A pediatric hospital known for its collaboration with international organizations.

- **Indira Gandhi Children's Hospital:** Focuses on children's healthcare and is a leading facility in this regard.

- **Afghan-Japan Hospital:** A modern hospital offering a variety of medical services, including surgery and emergency care, frequented by expatriates.

- **Maisondieu Hospital:** Caters specifically to expatriates, offering various medical services.

- **Rahmat Hospital:** Known for adequate medical services and interactions with international medical staff.

Beware that foreign nationals may encounter security concerns due to political instability. Also, many facilities require cash payments for services, and the economic situation may restrict the availability of medical supplies.

 ## Safety Precautions for LGBTQ+ Travelers

LGBTQ+ travelers to Afghanistan should prioritize safety by adopting several precautions to navigate the hostile environment. It is crucial to avoid public displays of affection and to use discreet language regarding sexual orientation. Dressing conservatively to blend in with local customs is important, as is being cautious in social settings to prevent unwanted attention or conflict. Digital security measures, such as using VPNs and limiting social media activity, can help protect personal information. Additionally, establishing a support network with local organizations and identifying safe locations for accommodation are essential steps in ensuring personal safety during travel in Afghanistan.

Emergency Contact Numbers

- **Police:** 119
- **Ambulance:** 112
- **Fire Department:** 119
- **U.S. Embassy in Kabul:** +93 (0) 700 10 400
- **ICRC:** +93-7-995-50-055 / +93-7-011-50-000

Useful Emergency Phrases in Pashto and Dari

Afghanistan has two official languages. **Pashto** is spoken primarily by the Pashtun ethnic group, it is one of the most widely spoken languages in the country, while **Dari,** a variety of Persian (Farsi), is spoken by many ethnic groups in Afghanistan and is the most commonly used language in government and education. Both Pashto and Dari are used in everyday life, with Dari being the dominant language in the capital, Kabul, and in urban areas.

Pashto:

HELP! – مرستـه! *(mas-TAH)*

CALL AN AMBULANCE! – امبولانس ته زنـگ ووهه! *(am-boo-LAANS ta zang wo-HAH)*

I NEED A DOCTOR – زه ډاکتر ته اړتیا لرم *(za DAHK-tar ta ar-TEY-ah lar-um)*

POLICE – پولیس *(po-LEES)*

I'M LOST – زه ورک شوی یم *(za WARK shoi yam)*

IT'S AN EMERGENCY – دا بیرنی حالت دی *(da BEER-nee HA-laat dee)*

Dari:

HELP! – کمک! *(ko-MAK)*

CALL AN AMBULANCE! – امبولانس را بخواهید! (*am-boo-LAANS ra bekh-wah-YEED!*)

I NEED A DOCTOR – من به یک دکتر نیاز دارم (*man ba yak DAHK-ter nee-AZ dar-am*)

POLICE – پولیس (*po-LEES*)

I'M LOST – من گم شده‌ام (*man gom sho-DEH-am*)

IT'S AN EMERGENCY – این یک حالت اضطراری است (*een yak HA-laat ez-TER-aree ast*)

EGYPT

Egypt is a strategically important country in North Africa, with a rich cultural and historical legacy as one of the world's oldest civilizations. Its geopolitical significance is bolstered by its control over the Suez Canal, a vital global trade route. While it is predominantly a conservative nation with 90% of its population identifying as Sunni Muslims, the country also harbors a small but vibrant Christian community. Politically, Egypt is largely conservative, with an authoritarian government that emphasizes stability and traditional values, though there is also a growing liberal movement, particularly among younger generations.

Politics and LGBTQ+ Legislation

Egypt's political climate under President Abdel Fattah al-Sisi is characterized by a **strong conservatism** rooted in historical nationalism and intertwined with military dominance. The government promotes a narrative that aligns state power with religious values, reinforcing a conservative ideology perceived as essential for national unity, significantly impacting the rights of the LGBTQ+ community. Same-sex sexual activity is criminalized under the Penal Code of 1937 and Law 10/1961, which prohibit acts deemed as 'indecency,' 'scandalous behavior,' and 'debauchery', carrying a maximum penalty of three years' imprisonment and a fine.

Tactics such as entrapment through dating apps by police create an environment of fear and heightened risks for those in the LGBTQ+ community. Furthermore, the absence of legal protections renders individuals vulnerable to discrimination and violence without recourse.[183]

True Story

In Egypt, the stigma surrounding homosexuality fosters a hostile environment for LGBTQ+ individuals, further complicated by police tactics that use dating apps for entrapment. "In Egypt, homosexuality is highly stigmatized, and there have long been allegations that police are hunting LGBT people online." Authorities utilize laws against "debauchery" to prosecute LGBTQ+ individuals, with undercover officers manipulating users on apps like WhosHere by pressuring them to meet in person. Foreigners are not exempt from this danger; a victim named Matt was targeted on Grindr and arrested after confessing to "his perversion." These actions highlight how Egyptian authorities exploit technology to enforce antiquated moral laws, perpetuating discrimination against the LGBTQ+ community.[184]

 **LGBTQ+ Scene**

The LGBTQ+ scene in Egypt operates under severe repression, characterized by significant discrimination and legal ambiguity. Despite these

---

183 https://www.humandignitytrust.org/country-profile/egypt/

184 https://www.bbc.com/news/world-middle-east-64390817

challenges, the community has demonstrated resilience through activism and solidarity at notable events. The 2017 concert by the Lebanese band Mashrou' Leila marked a pivotal moment when audience members raised rainbow flags, leading to a harsh governmental crackdown with over 100 arrests under vague laws against "debauchery."[185] Grassroots organizations like Bedayaa work to provide legal support and promote awareness, often discreetly due to the risks involved.[186] Social media plays a crucial role in connecting LGBTQ+ individuals, though it also exposes them to surveillance by authorities.

 **LGBTQ+-Related Crime**

Statistical data reveals an alarming rise in such incidents in Egypt, with the FBI reporting 2,402 hate crimes motivated by sexual orientation bias in 2022, highlighting the vulnerability of LGBTQ+ individuals, especially transgender women and people of color.[187] Further emphasizing this trend, a Human Rights Campaign report noted that LGBTQ+ individuals represent about 22.8% of all hate crime victims, a significant proportion given the overall crime rates. Research indicates that many of these incidents are committed by individuals who are strangers to the victim, suggesting a broader societal bias rather than personal grievances. Furthermore, LGBTQ+ individuals, particularly transgender women and people of color, are disproportionately affected by the most violent forms of hate crimes, often resulting in severe injuries or fatalities.

LGBTQ+ and Prostitution

In Egypt, prostitution itself is not explicitly named in the penal code; however, various related activities are criminalized under laws that

---

185 https://foreignpolicy.com/2017/12/28/2017-was-a-bad-yea-for-egypts-lgbt-community-2018-could-be-even-worse/

186 https://www.cloudflare.com/case-studies/bedayaa/

187 https://www.hrc.org/press-releases/new-fbi-data-anti-lgbtq-hate-crimes-continue-to-spike-even-as-overall-crime-rate-declines

address "debauchery," "immorality," and public morality offenses. Law No. 10 of 1961, titled "Law on the Combating of Prostitution," outlines several offenses related to prostitution. This law aims to penalize individuals who incite, assist, or engage others in activities deemed immoral or prostitution-related, leading to sentences that range from imprisonment for several months to several years depending on the severity of the offenses with even harsher penalties in cases involving minors.[188]

While precise statistics regarding the percentage of LGBTQ+ individuals involved in prostitution in Egypt are absent, estimates suggest that a significant number of LGBTQ+ identifying individuals may engage in sex work. Some reports indicate that after the 2017 crackdown following the Mashrou' Leila concert, which saw numerous LGBTQ+ individuals arrested, there was an observable uptick in individuals turning to sex work as a means of financial stability due to overwhelming job loss and societal rejection[189]

LGBTQ+ and Jail System

Egypt's prison system faces severe overcrowding, holding about 114,000 inmates—more than double its intended capacity. Overcrowding results in poor ventilation, sanitation, nutrition, and lack of basic necessities. Healthcare is inadequate, with unsanitary facilities, limited medical staff, and insufficient mental health services, causing preventable illnesses and deaths. LGBTQ+ prisoners experience extreme abuse, including physical violence, sexual assault, psychological harassment, and denial of medical care. Transgender women are particularly at risk, often denied hormone therapy and subjected to placement in male facilities, worsening both physical and mental health outcomes. Overall, conditions violate international human rights standards.

---

188 https://www.refworld.org/legal/legislation/natlegbod/1961/en/102795

189 https://outrightinternational.org/our-work/middle-east-and-north-africa/egypt

 **Arrested in Egypt**

Foreign nationals in Egypt are subject to local laws, which can differ greatly from their home countries. Although they are legally entitled to contact their embassy and obtain legal representation, in practice access to lawyers is often delayed or denied, especially in politically sensitive cases.

Arrests can occur with or without a warrant, and detainees are supposed to be informed of charges and brought before a prosecutor within 24 hours, but extended pretrial detention—sometimes lasting months or years—is common, particularly under anti-terrorism laws. Trials may be unfair, with reports of torture to extract confessions, especially in military or emergency courts. In some cases, foreigners may be deported instead of being tried, often with minimal legal process or notice.

Bail

In Egypt, bail is governed by the Criminal Procedures Law, with Article 201 allowing bail for minor offenses, but requiring specific conditions for offenses punishable by over three years in prison. The decision to grant bail is at the discretion of the judiciary, considering factors like the offense's severity, flight risk, and public interest. The process involves a bail petition, usually made during the first court appearance, and the amount varies based on the offense and the judge's assessment. However, the bail system faces challenges, especially for individuals accused of political offenses, who are often denied bail or subjected to prolonged pretrial detention without charges. Political influence and public attitudes can also lead to unfair bail decisions, particularly for dissenters or activists.

Legal Representation

In Egypt, foreign nationals have a legal right to counsel and embassy contact, crucial for fair trials and defense. However, accessing legal representation can be difficult due to language barriers, political sensitivities, and limited resources. Foreigners can hire local attorneys, many of whom are English-speaking and experienced with international clients, or seek assistance from NGOs and legal aid clinics offering pro bono support. Specialized organizations also provide legal aid for marginalized groups, such as women and refugees.

U.S. Embassy in Cairo

8 Kamal el-Din Salah Street, Garden
City, Cairo, 11519 Egypt
Phone: +20-2-2797-3300
Email: ConsularCairoACS@state.gov

If you are arrested, you may also need to contact local authorities directly. You can request to speak with your embassy representative or to have them notified of your arrest.

It is advisable to contact an attorney who specializes in legal matters in Egypt, especially one who speaks English if that is your preferred language. Many law firms in Egypt have attorneys fluent in English who can help navigate the legal system. You can find a list of English-speaking attorneys in Egypt at **https://eg.usembassy.gov/wp-content/uploads/ sites/156/2016/10/att_list.pdf.**

Healthcare System and Medical Facilities

Egypt's healthcare system struggles with limited resources and variable quality. Public hospitals provide affordable care but often face overcrowding, long wait times, and inconsistent services, especially outside major cities. Private hospitals offer higher-quality care, shorter wait times, and internationally trained staff, but at greater cost. Foreign visitors are advised to obtain comprehensive travel insurance. Notable facilities catering to international patients include the As-Salam International Hospital, Cairo University Hospitals, and Cleopatra Hospital, all of which provide a broad range of medical services and English-speaking support.

 ## Safety Precautions for LGBTQ+ Travelers

LGBTQ+ travelers in Egypt must prioritize safety due to local laws and widespread societal attitudes that are often hostile towards their identity. Key precautions include maintaining discretion by avoiding public displays of affection and dressing modestly to blend in with local customs. It is wise to refrain from using LGBTQ+ symbols or dating apps, as these can attract unwanted attention and lead to entrapment by authorities. Choosing international hotel chains known for their acceptance and connecting with local LGBTQ+ support networks are also recommended for a safer stay. Lastly, travelers should be prepared for emergencies by knowing the location of the nearest embassy and keeping reliable contacts and emergency numbers accessible.

Emergency Contact Numbers

- **Police:** 122
- **Ambulance:** 123
- **Fire Department:** 180
- **U.S. Embassy in Cairo:** +20-2-2797-3300

Useful Emergency Phrases in Arabic

HELP! – مساعدة! *(mu-sa-AH-dah!)*

CALL AN AMBULANCE! – اتصل بالإسعاف! *(it-tasl bil is-'aaf!)*

I NEED A DOCTOR – أحتاج إلى طبيب *(ah-TAJ ila TAH-beeb)*

POLICE – شرطة *(SHOR-tah)*

I'M LOST – أنا ضائع *(ana DAA-ih)* [for males]

أنا ضائعة *(ana DAA-i-ah)* [for females]

IT'S AN EMERGENCY – إنه حالة طوارئ *(in-nahu HA-lah-tah TAW-ah-ree)*

246

UGANDA

Uganda, a landlocked country in East Africa, is home to over 50 ethnic groups, with a population divided between Christianity and Islam. Uganda has been criticized for human rights violations; concerns include restrictions on political freedoms, suppression of opposition, media censorship, and its treatment of LGBTQ+ individuals. Human rights organizations have frequently reported on the repression of dissent, arbitrary arrests, and the use of force by security forces. Geopolitically, Uganda is strategically significant for its location, oil reserves, and role in regional peacekeeping, especially in South Sudan and the Democratic Republic of Congo.

 ## Politics and LGBTQ+ Legislation

Uganda's political environment is characterized by conservatism and authoritarianism, shaped by President Yoweri Museveni's extended leadership since 1986. His rule, which is expected to continue at least until 2026 barring unexpected political shifts, has maintained tight control over the government, restricting political opposition. The government upholds strict social norms, largely influenced by Christianity and Islam, resulting in **conservative** policies, particularly regarding LGBTQ+ rights and gender roles.

Homosexuality in Uganda has been criminalized since colonial times, with laws prohibiting same-sex relations retained after independence. The political climate became more hostile in the 2000s, marked by the introduction of the 2009 *Anti-Homosexuality Bill*. In 2023, the *Anti-Homosexuality Act* was enacted, imposing harsh penalties, including life imprisonment and the death penalty for "aggravated homosexuality."[190] The enforcement of these laws has led to human rights violations, with authorities using vague charges like "debauchery" and "immorality" to target LGBTQ+ individuals through tactics like online entrapment. Public attitudes, heavily shaped by Christian religious values, fuel stigma and discrimination, causing widespread violence and forcing many LGBTQ+ individuals to live in fear and isolation.

 ## LGBTQ+ Scene

The LGBTQ+ scene in Uganda operates under the shadow of intense repressio n due to legal frameworks like the *Anti-Homosexuality Act of 2023*, which criminalizes same-sex relationships and enforces severe penalties, fostering an environment of fear and hostility. Despite these challenges, underground communities and organizations such as *Sexual Minorities Uganda* (SMUG) have emerged to provide support, resources, and advocacy efforts, often working covertly to navigate risks associated with activism. Public LGBTQ+ events are virtually nonexistent, as attempts to organize celebrations like Pride have been met with government crackdowns and societal backlash; however, private gatherings and online initiatives allow community members to commemorate significant days and build solidarity. International support from human rights organizations plays a crucial role in raising awareness and advocating for legal reforms.

True Story

The Ugandan Appeals Court recently ruled to shut down Sexual Minorities Uganda (SMUG), a prominent LGBTQ+ rights organization, by rejecting its petition to register its name. The court claimed the organization's name violated "public interest" due to its association with LGBT advocacy, which is criminalized under Uganda's harsh Anti-Homosexuality Act. Human rights advocates criticized

190 https://2009-2017.state.gov/outofdate/bgn/uganda/55917.htm

the decision, with one stating, "This is invalidating all the advocacy work that has been done for years and gives the Anti-Homosexuality Act and all homophobes more power over people's lives, bodies, and rights." This ruling further strengthens state-sanctioned homophobia and undermines fundamental freedoms of association and expression in Uganda.[191]

 ## LGBTQ+-Related Crime

A slew of violent incidents has been documented since the enactment of the *Anti-Homosexuality Act*, illustrating the climate of hostility toward LGBTQ+ individuals. For instance, following the law's passage, prominent LGBTQ+ activist Steven Kabuye was attacked by assailants in a hate crime that left him critically injured.[192] Such targeted acts of violence are not isolated; they occur amidst a broader trend of harassment and persecution. Reports indicate that LGBTQ+ individuals have faced beatings, mob violence, and even murder, as seen in the case of Brian Wasswa, a gay rights activist who was brutally murdered in 2019 amid escalating anti-LGBTQ+ fervor.[193]

In a broader survey referenced by the Strategic Response Team, over 110 reports of various forms of violence, including arrests, sexual violence, and evictions, were documented in February 2023 alone.[194] The systematic nature of this violence points to a coordinated effort to marginalize and intimidate LGBTQ+ individuals, often backed by state institutions that perpetuate discrimination through inaction or complicity.

---

191 https://www.hrw.org/news/2024/03/21/
   ugandan-appeals-court-shutters-lgbt-rights-group

192 https://www.africanews.com/2024/01/04/
   ugandan-lgbtq-rights-activist-stabbed-in-hate-crime

193 https://www.hrw.org/news/2019/10/15/uganda-brutal-killing-gay-activist

194 https://www.theguardian.com/global-development/2023/mar/14/
   lgbtq-crackdowns-uganda-environment-hostile

LGBTQ+ and Prostitution

In Uganda, prostitution is illegal, forcing sex workers—including LGBTQ+ individuals—into an unregulated underground economy, exposing them to arrest, violence, and exploitation. LGBTQ+ sex workers face heightened risks due to stigma and legal barriers, with high rates of HIV and widespread employment discrimination, pushing many into sex work and increasing their vulnerability to abuse and limited healthcare access.

LGBTQ+ and Jail System

Uganda's jail system, part of the broader criminal justice framework, faces significant challenges related to overcrowding, poor conditions, and human rights violations. According to current statistics, the Uganda Prison Service is designed to accommodate approximately 20,996 inmates, yet the actual prison population has ballooned to around 76,946, resulting in an overcrowding rate of approximately 366.5%.[195] Within these facilities, inmates frequently face dire conditions, including inadequate access to healthcare, hygiene, and nutrition, which exacerbate health risks and contribute to deteriorating well-being.

LGBTQ+ individuals in Ugandan prisons face severe challenges, including isolation from the general inmate population to protect them from violence, leading to mental distress and a lack of social support. In addition to overcrowded and inadequate conditions, LGBTQ+ inmates often encounter significant barriers to healthcare, with many prison health professionals lacking training in LGBTQ+-specific care, exacerbating neglect and health risks. Human rights organizations report instances of abuse, such as forced anal examinations, which are condemned as torture and further stigmatize LGBTQ+ individuals within the prison system.[196]

---

195 https://www.prisonstudies.org/country/uganda#:~:text=Official%20 capacity%20of%20prison%20system%2020%20996

196 https://www.hrw.org/news/2024/04/04/ uganda-court-upholds-anti-homosexuality-act

 **Arrested in Uganda**

In Uganda, foreign nationals can be arrested under the Criminal Procedure Code and Immigration laws, sometimes without a warrant for criminal or immigration violations. Legally, they must be informed of their rights, allowed legal counsel, and have their consulate notified, with a required appearance before a magistrate within 48 hours. Minor offenses or visa issues may result in deportation rather than prosecution. However, human rights reports indicate that foreign detainees often face arbitrary detention, inhumane treatment, torture, and lack of legal access, sometimes in unregulated "safehouses," with discrimination and politically motivated charges exacerbating their vulnerability.

Bail

Uganda has a structured bail system regulated by the Constitution and various statutes that can take two primary forms: cash bail and non-cash bail. Cash bail requires the accused to pay a specified sum of money to secure their release, while non-cash bail involves the provision of sureties—individuals who guarantee that the accused will appear in court for the trial. The decision to grant bail is primarily at the discretion of the court and hinges on several considerations, including the nature of the offense, the likelihood of the accused appearing for trial, and the risk to public safety.[197]

Despite the established legal structure, several challenges persist within Uganda's bail system. One significant issue is the inconsistency in the application of bail across different cases and jurisdictions, leading to disparities in how courts grant bail. Factors such as the profile of the accused and public perception of the alleged offense can influence bail decisions, often resulting in more lenient treatment for some individuals compared to others.[198]

---

197 https://www.refugeelawproject.org/files/others/Bail_flyer.pdf

198 https://asf.be/bail-in-uganda-a-right-or-a-privilege/

Legal Representation

In Uganda, the Constitution and international agreements guarantee the right to legal representation for all, including foreigners. However, access is often hindered by lack of awareness, language barriers, limited legal aid, and potential discrimination. Many attorneys are trained in English law, and urban law firms often provide services for foreigners, including English-speaking lawyers. Arrested visitors are advised to promptly contact their embassy or consulate to secure legal support and ensure their rights are upheld.

U. S. Embassy Kampala

Plot 1577 Ggaba Road, P.O. Box 7007, Kampala, Uganda

Phone: +256-312-306-001 or 256-414-306-001

Email: KampalaWebContact@state.gov

Website: https://ug.usembassy.gov/embassy/kampala/

Additionally, you should seek local legal counsel, preferably an attorney experienced in criminal law, to represent you in court and guide you through the legal process. For the Uganda government-approved list of English-speaking attorneys, refer to **https://uls.or.ug/wp-content/uploads/2024/11/LIST-OF-APPROVED-LAW-FIRMS.pdf.**

Knowing the contact information for the Uganda Police Force and the specific station where you are held can also be beneficial. The primary emergency contact number for the Uganda Police Force is **999**, which can be dialed for immediate assistance. For specific inquiries or non-emergency situations, you may also reach out to the Uganda Police Force Headquarters at 0414233814 or 0414250613. Furthermore, local non-government organizations offering legal aid can provide extra support to ensure you receive fair treatment during your detention. These include *Uganda Law Society* (ULS), *Foundation for Human Rights Initiative* (FHRI), and *Legal Aid Service Providers' Network* (LASPNET).

Healthcare System and Medical Facilities

Uganda's healthcare system is decentralized, comprising health centers, general hospitals, and specialized referral hospitals. While the country has made progress in areas like HIV/AIDS, challenges such as under-funding, staff shortages, and limited infrastructure affect care quality. Foreign visitors can access services, but many prefer private facilities, and comprehensive health insurance is strongly advised due to upfront payment requirements and limited care in remote areas.

Notable hospitals catering to international patients include Nakasero Hospital, Aga Khan University Hospital, and International Hospital Kampala, all offering advanced diagnostics, specialized treatments, and services tailored to foreigners, including language support through services like Miratude Interpreters.

 ## Safety Precautions for LGBTQ+ Travelers

To ensure safety while visiting Uganda, LGBTQ+ travelers should familiarize themselves with local laws, practice discretion in their behavior and conversations, and choose inclusive accommodations known for respecting LGBTQ+ guests. Traveling with a companion or joining LGBTQ+-friendly tour groups can provide additional support, while establishing a crisis plan, including contacts for local LGBTQ+ organizations and embassies, is crucial for emergency preparedness.

Emergency Contact Numbers

- **Police/Ambulance/Fire Department:** 999 or 112
- **U.S. Embassy in Kampala:** +256-312-306-001 or 256-414-306-001

Useful Emergency Phrases in Swahili

The official languages of Uganda are English and Swahili. **English** is used in government, education, and formal communication, while **Swahili** was declared the second official language in 2005, and it is widely spoken as a lingua franca, particularly in urban areas and among different ethnic groups.

HELP! – Msaada! *(m-saa-DAH!)*

CALL AN AMBULANCE! – Piga simu kwa ambulensi! *(pee-ga SEE-moo kwa am-boo-LEN-see!)*

I NEED A DOCTOR – Nahitaji daktari *(na-hee-TAH-jee dak-TAH-ree)*

POLICE – Polisi *(po-LEE-see)*

I'M LOST – Nimepotea *(nee-meh-po-TEH-ah)*

IT'S AN EMERGENCY – Ni dharura *(nee dha-ROO-rah)*

NIGERIA

Nigerian society is deeply rooted in traditional values that emphasize family, respect for elders, and communal ties, with practices like arranged marriages and patriarchal structures common, especially in rural areas. The country's cultural conservatism is also reflected in the preservation of indigenous religions, which resist liberal ideologies. As Africa's most populous nation, Nigeria is a complex blend of over 500 ethnic groups and more than 500 languages, with a rich cultural and religious diversity. The country's mixed economy is largely driven by its oil and gas industry, making it a key player in Africa's economic landscape.

 ## Politics and LGBTQ+ Legislation

Nigeria is a conservative country, heavily influenced by religious and traditional values, with a stark divide between the predominantly Muslim north and the more liberal Christian south. Its legal system blends secular and Sharia law, especially in northern states, reinforcing conservative social norms. Politically, Nigeria faces corruption, insecurity, and ethnic tensions that complicate governance. LGBTQ+ rights are severely restricted under the Same-Sex Marriage (Prohibition) Act of 2014, which criminalizes same-sex marriage, public displays of same-sex affection, and LGBTQ+ advocacy, with penalties up to 14 years in prison. In **Sharia-governed northern states, punishments can be even harsher, including the death penalty.**

 ## LGBTQ+ Scene

The LGBTQ+ scene in Nigeria largely operates underground, shaped by societal stigma and strict legal restrictions. Despite the criminalization of same-sex relationships, vibrant LGBTQ+ communities have emerged, particularly in urban areas like Lagos and Abuja. These communities organize secretive gatherings and events that provide safe spaces for self-expression, with notable examples including the *Fola Francis Ball*, which celebrates gay culture and honors activists within the community. Organizers of such events often rely on measures like invite-only guest lists and last-minute venue changes to ensure safety from potential police raids and societal violence.

Annual events like Pride in Lagos highlight the courage of the LGBTQ+ community in advocating for rights and visibility. Various organizations, including the *Bisi Alimi Foundation* and *Rainbow Alliance Nigeria*, work tirelessly to promote acceptance and support for LGBTQ+ individuals by providing essential services, education, and advocacy efforts.

True Story

The murder of "Abuja Area Mama," a well-known Nigerian cross-dresser, has raised serious safety concerns among LGBTQ+ activists in Nigeria. Franklin Ejiogu, founder of Creme De la Creme, described the shock within the community as police began investigating the killing, which involved a gunshot wound to the victim's head. Ejiogu linked the surge in violence to the signing of the controversial Samoa Agreement, claiming it has emboldened attacks on LGBTQ+ individuals.

Activist Promise Ohiri, known as Empress Cookie, warned that failing to hold perpetrators accountable would encourage more homophobic offenses, stating, "This is a gateway to uncivilized injustices against the queer community". Given Nigeria's harsh laws that impose prison sentences for same-sex relationships and potential death sentences in some areas, the precarious situation for LGBTQ+ individuals underscores the need for protective measures and legal reforms to ensure their safety and rights in the country.[199]

 LGBTQ+-Related Crime

Nigeria's legislative environment not only fosters discrimination against LGBTQ+ individuals but also legitimizes violence, as perpetrators often act under the guise of defending societal norms. The introduction of the SSMPA has led to a disturbing increase in hate crimes, including physical attacks, mob violence, extortion, and even murders. Notably, a high-profile case that shocked many occurred in August 2023, when a popular Nigerian cross-dresser, known as "Area Mama," was murdered under undisclosed circumstances, sparking fears among the community of escalating violence against LGBTQ+ persons.[200]

199 https://www.voanews.com/a/fear-grips-nigeria-s-lgbtq-community-after-popular-cross-dresser-killed/7737203.html

200 https://www.voanews.com/a/fear-grips-nigeria-s-lgbtq-community-after-popular-cross-dresser-killed/7737203.html

Violence against LGBTQ+ individuals in Nigeria stems from both state-sponsored discrimination and vigilante actions, with law enforcement exploiting their authority to harass and extort victims, while community members carry out violent acts with little fear of repercussions. The threat of legal penalties and societal ostracism discourages many victims from reporting these hate crimes, perpetuating a culture of impunity. As a result, human rights abuse often go unaddressed, with law enforcement agencies dismissing such incidents as acts of moral rectitude rather than crimes.

LGBTQ+ and Prostitution

In Nigeria, the legality of prostitution is marked by a complex framework where, while not explicitly legalized, the criminal code punishes practices associated with it, particularly in the southern regions, whereas northern states enforce strict prohibitions under Islamic law.[201]

Many individuals, particularly women and LGBTQ+ individuals, resort to sex work as a means of survival. For LGBTQ+ individuals, the stakes are even higher. Marginalized by both society and the law, these individuals often find themselves with limited options, leading many into underground sex work.

Statistics surrounding the involvement of LGBTQ+ individuals in prostitution highlight the extent of vulnerability within this population. A report by the Initiative for Equal Rights (TIER) indicated that a staggering 70% of LGBTQ+ respondents had experienced violence related to their sexual orientation, and among these, many reported turning to sex work as a last resort Moreover, research conducted by the U.S. State Department reported that 30% of LGBTQ+ individuals in Nigeria had engaged in sex work due to economic necessity, pointing to a direct correlation between financial insecurity and involvement in prostitution.[202]

---

201 https://sabilaw.org/the-legality-of-prostitution-in-nigeria

202 https://www.humandignitytrust.org/country-profile/nigeria/

LGBTQ+ and Jail System

The jail system in Nigeria, under the purview of the Nigerian Correctional Service (NCoS), has historically been plagued by significant challenges, including overcrowding, inadequate infrastructure, and a lack of rehabilitation programs. As of 2024, Nigerian prisons have an official capacity of approximately 50,153, yet the inmate population exceeds 80,000, leading to an occupancy rate of around 136.7%. The system is characterized by a high percentage of pre-trial detainees, with about 67.7% of inmates awaiting trial, often due to slow judicial processes.[203] Conditions in many facilities are dire, marked by insufficient healthcare, poor nutrition, and rampant human rights abuses. Moreover, the prison system often struggles with underfunding and corruption, which hinder efforts to improve conditions and provide meaningful rehabilitation for inmates.

LGBTQ+ individuals in Nigerian prisons face severe discrimination, often isolated from the general population for their safety, which worsens their vulnerability and mental health issues. Many endure physical violence, sexual assault, and psychological abuse. Healthcare access is limited, with LGBTQ+ inmates fearing that seeking help could lead to further stigmatization. The lack of sensitivity to their specific health needs, particularly regarding HIV/AIDS, exacerbates their risks. The legal environment fosters impunity, allowing law enforcement and prison staff to harass and extort LGBTQ+ prisoners, underscoring the urgent need for reform.

 **Arrested in Nigeria**

In Nigeria, foreigners can be arrested by police or immigration authorities based on evidence or suspicion of an offense. They have the right to be informed of the charges and to contact their embassy. After arrest, they are taken to a police station for questioning and can be detained up to 24 hours without charges, though this period can extend in serious cases. Following detention, they must either be formally charged and

---

203 https://www.prisonstudies.org/country/nigeria

brought to court or released. The legal process can be lengthy, so consular assistance is crucial for coordinating legal support and guidance throughout proceedings.

Bail

In Nigeria, bail can take several forms. Bail on self-recognizance allows an accused individual to be released based solely on their promise to appear in court, without providing financial collateral. Bail with sureties requires one or more individuals to guarantee the accused's court appearance, often needing to meet qualifications such as property ownership. Police bail is a temporary release granted at the police station until formal charges are filed, while court bail is requested during court proceedings, with judges evaluating the application based on factors such as the severity of the offense, the likelihood of the accused fleeing, and the character of the individual.

Bail applications can be submitted either at the police station or during arraignment. Police bail allows for a quicker response, whereas court bail requires a formal hearing. Judges in Nigeria exercise broad discretion in granting bail, and serious offenses—particularly violent crimes—frequently result in denials. This discretionary power can lead to inconsistent applications of the law, with some bail requests being denied without a thorough examination of the evidence.

Legal Representation

In Nigeria, the right to legal representation is guaranteed by the 1999 Constitution, ensuring all individuals, including foreigners, have access to a fair hearing and legal counsel of their choice. The *Legal Aid Act* of 2011 provides legal assistance to indigent persons, but its applicability to foreigners is limited, creating a need for specialized legal support organizations. Foreigners can access legal representation through law firms specializing in immigration and international law, as well as through initiatives by the Nigerian Bar Association (NBA), which promotes pro bono services and raises awareness of legal rights.[204] However, challenges such as a lack of awareness, language barriers, and corruption hinder foreigners' ability to fully access legal representation in Nigeria.

When foreign nationals are arrested in Nigeria, it is crucial for them to know whom to contact for assistance. Key contacts include the Nigeria Police Force, which oversees law enforcement, and the Federal Ministry of Foreign Affairs, which can provide guidance on legal procedures.

Engaging a local lawyer with expertise in criminal law is essential. Nigeria boasts a substantial number of English-speaking attorneys due to its colonial history, where British rule established the foundation for the legal system and language used in court proceedings. Many law firms across the country employ attorneys who are fluent in English, providing services to national and multinational clients alike. Firms such as Vassalcrest Attorneys, Dentons, and Banwo & Ighodalo offer robust legal services, with teams proficient in English addressing various legal needs. You can also find a list of English-speaking attorneys in Nigeria at: **https://ng.usembassy.gov/legal-assistance/**

Contacting your home country's embassy or consulate is vital, as they can assist with limited legal advice, monitor detention conditions, and facilitate communication with family.

U.S. Embassy in Abuja
Plot 1075 Diplomatic Drive
Central District Area, Abuja, Nigeria
Phone: +234-209-461-4000 or 0209-461-4000

Healthcare System and Medical Facilities

Nigeria's healthcare system is underdeveloped, ranking among the lowest globally, with many public hospitals overcrowded and lacking

---

204 https://nigeria.action4justice.org/legal_areas/detention-and-bail/
legal-aid-and-where-to-find-support

essential equipment. Foreign visitors often face practical challenges in accessing care, including high costs, upfront payment requirements, and limited insurance coverage. Public facilities frequently cannot meet local demands, so private hospitals are generally recommended, although they may still fall short of international standards. Health risks are elevated due to poor indicators and prevalent diseases like cholera and malaria, making comprehensive travel insurance essential. Several private and specialized hospitals cater to expatriates and international patients, including Cedarcrest Hospitals in Lagos and Abuja, First Consultant Medical Centre in Lagos, and Lagos University Teaching Hospital (LUTH), which offers advanced care and serves as a major referral and teaching center.

 ## Safety Precautions for LGBTQ+ Travelers

LGBTQ+ travelers to Nigeria should exercise caution due to the country's strict laws and cultural hostility toward LGBTQ+ individuals. Travelers should avoid public displays of affection, keep their sexual orientation or gender identity discreet, and be cautious in interactions with local authorities. It is also advisable to stay in international hotels, avoid LGBTQ+ gatherings, and have emergency contact information for their embassy or consulate. Being discreet and informed about the local legal and social climate is key to ensuring safety in Nigeria.

Emergency Contact Numbers

- **Police:** 199
- **Ambulance:** 112
- **Fire Department:** 01-7944929
- **U.S. Embassy in Abuja:** +234-209-461-4000 or 0209-461-4000

Useful Emergency Phrases

Nigeria is a multilingual country with over 500 languages spoken. However, the official language is **English**, which is used in government, education, and formal communication.

RUSSIA

Russia's geopolitical status is marked by its assertive foreign policy, often positioned in opposition to Western influence through military actions in Ukraine and strategic alliances with countries like China. Culturally, Russia boasts a rich heritage defined by its contributions to literature, art, and music, predominantly shaped by Orthodox Christianity, which plays a significant role in its national identity. However, the country's attitude toward LGBTQ+ rights and human rights is notably conservative, characterized by strict laws that criminalize expressions of non-heteronormative identities and significant repression of civil society, reflecting a prioritization of state control over individual freedoms.

 ## Politics and LGBTQ+ Legislation

Russia's political scene is dominated by President Vladimir Putin, whose administration has increasingly centralized power and suppressed dissent through various legal and extralegal means. The political landscape is characterized by the absence of genuine opposition, with many critics incarcerated, exiled, or removed from the political process entirely under the guise of national security and anti-terrorism measures. Additionally, the government's close association with the Russian Orthodox Church reinforces **conservative** values, impacting legislation and societal attitudes towards issues such as LGBTQ+ rights and civil liberties.

Russia's LGBTQ+ legislation has seen a significant regression in rights since the initial decriminalization of homosexuality in 1993. The 2013 federal law banning the "propaganda of non-traditional sexual relationships" has criminalized any promotion of LGBTQ+ rights, fostering widespread discrimination and hostility against sexual minorities. Societal attitudes remain largely negative, exacerbated by the influence of the Russian Orthodox Church, which advocates traditional family structures continues to classify LGBTQ+ identities as threats to societal norms, leading to an increasingly hostile environment for those seeking equality and justice.

True Story

Russia's Supreme Court has labeled the "international LGBT movement" an "extremist organization," jeopardizing LGBT rights activism in the country. This ruling allows authorities to prosecute anyone involved in LGBT rights activities, even though the "international LGBT movement" does not exist. The decision is seen as a tactic to gain support for the Kremlin ahead of the 2024 elections and suppress rights groups.

Under Russian law, participating in an extremist organization can lead to long prison sentences, and the ruling adds to a pattern of using anti-extremism laws to target critics. The government has also expanded its "gay propaganda" law and passed restrictive legislation against transgender people.

Human Rights Watch urges international support for Russian LGBT activists, including safe haven and visas, as they face increasing persecution. This move reflects Russia's broader rejection of universal human rights in favor of "traditional values."[205]

---

205 https://www.hrw.org/news/2023/11/30/
    russia-supreme-court-bans-lgbt-movement-extremist

LGBTQ+ Scene

The LGBTQ+ scene in Russia has faced increasing repression in recent years, particularly following the enactment of the federal law banning "propaganda of nontraditional sexual relationships." This law has fundamentally restricted public visibility and activism for the LGBTQ+ community, leading to an atmosphere of fear and intimidation.[206] Events such as pride marches have been largely stifled, and many LGBTQ+ venues have been raided. Nevertheless, underground networks and online communities have emerged, allowing individuals to connect, share experiences, and mobilize for rights despite the dangers. Notable organizations like the *Russian LGBTQ+ Network* and *Centre T* strive to provide legal assistance, psychological support, and advocacy, aiming to preserve their community even amidst harsh government crackdown.[207]

LGBTQ+-Related Crime

LGBTQ+ hate crimes in Russia have seen a disturbing rise, particularly following the introduction of the "gay propaganda law" in 2013. Research indicates that incidents of violence against the community have tripled between 2010 and 2015, with documented cases increasing from 34 to 138. The law not only criminalizes the promotion of LGBTQ+ rights but also reinforces societal stigma, leading to more hostile conditions. Notably, groups like "Occupy Pedophilia" have emerged, utilizing online platforms to perpetrate violence against LGBTQ+ individuals.[208] Despite a 2017 European Court of Human Rights ruling deeming the law a violation of the European Convention on Human Rights, authorities have largely ignored the escalating violence, resulting in significant

---

206 https://apnews.com/article/russia-lgbtq-crackdown-putin-moscow-aef-5650c6fdadbe1ac13e0d0b9f93f3b

207 https://www.equaldex.com/organizations/russia

208 https://hatecrime.osce.org/russian-federation

underreporting of hate crimes. Between 2010 and 2020, over 1,056 hate crime incidents were identified, including 365 fatalities, underscoring the urgent need for legal protections and advocacy for LGBTQ+ rights in Russia.[209]

LGBTQ+ and Prostitution

The legal context surrounding prostitution is compounded by Russia's increasingly hostile environment toward LGBTQ+ rights. Prostitution remains criminalized, and police enforcement often targets sex workers, particularly those who identify as LGBTQ+. Research indicates that law enforcement practices frequently involve harassment and discrimination, which further exacerbate the vulnerabilities of LGBTQ+ sex workers who already face significant stigma.[210]

The disempowerment faced by LGBTQ+ individuals in Russia is a critical factor contributing to their involvement in sex work. Many members of this community experience societal rejection, familial disownment, and employment discrimination, which may render them economically vulnerable and desperate for financial support. Studies have indicated that a significant proportion of male sex workers identify as gay and often engage in sex work not merely as a choice but as a necessity for survival. Notably, since the dissolution of the Soviet Union, the economic situation for many has become precarious, driving some into clandestine work to make a living.[211]

---

209 https://www.tandfonline.com/doi/full/10.1080/15564886.2023.2167142#d1e113

210 https://en.zona.media/article/2023/02/27/propaganda-trl#:~:text

211 https://pmc.ncbi.nlm.nih.gov/articles/PMC3595126/#:~:text=Another%20study%20also%20conducted,these%20risks.&text

LGBTQ+ and Jail System

Russia's prison system includes 869 penal colonies, eight prisons, and 315 remand centers, with inmates typically housed in barrack-style accommodations rather than cells. Penal colonies are classified by regime severity—settlement, ordinary, strict, and special—which dictates levels of freedom, supervision, and living conditions. With around 467,000 inmates, Russia has one of Europe's highest incarceration rates. Many facilities are overcrowded, poorly maintained, and lack adequate sanitation and healthcare, leading to outbreaks of diseases like tuberculosis and HIV. Inmates face systemic abuse, including police brutality, torture, and harassment, which hampers rehabilitation and contributes to high recidivism. LGBTQ+ prisoners are particularly vulnerable to violence, isolation, and humiliation, but limited data and a hostile social and political climate obscure the full extent of their mistreatment.

 **Arrested in Russia**

In Russia, the arrest of foreign nationals is governed by the Criminal Procedure Code and relevant international treaties. Authorities must notify the individual's embassy or consulate within 12 hours. Arrests occur based on reasonable suspicion, and detainees must be informed of their rights, including the right to remain silent and access legal representation. A custody report detailing the arrest and detainee rights must be compiled within three hours. During interrogation, foreigners can request a lawyer and consular presence. Authorities then decide whether to formally charge the individual, and if charged, legal proceedings begin. Depending on the case, bail may be granted, but pre-trial detention can last several months or longer.

Bail

In Russia, bail for foreign nationals is granted at the court's discretion, considering factors like the crime's severity and flight risk. Foreigners often face extra scrutiny due to non-residency, and language barriers, inconsistent court practices, and procedural challenges can complicate the process. Securing legal representation and consular support is crucial to improve the chances of favorable bail and protect detainees' rights.

Legal Representation

In Russia, detainees—including foreigners—have the right to legal counsel under Article 48 of the Criminal Procedure Code. In practice, foreign nationals often face difficulties due to language barriers, limited knowledge of Russian law, and challenges finding lawyers experienced in both domestic and international law. Consulates play a key role in connecting detainees with legal support and advocating for their rights, though political factors can limit effectiveness. Visitors detained in Russia should promptly request legal counsel and contact their embassy to ensure proper representation and assistance.

U.S. Embassy in Moscow

Bolshoy Devyatinsky Ln, 8,
Moscow, Russia, 121099
Phone: +7-495-728-50-00

There is a notable presence of English-speaking attorneys in Russia, particularly in major cities like Moscow and St. Petersburg, where law firms cater to the needs of foreign nationals and expatriates. These attorneys specialize in various legal fields, including corporate law, family law, criminal defense, immigration law, and real estate law. You can access a list of local attorneys at **https://ru.usembassy.gov/wp-content/uploads/sites/138/acs-attorneys-list.pdf**.

Healthcare System and Medical Facilities

Russia's healthcare system is primarily state-funded and designed to provide universal coverage, but significant disparities exist, especially between urban and rural areas, with many facilities are under-resourced and understaffed. Bureaucratic hurdles, long wait times, and inconsistent quality make public healthcare challenging for foreigners. Most visitors rely on private hospitals, which provide higher-quality care but require upfront payment or comprehensive insurance, which is also needed for visa purposes. Major cities like Moscow and St. Petersburg have private facilities catering to foreign patients, including the European Medical Center, the American Medical Clinic, and the Almazov National Medical Research Centre, offering international-standard services and English-speaking staff.

 ## Safety Precautions for LGBTQ+ Travelers

LGBTQ+ travelers in Russia should remain vigilant and adopt several safety precautions to navigate the country's challenging social landscape. It is advisable to avoid public displays of affection and to refrain from openly discussing sexual orientation or gender identity, especially in rural areas where conservative attitudes prevail. Researching local LGBTQ+-friendly establishments and connecting with expatriate communities can provide valuable support and resources. Additionally, using a reliable VPN for online activities is essential to protect privacy, given increasing government surveillance. Lastly, staying informed about local laws and customs and having emergency contact information for local embassies or consulates can significantly enhance personal safety during travel.

Emergency Contact Numbers

- **Police:** 112 or 102
- **Ambulance:** 113 or 103
- **Fire Department:** 101
- **U.S. Embassy in Moscow:** +7-495-728-50-00

Useful Emergency Phrases in Russian

HELP! – Помогите! (pa-ma-GHEE-tye!)

CALL AN AMBULANCE! – Вызовите скорую! (VY-za-vee-tye SKO-roo-yu!)

I NEED A DOCTOR – Мне нужен врач (mnye NOO-zhen vrach)

POLICE – Полиция (pa-LEE-tsi-ya)

I'M LOST – Я потерялся (ya pa-tye-RYAL-sya) [male]

Я потерялась (ya pa-tye-RYA-las) [female]

IT'S AN EMERGENCY – Это чрезвычайная ситуация (E-ta chrez-vy-CHA-ynaya si-tu-A-tsi-ya)

GLOSSARY

ACQUITTAL: A jury verdict that a criminal defendant is not guilty, or the finding of a judge that the evidence cannot support a conviction.

ADVERSARY PROCEEDING: A lawsuit arising from a controversy that begins with filing a complaint.

AFFIDAVIT: A written statement made under oath.

APPEAL: A request made after a trial court has decided against one party in which the losing party asks a higher court to review the decision for legal error.

ARRAIGNMENT: A proceeding in which a criminal defendant is brought to court, told of the charges, and asked to plead guilty or not guilty.

BAIL: The temporary release of a person from jail when awaiting trial, on condition that a sum of money be lodged or deposited to guarantee an appearance in court.

BARRISTER: A lawyer admitted to plead at the Bar and who may try cases in superior court.

BURDEN OF PROOF: The duty to prove disputed facts.

CAUSE OF ACTION: A legal claim in a civil action.

COMPLAINT: A written statement that begins a civil lawsuit in which the plaintiff details the claims.

CONTRACT: An agreement between two or more persons to do something or to not do something.

CONVICTION: A judgment of guilt against a person charged with a crime.

CUSTOMS DUTY: A tariff or tax imposed on goods when transported across international borders.

COURT LIAISON: A person that coordinates with attorneys to perform administrative duties, such as scheduling witnesses, sharing information with law enforcement, and overseeing the reporting of cases to foreign embassies when applicable.

DAMAGES: Money that a defendant pays to a plaintiff in a civil case if the plaintiff wins.

DEFENDANT: 1) The individual against whom a civil claim is filed; 2) The individual against whom a criminal claim is filed.

FELONY: A serious crime, punishable by more than one year in prison.

MAGISTRATE: A judicial officer of a district court, who conducts initial proceedings in criminal cases, decides criminal misdemeanor cases, conducts many pretrial civil and criminal matters on behalf of district judges, and decides civil cases with the consent of the parties.

MISDEMEANOR: An offense punishable by one year or less in jail.

PLAINTIFF: A person or business that files a formal complaint with the court.

PLEA: In a criminal case, the answer of "guilty," "not guilty," or "no contest" in response to a criminal charge.

SOLICITOR: A lawyer who advises clients, represents them in lower court, and prepares cases for barristers to try in higher courts.

SOVEREIGN IMMUNITY: A legal doctrine by which the sovereign or the state (i.e. government) cannot commit a legal wrong and thus, it is immune from criminal and civil liability and cannot be sued.

STATUTE: A written law passed by a legislative body.

STATUTE OF LIMITATIONS: A statute prescribing a period of limitation to bring certain types of legal actions. If the action is not brought within that time, the person or entity (in a criminal context) is permanently barred from suing in court.

SUBPOENA: A command, issued under court authority, for a witness to appear and to give testimony.

TESTIMONY: Evidence presented orally by witnesses.

VERDICT: The decision of a judge or jury in a case.

WARRANT: Court authorization to conduct a search or to make an arrest.

ACKNOWLEDGMENTS

This book series would never have seen the light of day without the able assistance of the following people:

Kathy Adams, my paralegal for over 22 years, who is the "Best" I've ever worked with during my entire legal career because of her amazing work ethic, organizational skills, and her ability to think outside of the box in unique and creative ways;

Ally Knez-Siddique, a professional writer, and one of my paralegals, whose eye for detail, according to her, is both a blessing and a curse;

Gino Ibanez, my former law clerk, whose exceptional research skills helped move this book series along in its early stages;

Rosa Diaz Graham, my legal assistant who helped with research and word processing at the very beginning of this project;

Shelia Martin, one of my former paralegals, worked diligently on this series of books, even after taking on another job. Her organizational skills are reflected throughout;

Oliver Clark, whose hard work and diligence researching and writing, helped bring this book to life.

Mindy Scarlett, my marketing and publishing "Guru"! Her creativity and vision has no boundaries!

ABOUT THE AUTHOR

Michael L. Moore practices in Orlando, Florida, the city where he spent his formative years. He credits the trauma of having his brother murdered when he was only 10 years old, as the catalyst that drew him into the practice of law.

Moore attended Florida State University, where he was a member of the FSU debate team. Upon graduating, he was awarded a full scholarship to attend the University of Tennessee College of Law, where he was elected President of the Student Bar Association. He further honed his advocacy and public speaking skills by participating in 'moot court' competitions.

After clerking at the Tennessee Attorney General's office while in law school, Moore moved back to Orlando, Florida, to work at the State Attorney's Office as a prosecutor, and where he was fortunate enough to meet the young lady that would eventually become his wife. Moore moved on to working for private law firms, both local and national, and eventually established his own law firm in 1999. He continues to make Orlando his home base.

It was the murder of a close friend and client in Jamaica that caused Moore to realize that books on laws in other countries were few and far between, and he was inspired to create Law of the Land Publishing. Moore launched Law of the Land Publishing to provide a series of guidebooks and a membership site for tourists and business travelers to stay up to date on the laws in each country they travel to, as well as having access to assistance if they run into legal issues.

"My vision is to educate people on what their legal rights are, and how they can access legal assistance, no matter where they have to travel to in the world," said Moore. "As Americans, we have a right to due process, but in some countries, you don't even have the right to access a square meal when incarcerated. My goal is to provide the information needed to stay out of trouble, as well as having access to assistance if trouble finds you."